EGYPT

FODOR'S TRAVEL GUIDES

are compiled, researched, and edited by an international team of travel writers, field correspondents, and editors. The series, which now almost covers the globe, was founded by Eugene Fodor in 1936.

OFFICES

New York & London

FODOR'S EGYPT:

Editor: LISA A. CHECCHI
Editorial Associate: FRAN SNYDER
Maps: DYNO LOWENSTEIN
Drawings: EDGAR BLAKENEY

FODOR'S®
EGYPT
1984

KAY SHOWKER

FODOR'S TRAVEL GUIDES
New York

ISBN 0-679-01000-9
ISBN 0-340-34067-3 (Hodder & Stoughton edition)

MANUFACTURED IN THE UNITED STATES OF AMERICA
10 9 8 7 6 5 4 3 2

CONTENTS

APPENDIX

AUTHOR'S FOREWORD

In preparing a guide on a country 7,000 years old, the biggest problem facing a writer is deciding what to leave out. Egypt's antiquities alone fill volumes. After examining the current literature, I found that much of it tends to be of two types: history books, scholarly treatises and art books—all serious in tone and profuse in detail—or nostalgic ramblings by former European residents, which are entertaining and charming but somewhat irrelevant.

The scholarly books can be invaluable when one is standing in front of a strange drawing on the wall of an ancient tomb or temple, but are not much help for planning a trip from a distance of 6,000 miles. The sentimental type of book offers its readers the vicarious enjoyment which helps get today's travelers out of their armchairs and into plane seats but they are neither practical nor timely.

This book is meant to bridge the gap. I have tried to give readers enough historical background to understand the broad changes that took place in the long span of Egypt's history without becoming lost in its maze. For those interested in more detail, I have, where appropriate, mentioned books which will provide this type of information.

At the same time, Egypt is a bustling modern country where a visitor can have fun, eat well, enjoy sports, shop and spend time among warm and generous people who will become lifelong friends. I have devoted a great part of this book to making this facet of the country more approachable and accessible to a newcomer.

Yet, more than anything else, this book is aimed at being concise and practical—to help you plan your trip before you go and to help you enjoy your visit after you arrive.

Reading about Egypt's history in advance will greatly augment the pleasure and meaning of your visit, and I urge you to do so. The *Suggested Reading List* later in the book is intended as an aid in selecting books. I have relied heavily on these sources myself.

Egypt is the result of my personal experience and impressions as a traveler. The choice of information and opinions are mine without any obligations whatsoever. I welcome suggestions from readers for information to be included in any future edition, and I will be grateful to learn about any experience that did not match my description encountered by a reader.

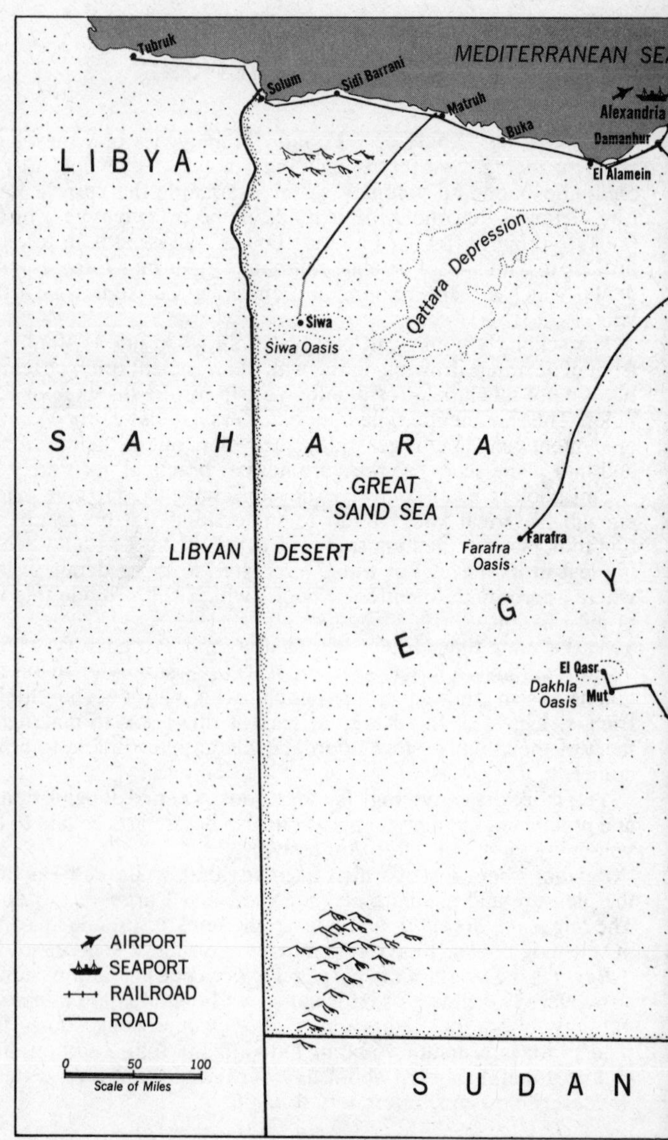

MEDITERRANEAN SEA
Tubruk
Solum
Sidi Barrani
Matruh
Buka
Alexandria
Damanhur
El Alamein
LIBYA
Qattara Depression
Siwa
Siwa Oasis
SAHARA
GREAT SAND SEA
LIBYAN DESERT
Farafra
Farafra Oasis
EGY
El Qasr
Dakhla Oasis
Mut
AIRPORT
SEAPORT
RAILROAD
ROAD
0
50
100
Scale of Miles
SUDAN

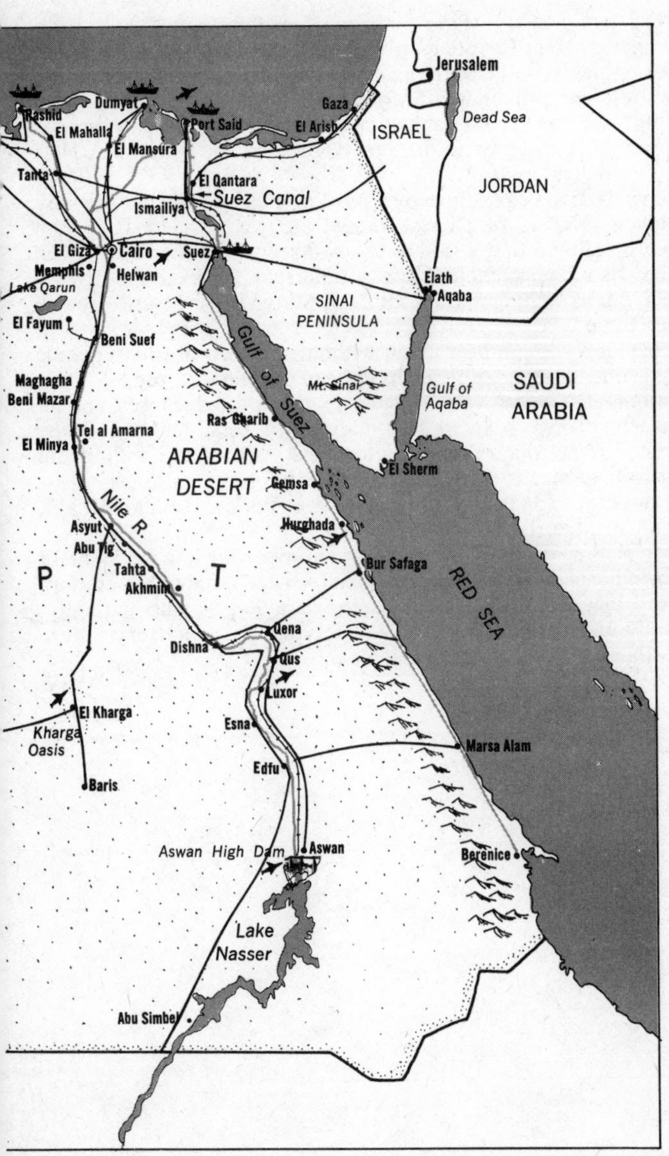

Jerusalem
Dead Sea
Gaza
El Arish
ISRAEL
JORDAN
Rashid
Dumyat
Port Said
El Mahalla
El Mansura
Tanta
El Qantara
Suez Canal
Ismailiya
El Giza
Cairo
Suez
Memphis
Helwan
Lake Qarun
El Fayum
Beni Suef
Elath
Aqaba
SINAI
PENINSULA
Gulf of Suez
Mt. Sinai
Gulf of Aqaba
SAUDI
ARABIA
Maghagha
Beni Mazar
Ras Gharib
Tel al Amarna
El Minya
ARABIAN
DESERT
El Sherm
Gemsa
Nile R.
Asyut
Hurghada
Abu Tig
Tahta
Bur Safaga
P
T
Akhmim
RED SEA
Qena
Dishna
Qus
Luxor
El Kharga
Kharga
Oasis
Esna
Marsa Alam
Edfu
Baris
Aswan High Dam
Aswan
Berenice
Lake
Nasser
Abu Simbel

Consistency in the transliteration of Arabic names and in the spelling of ancient Egyptian ones is an insurmountable problem. A few examples will illustrate the difficulty: the name of the Prophet is written as Muhammad, Mohammed, Muhamed, Mohamed, Mehmet. Among the pharaohs one encounters most often there is Ramesis or Ramses or Ramesses; Thutmosis or Tuthmose; Hatshepchut or Hatchapsut.

I have tried to be practical by using the spellings most commonly employed. Names of places, shops, etc. are rendered as they appear locally so that a newcomer will recognize them, but even this has its inconsistencies. It is not unusual, for example, to find the Egyptians writing Menia, Minia or Minya for the same town in Upper Egypt.

No guidebook can be written without the help of many people and this one is no exception. I have been dealing with the Egyptian Government Tourist Office, both in the United States and in Egypt, for twenty years and no matter how small or how big the request, I have found their directors and staff always willing and eager to help me. In particular, I am grateful to Dr. Shawki Hussein, director of the tourist office in New York and Samir Khalil, director of Misr Travel, in New York.

Special thanks are due to Celia Latimer Ochs, a resident of Cairo, whose invaluable research helped to update this edition, and my biggest thanks of all go to Tiara Pestal who patiently, carefully and graciously typed and retyped the manuscript more times than either of us can remember.

K.S.

EDITORS' FOREWORD

The lure of ancient Egypt is so great that travelers are seldom aware of the country's other attractions. But it is no exaggeration to say that if there were no Pyramids or Abu Simbel, no Valley of the Kings or Karnak Temple, Egypt would still be one of the most interesting countries in the world to visit.

Cairo has more magnificent Islamic treasures than any city in the world. They alone are well worth a visit.

Egypt's Christian history, which formed a bridge between the ancient world and the development of western civilization, is even less known and is almost completely overlooked by visitors today.

And none of these—ancient temples, old churches, magnificent mosques—acquaint the traveler with the Egypt of today: a nation of 45 million people that is growing and developing with a new sense of its destiny; a nation that has changed more in the last thirty years than it has in the past thirty centuries.

Yet, Egypt has not changed at all.

Egypt is the cradle of history and human culture. Few countries in the world can trace their beginnings to so remote a time as the civilization which developed along the banks of the Nile, the river which creates Egypt and makes it the most fertile country in North Africa.

It was the Nile that molded the character of the people, stimulating the ancient Egyptians to great physical and intellectual feats far in advance of their contemporaries. It was the bountiful Nile that made them the most prosperous, the most famous and the most civilized among the nations of antiquity.

Now, as then, Egypt without the Nile would not exist.

Egypt's location has made it unique in another way too. Situated as it is in the northeast corner of Africa, throughout history Egypt has been a bridge between Asia and Europe, Africa and Asia; a bridge over which have passed armies, commerce, people and ideas. It is no less true now than it was 4,000 years ago.

What a visitor will discover on a visit to Egypt is a country with a rich texture in which the constant fiber is the Nile, interwoven with Pharaonic, Christian, Islamic patterns and in colors that are African, Asian and European. Together, they create the tapestry that is Egypt.

***

We are proud to have as author of EGYPT the journalist and photographer Kay Showker, who has lived, worked and traveled extensively in the Middle East. Her publications include Pan American's *Complete Reference Guide to the Arab Middle East* (Simon & Schuster) and *Travel Lebanon, Travel Jordan* and *Travel Egypt,* published in Beirut. She is also the author of Fodor's JORDAN AND THE HOLY LAND.

FACTS AT YOUR FINGERTIPS

Horus, Son of Isis and Osiris

FACTS AT YOUR FINGERTIPS

WHEN TO COME. Egypt is a year-round travel destination, but October through May is the ideal time to visit. Winter is considered the high season, especially at Luxor and Aswan in Upper Egypt which has been a popular winter resort for wealthy Europeans since Edwardian aristocrats made it fashionable.

The year-round climate in Cairo is very dry. In the winter months it is warm and comfortable by day but at night it can be cool enough for a lightweight coat. April tends to be a month of unpredictable weather and can still be cool and windy.

From June through September, Cairo is hot and Upper Egypt is very hot. However, leading hotels in Cairo, Luxor and Aswan are air-conditioned, and if one is careful to sightsee in the early morning or late afternoon, it is not unbearable. On the other hand, those who suffer from exposure to intense, direct sun and heat should not attempt a trip to Abu Simbel during the summer months.

AVERAGE TEMPERATURES IN MAJOR TOURIST CENTERS

		Winter			*Spring*			*Summer*			*Fall*	
	Dec.	Jan.	Feb.	Mar.	Apr.	May	June	July	Aug.	Sept.	Oct.	Nov.
ALEXANDRIA:(high)	F. 69	66	67	70	75	80	83	86	87	86	83	77
(low)	F. 54	51	51	54	58	63	69	73	74	72	68	62
CAIRO:	F. 69	66	69	75	83	90	95	96	95	89	85	78
	F. 49	45	47	51	56	62	68	71	71	68	63	57
LUXOR:	F. 78	74	79	86	95	103	106	107	106	103	98	87
	F. 45	42	44	50	59	69	70	72	73	71	65	54
ASWAN:	F. 78	75	79	88	97	103	108	107	106	103	99	88
	F. 52	49	51	57	65	73	77	78	80	74	71	61

EGYPTIAN MONTHS OF THE YEAR COMPARED TO THE GREGORIAN CALENDAR

Gregorian (A)	Solar (A)	Coptic (B)	Hijra (C)
January	Khanun II	Tuba	Moharram
February	Shabat	Amchir	Safar
March	Azar	Baramhat	Rabi I
April	Nizan	Barmuda	Rabi II
May	Ayar	Bashans	Gumada I
June	Haziran	Bauna	Gumada II
July	Thamuz	Abib	Ragab
August	Aab	Misra	Shaban
		Nasi (D)	
September	Aylul	Tut	Ramadan
October	Techrin I	Babeh	Shawal
November	Techrin II	Hatur	Thul-Kida
December	Khanun I	Kiyahk	Thul-Higga

(A) Solar and Gregorian months are same.
(B) Coptic month is 30 days.
(C) Hijra-month is 29 or 30 days, the year is 354 days.
(D) Nasi lasts 5 or 6 days.

HOLIDAYS. *National:* Feb. 22, Union Day; May 1, Labor Day; June 18, Evacuation Day; July 23, Revolution Anniversary; Oct. 6, Armed Forces Day; Oct. 24, Suez Day; Dec. 23, Victory Day. Festivals: Sham en Nessim (Celebration of Spring), first Monday following Eastern Orthodox Easter.

Religious: Moslem religious holidays are calculated by the lunar calendar and occur 11–12 days earlier each year. Ramadan is the Moslem month of fasting from sunrise to sunset. During these hours not even water may be taken. In 1984, Ramadan begins about June 1. The fast is particularly hard on those devout Moslems who observe it during the hottest summer months, and you will do yourself a favor by avoiding a visit during this time.

Ramadan ends with the Id al Fitr, or Small Bairam. The Id al Adha, or Big Bairam, comes 70 days later at the end of the period of the pilgrimage to Mecca, and commemorates Abraham's sacrificing his son to God.

Islamic New Year's Day is the first day of the Hijrah year, and marks the flight of the Prophet Mohamed and his followers from Mecca to Medina in an effort to save his prophetic mission. The Moulid El Nabi celebrates the birth of the Prophet.

On major holidays Egyptians tend to take 3–5-day vacations. Government offices are open only from 10 A.M. to 2 P.M. during Ramadan, and most offices and many businesses close for several days during the Bairam feasts. Businessmen in particular should try to avoid visiting Egypt during Ramadan and the Bairam feasts as they will accomplish little.

HOW TO GET THERE. Cairo is today as it has been throughout its history—a crossroad. The air routes between Europe, Asia and Africa crisscross at the Egyptian capital, making it readily accessible by the major international airlines from almost any country of the world. Following the reopening of the Suez Canal in June, 1975, Egypt quickly regained its preeminence on the sea routes and now several steamship companies offer a voyage through the canal as part of a Mediterranean or Red Sea cruise or on around-the-world itineraries.

By Air: *Pan Am* has daily 747 service from New York to Rome with a change of plane for the onward non–stop flight to Cairo four days of the week or via Beirut on the remaining three days. *TWA*'s daily 747 direct flights from New York to Cairo stop in Rome and Athens. *PIA*'s twice weekly service flies via Paris. Other international airlines fly from major U.S. gateways with interim stops and connecting flights to Cairo via almost any European capital. *KLM,* for example, has daily service between New York and Amsterdam with same day connections between Amsterdam and Cairo.

From London, *British Airways* and *EgyptAir* have direct flights, and from the Continent, *EgyptAir* and the leading carriers of Europe offer regular flights from their capitals to Cairo.

The airlines of the Middle East also have daily connections between Cairo and the capitals of the region.

Although Cairo is easily accessible from the U.S. and almost any European or Middle Eastern capital, travelers should be aware that demand for airline seats is sometimes greater than supply. Book early, reconfirm and get to the airport early, especially when you are traveling to Egypt from any other capital in the Middle East.

Regularly scheduled air service between Cairo and Tel Aviv is available from *El Al Airlines* and *Air Sinai.* The flight takes 1¼ hours.

AIR FARES

Among the more confusing aspects of travel these days is the matter of air fares, and perhaps none are more confusing than those that apply to Egypt. The following fares were valid at the time of writing but, based on past experience, the list will not be valid by the time the ink is dry on the page. All prices are round-trip between New York and Cairo:

Individual Fares

First Class: $3986—available year round.

TWA Ambassador Class: $2306—basic (Sept. 15–May 14); $2660—peak (May 15–Sept. 14).
Economy Class: $1590—basic fare (Sept. 15–May 31); $1748—peak months.
6–60 days APEX: $774 winter; $980 peak.
14–90 day Excursion: $1235—basic fare; $1341—peak.
Youth (*12–21 years*): $996—basic; $1033—peak.

Group Fares

Many group fares are being phased out in favor of the lower individual fares. However, there are still a few which can be advantageous for as few as 5 or 10 persons traveling together. Ask your travel agent to check; these fares change too rapidly to be included here.

By Sea: At present, there are no all-passenger ships in regular service from the U.S. to the Mediterranean. However, European steamship companies that offer Mediterranean cruises have combined air-sea programs which include a stopover in Alexandria with an excursion to Cairo. Local travel agents arrange to meet passengers at the port and provide them with a sightseeing program to Cairo while their ship passes through the Canal. Afterward, passengers travel to another port to rejoin their ship. For example, they might disembark in Alexandria, journey overland to Cairo while the ship transits the Canal, and pick up their ship again in Suez. Others offer day tours to Cairo, usually by motor coach, for a very quick look at the Pyramids and bazaars. These tours tend to be very hurried and much over-priced. Many such combined air-sea programs can be purchased in the United States.

The cruiselines that call at Egyptian ports are *Cunard, Epirotiki, Karageorgis, Norwegian America, Royal Viking Line* and *Sun Line Cruises*. Your travel agent can give you more details.

The *Egyptian Maritime Company,* 1 El Hurreya Avenue, Alexandria, Egypt, has departures from Piraeus, Naples, Genoa, Marseilles, Beirut to Alexandria and vice versa. For booking information, contact their agents:

England: *Alexandria Navigation Co.,* 35 Piccadilly, London W1.

Greece: *George A. Callitsis,* Stadiou Street No. 10, Athens.

Italy: *Italafric Spa,* Piazzetta Lacopo da Varagine 2/6, 1 16124 Genoa, and Dorsoduro 3500/1, 30123 Venice.

Car ferries from Athens make it possible to drive from Europe to the Middle East, covering the leg to Egypt by sea. *Menatours,* Egyptian agents for the European ferry service of *DFDS,* has two weekly deluxe ferries between Italy or Greece and Alexandria, as well as between Israel, Jordan and Saudi Arabia. *Adriatica Lines* has several ferry ships connecting Venice and Alexandria. Their offices are at 5 World Trade Center, New York.

By Land: The road between Egypt and Israel is open; transportation is available by motorcoach, taxi and private vehicles. Buses go between Cairo and El Areesh, where passengers cross the border and continue into

Israel via Israeli bus. Or, if one is starting out in Israel, transportation is available from Tel Avis and Jerusalem to Cairo via El Areesh.

Travel time from Cairo to El Areesh is about six hours. There, the wait for the bus from Israel to pick up passengers and clearance through customs for the onward trip to Tel Aviv can add three to four hours to the trip.

Passengers who plan to make a round trip from Egypt must have a multi–entry visa for returning to Egypt *before* departing Cairo as there are no visa issuing facilities at the border. You should take food and water, as there are no facilities enroute in Sinai. (If you are a member of a tour, food and formalities are provided by the operator.) This trip is long and tiring. *Do not undertake it unless you are prepared to withstand delays and inconveniences.*

Three companies offer seat–in–bus service from Cairo. Individual travelers must book in advance. *Emeco Travel,* 2 Talaat Harb, has a bus leaving from its office on Wed. and Sun. at 4 A.M. Cost is $25 one–way.

Oasis Travel, 928 Broadway, NYC 10010 (Egged Tours/Israel representative) has daily except Fri. and Sat. motorcoach departures from the Nile Hilton at 5 A.M. Cost is $24 one–way; $40 round trip, if purchased in conjunction with a package; or $25, plus $15 service charge, if bought separately.

Travco Egypt, 3 Ishaak Yacoub, Zamalek, Tel. 803-448, Telex 92926, has daily, except Sat., motorcoach departures from the Cairo Sheraton at 4 A.M. and from the Continental Savoy at 4:15 A.M. to Tel Aviv and Jerusalem. Price is L.E. 25 one–way and L.E. 40 round trip.

Another possibility, but only for students and others prepared for long inconvenience, is to take a three-stage taxi—from Ramses Sq. in Cairo to Suez; ferry to Qantara; taxi to El-Areesh; cross border; and taxi to Tel Aviv or Jerusalem. Total cost is about $20 and trip takes up to 12 hrs. depending on border delays. As with bus, one should take food and bottled water.

It is next to impossible to drive across North Africa from Morocco to Egypt because there are no diplomatic relations between Libya and Egypt. The distance from Casablanca to Cairo is approximately 3,000 miles.

PACKAGED TOURS AND COSTS. Many American tour operators offer packaged tours to Egypt which for one price include transportation, hotels, sightseeing and most meals. Such inclusive packages are the most economical and convenient way to visit Egypt and are strongly recommended, particularly for first-time visitors.

A large number of packages combine Egypt with several other Mediterranean or Middle Eastern destinations. For a first-time traveler to this part of the world, multistop packages are enticing, but are not recommended. On such a tour, you will see the Pyramids and Sphinx, visit the Egyptian Museum and the old bazaars of Cairo—*but you will not see Egypt*. There is too much to enjoy in Egypt to combine it with a hurried trip through four or five countries in two or three weeks. Of necessity, the emphasis of any Middle East tour is on history, monuments and antiquities, and even the most avid history buff or amateur archaeologist may tire of too many museums and temples in a day. Moreover, if you combine too many countries on one tour the impressions run together. Egypt alone is more than worth a visit.

The following examples of tours are meant as an indication, not a complete list, of what is currently on the market. Every effort has been made to provide the most current prices but *all prices* are subject to change. The information should give readers a reasonable idea of the types of tours available and the approximate costs of a trip to Egypt. You should consult a travel agent for the most up-to-date information, as new programs are being added all the time. Prices listed here are for one person sharing a hotel room with another. In most cases, a high season supplement will increase the airfare in June, July and August. (See *Getting There*.)

The tour operators are listed here in alphabetical order. No other criteria have been used nor have we attempted to evaluate their products. The purpose of the list is to give readers as complete a guide to the tours as possible. Recently so many new programs have been added it is difficult to keep up with them, and we may have inadvertently omitted a few. All prices are land arrangements only, per person for two sharing a double room; airfare is additional, unless otherwise stated. The airline named is the principal one for the program; it or your travel agent should have the program's brochure.

Abercrombie & Kent International, 1000 Oak Brook Road, Oak Brook, IL 60521; 312-887-7766; 800-323-7308. Four year-round programs, one exclusively Egypt, and the others combinations of Egypt, Kenya, Israel and Ethiopia; ranging from 12 to 19 days; departures are twice monthly. Prices start at $1,996. Two special tours operate from Oct. through Apr. featuring seven- and 14-night Nile cruises on *M.S. Abu Simbel,* a 20-passenger vessel. Tours include all meals, sightseeing, deluxe accommodations and internal Egypt flights. *British Airways.*

American Express Co., American Express Plaza, NYC 10004; 800-241-1700 (except Georgia). Six escorted programs visit Egypt; two are Egypt only, the others combine Egypt with Greece and/or other Middle Eastern destinations. The 10-day Egypt covers Cairo, Luxor, overland to Aswan, plus Abu Simbel, from $960. It can be combined with a 7-day Israel package. Ancient Wonders and Nile Cruise is also 10 days and includes a 5-day Sheraton Nile cruise, from $1,165. The 15-day Egypt plus Aquarius Cruise combines four days in Cairo with a seven-day Greek Islands cruise; two 15-day programs offer Egypt ports-of-call on cruises of the *Stella Solaris.*

The Cortell Group, 3 East 54th St., NYC 10022; 212-751-3250. Four year-round programs ranging from nine to 15 days. Three are Egypt-only programs, and one combines Egypt with Jordan and Israel. "Egypt With A Five-Day Nile Cruise" is a nine-day tour, featuring three nights in Cairo and a cruise from Luxor to Aswan, (Abu Simbel is available as an option), from $989 land. Ancient and Modern Egypt, 10 days, highlights Cairo, Aswan and Luxor, from $766 land.

Exprinter (rep. Swan Hellenic Ltd.), 500 Fifth Ave., NYC 10110; 212-719-1200; 800-221-1666. Year-round 18-day Nile cruises cover 600 miles between Cairo and Aswan, escorted by lecturers and cruise manager. Prices start at $2,654, and include outside twin on *M.S. Nile Star;* local transportation, meals, sightseeing, gratuities, taxes, and round trip airfare from London. *British Airways.* Four 14-day programs combine Egypt and Israel.

Four Winds Travel, 175 Fifth Ave. NYC 10010; 212-777-2711. Six itineraries, two exclusively Egypt, two combining Egypt with East and South Africa, and two with Israel and Jordan. All are escorted and include all land arrangements, sightseeing, tips and most meals. The nine-day "Best of Egypt" covers Cairo, Luxor, Aswan and Abu Simbel, from $1,188. The 15-day Egypt and the Great Nile Cruise adds a four-day Nile cruise. *Swissair.*

General Tours, 711 Third Ave. NYC 10017; 212-687-7400; 800-221-2216. There is an exclusively Egypt tour: the 10-day "Egypt in Brief" visits Cairo, Aswan, Luxor and has a four-day Nile cruise on the *M.S. Horus,* from $1,882. It includes all transportation within Egypt, deluxe hotels, Nile cruises, full breakfast daily and other meals, sightseeing, the sound and light performance at Karnak, transfers, baggage handling, taxes and service charges, and tour escort. *Olympic Airways.*

Hemphill Harris Travel, 16000 Ventura Blvd., Encino CA 91436; 800-421-0454; 213-906-8086. Three deluxe programs ranging from 11 to 22 days, include three meals daily, accommodations, sightseeing and all gratuities. The 11-day "Egypt Explored" includes a five-day Nile cruise from Luxor to Aswan, for $1,380. It is limited to 25 persons.

Lindblad Travel, 8 Wright St., P.O. Box 912, Westport, Conn. 06881; 203-226-8531; 212-751-2300. A new two-week tour, "Wonders of Egypt," is specifically designed for summer, off-season travel and features a seven-night Nile cruise between Luxor and Aswan on the Sheraton vessels. The tour proceeds from New York via London to Luxor and by ship to Dendera, Abydos, Esna, Edfu, Kom Ombo and Aswan, plus an excursion to Abu Simbel, from $1,730. Other tours are the 15-day "A Thousand Miles up the Nile," from $2,150; and Egypt combined with Kenya.

Maupintour, Inc. 1515 St. Andrews Dr., P.O. Box 807, Lawrence, Kansas 66044; 913-843-1211; 800-255-4266. One of the most long-established, most reliable operators offering Egypt tours has six year-round escorted programs, ranging from 14 to 22 days, plus the seventh annual program that makes the longer cruise from Aswan to Cairo. Three itineraries are exclusively Egypt; others combine Egypt with Greece or Israel, and one itinerary includes Jordan. Prices start at $1,698 and include sightseeing, most meals, internal transportation where applicable. The 14-day "Egypt Exclusively" is a comprehensive tour of Cairo and environs, Luxor, Abydos, Dendera, Aswan and Abu Simbel. Two of the 17-day tours add Alexandria, El Alamein, a four-day Nile cruise, and begin with two days in London; the third departs May 30, and includes a 10-day Nile cruise on Hilton's ship, *Orisis,* from Aswan to Cairo, plus Abu Simbel and five days in Cairo. *TWA.*

Metco Tours, 295 Madison Ave., NYC 10017; 800-422-1211; 212-686-6622. "Plan Your Own Egypt" is a basic package to which participants can add sightseeing tours, each priced separately. The operator also has two unusual programs: an 11-day "Arabian Horses in Egypt" with lectures by specialists and visits to stables and to important historical sites; the other is the annual Senior Tennis Tournaments in Egypt and Kenya with playing time in both countries.

Nawas International Travel, 20 East 46th St. NYC 10017; 800-221-4984; 212-682-4088. Seven year-round programs range from 10 to 18 days; departures are weekly and twice monthly. Four itineraries include a Nile cruise on Sheraton ships, two of them cover Egypt exclusively. The others combine Egypt with Petra, Israel and/or Greece. Prices start at $1,098 and include accommodations in deluxe hotels, full sightseeing, most meals, domestic flights and local escorts. Tours are handled by Nawas's own offices in Cairo and Luxor. The 11-day "Pharaoh's Treasures" is a comprehensive tour of Egypt, including a four-day Nile cruise from Aswan to Luxor, sightseeing in Cairo, sound and light show, plus excursion to Abu Simbel. *TWA.* Nawas Tourist Agency, 19/21 Great Portland St., London W1, has similar programs with departures from the U.K.

Nefertiti Travel, 3000 Biscayne Blvd., Miami, FL 33137; 305-573-8864; 800-327-7854. Twelve programs are offered on a year-round basis. Three are combined with visits in England ranging from three to seven nights; the other nine offer both condensed and comprehensive tours of Egypt. A 13-night program is the most extensive, covering Cairo and environs, Abu Simbel, Aswan, Luxor, Fayoum, Wadi el Natroun and Alexandria. Another utilizes the overnight sleeper train to Upper Egypt, thus eliminating two hotel nights and reducing land costs while ensuring dependable transportation. It offers five days in Cairo, with an excursion to Fayoum, and optional tour to Alexandria or the Suez Canal. *British Airways* and *KLM.*

Park East Tours, 1841 Broadway, NYC 10023; 212-765-4870. The 12-day "Nile Odyssey" featuring Egypt exclusively, has guaranteed bi-monthly year-round departures from New York, $1,349 for air travel and land arrangements. The program includes a five-day Sheraton Nile cruise, Abu Simbel, Aswan and Luxor with comprehensive sightseeing, American breakfast, most lunches and dinners, and domestic air travel. There is a luncheon in Cairo on Oberoi's *M.S. Nile Pharoah* and a gala farewell Arabian tent party. A 20-day African Odyssey combines Egypt with Kenya.

Persepolis Tours, 667 Madison Ave., NYC 10021; 212-838-8585; 800-221-1680. Seven year-round programs, ranging from eight to 18 days, with monthly departures. Three are to Egypt only; others combine Egypt with Kenya, Turkey, Greece or Israel. Rates include most meals, domestic air ticket, sightseeing. "Egypt in Depth" is a 12-day program visiting Cairo, Aswan, Luxor and Abu Simbel, from $1,140. "Egypt with Cruise" is 12 days and includes a Sheraton or Hilton cruise, Cairo and Abu Simbel; and "Egypt Compact" is an eight-day tour of Cairo, Luxor and Aswan, from $559. *KLM*.

Sunny Land Tours, 166 Main St., Hackensack, N.J. 07601; 201-487-2150; 800-631-1997. This operator has been offering tours in the Middle East since 1965, ranging from 10- to 22-days with weekly departures. Five itineraries are exclusively Egypt and feature Cairo and Upper Egypt Nile cruises between Aswan and Luxor; others combine Egypt with Jordan and Israel, with a Kenya safari, and other Middle East destinations. Tours are locally hosted, provide extensive touring, most meals, and most of them include three- or four-day Nile cruises. New this year is the "FunFair AirFair Tour of Egypt," a one-week program for $874, including air travel from New York.

Tours Specialists, 1440 Broadway, NYC 10036; 800-223-7552; 212-840-4356. Four programs ranging from 11 to 22 days, with weekly or twice-monthly departures year-round. Two programs visit Egypt only; others combine Egypt with Greece or Kenya. The 11-day "Egypt's Best" visits Cairo, Luxor and Aswan, and is priced from $965; a Nile cruise is optional. The 15-day "Egypt in Depth" covers Cairo, Abu Simbel, a Hilton or Sheraton Nile cruise from Aswan to Luxor, plus Abydos, Denderah, and Alexandria. The operator has three- to seven-night packages for individual travelers. *TWA*.

Travcoa, 4000 MacArthur Blvd., Newport Beach, CA 92660. 714-975-1152; 800-432-8373. All tours are fully escorted and limited to 25 participants. They include a Nile cruise, deluxe accommodations, three meals including wine and mineral water daily (á la carte in Cairo), sightseeing with an Egyptologist, entertainment and cultural events. The 10-day program includes four nights in Cairo, plus a four-night Nile cruise and visits to Abu Simbel, Aswan, Kom Ombo, Edfu and Luxor, $1,495.

Travelink Tours International, 9675 W. Higgins Road, Rosemont, IL 60018; 312-692-5790; 800-323-0164. Ten year-round programs and two air-land-sea cruises from Mar. to Oct. ranging from four to 14 days. Eight programs are exclusively Egypt; one combines Egypt and Israel. *Alitalia*. All tour prices include airport transfers, hotel, internal transportation, tour escort, all sightseeing, local entrance fees and taxes, and most meals. Prices range from $269 for 3 nights to $2,698 for the 18-day air/sea package that includes round trip air and four-day Aegean cruise. *KLM* and *Epirotiki Lines*. Another program offers Egypt by private car.

Travel Plans International, 1200 Harger Road, Oak Brook, IL 60521; 312-655-5678; 800-323-6-7600. Three year-round tours of 13, 15, and 19 days have monthly departures and are escorted by resident Egyptologists

Nabil and Tarek Swelim. All feature air trip to Abu Simbel and á la carte meals. The 13-day "Kingdom of the Pharaohs" visits Luxor and Aswan, with a 5-day Sheraton steamer cruise. *KLM*.

TWA Getaway, 605 Third Avenue, NYC 10017; dial 800-GETAWAY. In its dozen Middle East programs, most including a Nile cruise, Egypt is offered exclusively in five tours ranging from 10 days to two weeks. Others combine Egypt with Israel, the Holy Land, Jordan or Greek Island cruises and range from 10 days to three weeks. Deluxe and first-class hotels are used throughout. New this year are the "top value" itineraries offering accommodations in new hotels and cruise ships at low prices: "Egyptian Discoverer," a 10-day tour that visits Cairo, Luxor, Karnak, Denderah, Abydos with a 3-day Nile cruise, from $648, including overnight train with sleeping compartment from Cairo to Luxor, air travel from Luxor to Cairo, all meals and shore excursions on the cruise plus other sightseeing.

BRITISH OPERATORS

British tour operators offer similar programs; however, some of the best have the added feature of an Egyptologist or well-known archeologist to accompany the tour. Among the most outstanding and best known is *W. F. & R. K. Swan (Hellenic) Ltd.*, 237-238 Tottenham Court Road, London WIP CAL. Their programs are two-week Nile cruises starting from either Aswan or Cairo with stops at more archeological sites than are generally offered on programs by U.S. operators. The only problem with Swan's tours is that they are usually booked solid for a year in advance.

Bales Tours Ltd., Bales House, Barrington Road, Dorking, Surrey, has a similar 21-day version, priced from £1099. The operator also offers a 15-day program which flies to Luxor, where it picks up the Nile cruise to Aswan. It costs £994. Bales offers a 15-day economy package with weekly departures from London, traveling to Upper Egypt by air. It costs £599, and drops to £570 from May to August.

V.I.P. Travel Ltd., 42 North Audley Street, London W1A 4PY, has one-week packages. The price includes air fare, hotel with breakfast and two half-day sightseeing tours. Hotels are three-star and tourist class.

Among the other operators with program to Egypt are *Alta Holidays,* 57 Victoria St., London SW1H OHG; *Fairways & Swinford Travel,* 18 St. George St., Hanover Square, London W1R OEE; *Thomas Cook,* 45 Berkeley St., London W1A 1EB; *Thomson Holidays,* Greater London House, Hampstead Rd., London NW1 7SD; *Flairworld,* 104 New Bond St., London W1; *Pitt & Scott Ltd.,* 3 Cathedral Place, London EC4M 7DT; and *Orientours,* Kent House, 87 Regent St., London W1R 8LS.

PASSPORTS AND VISAS. All visitors to Egypt must hold a valid passport or document in lieu of passport. Egyptian Consulates abroad are authorized to issue entry visas for tourists valid for 30 days and renewable for six months.

Egyptian Consulates in the *U.S.* are located at 2310 Decatur Pl. N.W., Washington, D.C. 20008; 1110 Second Avenue, New York, NY 10022; and 3001 Pacific Avenue, San Francisco, CA 94115; in *Canada* at 3754 Cote de Nieges, Montreal, and 454 Laurier Avenue N.E., Ottawa; and in the *United Kingdom* at 19 Kensington Place Gardens, London W8.

When applying for a tourist visa you will need: a passport, 1 photo with application, \$9.00 for U.S. citizens; \$11.00 for others; in cash or certified check, if applying in person; money order or certified check if applying by mail, a self-addressed envelope with required registered mail postage.

Please note that although tourist visas are valid for one month, the visa application form at the Egyptian Consulate may ask you to state specifically the length of your visit. Your visa will be issued for the exact time you state, e.g., one week, two weeks, etc. To give yourself flexibility state "one month" even if you plan to stay a shorter time.

Visitors may also obtain a visa at the port in Alexandria and the airport in Cairo on arrival. The visa is valid for one month.

A group (collective) visa can be issued on personal passports or collectively to a group of tourists organized by a travel agency, steamship or airline. Such visas are only used when members of a group remain together as a group and do not separate.

A six months' extension of a tourist visa can be obtained by applying to the Passport Department, Government Building, Room 16 (first floor), Midan Tahrir (Liberation Square), Cairo.

Transit: If you are transiting by ship or plane and not remaining in Egypt, you do not need a visa. You will be given a landing permit valid for the time your ship or plane is calling at an Egyptian port or airport.

Transit passengers with three or more hours' delay may want to try *EgyptAir's* minitours of Cairo, which can be purchased at the airport.

Prices include car, driver, guides, entrance fees, visa formalities and are for three or four people.

Tour A: Pyramids and Sphinx—three hours. Price: L.E. (Egyptian pounds) 21

Tour B: Pyramids, Sphinx and Egyptian Museum—four hours. Price: L.E. 25

Tour C: Tour A and B plus Citadel and City tour—five hours. Price: L.E. 28

Student Visas are granted at the beginning of the academic year in October and are valid for one year. Inquire at the Egyptian Embassy in Washington for details.

Business Visas and Work Permits: Foreigners coming to Egypt to take up employment or residence require special permission. Inquire for details from the Egyptian Commercial Office, 2715 Connecticut Avenue, N.W., Washington, D.C., Egyptian Economic Mission, 529 Fifth Avenue, New York, NY 10017, or the Egyptian consular offices mentioned above, under *tourist visas*.

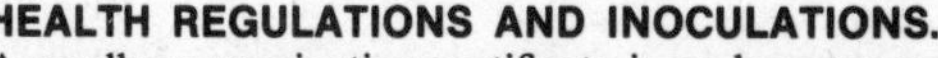

HEALTH REGULATIONS AND INOCULATIONS. A smallpox vaccination certificate is no longer necessary.

A valid vaccination certificate against cholera is required of all travelers (except children under one year of age) coming from or in transit through an infected area. A cholera vaccination certificate is valid for six months beginning six days from the date of inoculation.

Those coming from a yellow fever area must have had a yellow fever shot at least ten days prior to their arrival in Egypt.

If you are coming from or transiting an area internationally considered an infected one, you should inquire about current regulations from the nearest Egyptian Consulate in order to avoid delay upon arrival.

Egypt is a member of the World Health Organization and adheres strictly to its immunization requirements. Anyone who arrives in Egypt without proper records or inoculations will be quarantined.

Should you lose your international vaccination certificate, it can be replaced at the *Public Health Unit,* Continental-Savoy Hotel, Opera Square, Cairo.

WHAT TO TAKE. Pack with a plan so that you will not be burdened with useless items. Keep weight and luggage to what you can carry—and leave enough room for the gifts and souvenirs you are sure to buy in Egypt.

Although Egypt is thought of as having a hot climate, you will be surprised to discover how much the temperature varies within a given day or from one month to the next. Therefore, your wardrobe should be planned according to the time of the year and the extent of your itinerary.

In early summer and fall, cotton and dacron dresses and slacks for ladies and slacks and suits for men are comfortable, provided they are made of the type of fabric which breathes. In the dead of summer, only pure cotton dresses, blouses, and skirts and shirts and trousers are recommended, especially for those who suffer from the heat.

December through March, women will need light wool or knitted suits and dresses with long sleeves or jackets. Even April can be cool, especially in the evening, so be sure to include a versatile dress with jacket or polyester knits with long sleeves. Include a lightweight coat, a warm housecoat, nightgown and slippers, and a stole or a warm wrap for evenings the year-round. It is amazing how, in the middle of summer when the sun goes down after a scorching day, there is sometimes a chill in the air. You will feel it all the more because the day was so hot. Moreover, houses, old hotels and guest-houses are not centrally heated, and it is frequently cooler inside than outdoors. Hats, except as protection against the sun, are seldom worn.

Egyptians are accustomed to foreigners and to the bizarre ways some tourists dress. Nonetheless, Egypt is still a conservative country as far as women are concerned. Slacks are readily accepted; shorts and bare sunback dresses are not, except at the beach. Unless you are eager to attract attention to yourself, modesty in dress and decorum in manner are wise.

For men, most first class hotels and restaurants prefer tie and jacket during meals, although there is much less emphasis on formality of dress than in the past.

Hotel laundry service is fast and reasonable, so you do not need to burden yourself with a great deal of clothing. Also, don't forget that Egyptian cotton is among the finest in the world. You can buy shirts already made or have them tailored at reasonable cost.

As a reminder—the average rainfall in Cairo is 3.1 days in December and drops to zero on many days from July to October. In other words, it's dry.

Include in your suitcase: binoculars, a small flashlight (especially for visiting tombs and temples), a washcloth, disposable premoistened facecloths, insect repellent, collapsible hanger, face soap (kept in plastic bag), packaged soap powders, and a collapsible drinking cup. Always have an ample supply of facial tissues on hand—you will be amazed at their many uses. Only the better hotels supply facial tissues in your room.

Sunglasses are a MUST, and a shade hat for sightseeing rounds in the open and for the beach is useful. A raincoat and boots may be necessary in Alexandria during January and February. From April through October, bring a bathing suit for sunbathing or a swim in Alexandria and Cairo, year-round for a swim in Luxor and Aswan—and don't forget to pack the suntan lotion, or sun screen lotion for sensitive skin. A small canteen for water will be useful for sightseeing rounds in out-of-the-way places.

SOURCES OF INFORMATION. *Government Tourist Offices Abroad:* United States: Egyptian Government Tourist Office, 630 Fifth Ave., New York, NY 10020. Egyptian Government Tourist Office, 3001 Pacific Ave., San Francisco, CA 94115.

United Kingdom: Egyptian Ministry of Tourism, 62A Piccadilly, London W.1.

The Egyptian Government Tourist Office functions solely as an information center for tourists. For inquiries pertaining to subjects other than tourism, contact:

In U.S.A.: Press & Information Bureau, Egyptian Embassy, 2310 Decatur Place, N.W., Washington, D.C. 20008.

Egyptian Education and Cultural Program, 2200 Kalorama Road, N.W., Washington, D.C. 20008.

Egyptian Commercial Office, 2715 Connecticut Avenue, N.W., Washington, D.C.

Egyptian Economic Mission, 529 Fifth Avenue, New York, NY.

In Canada: Egyptian Consulate, 3754 Cote des Neiges, Montreal, P.Q. H3H.

In the United Kingdom: Egyptian Consulate, 19 Kensington Place Gardens. London W.8.

Arriving in Egypt

ARRIVING AT THE AIRPORT. Cairo's airport terminal, built over a decade ago, has recently been expanded to handle the increased flow of passengers. It has greatly facilitated arrival and departure procedures, but there is still a certain amount of confusion, especially if several large aircraft arrive at one time with hosts and ground personnel, tour escorts and customs officials babbling a bewildering number of languages at the many tourists from around the world visiting Egypt these days. You are likely to have the helpless feeling that you're not quite sure what to do next. But be patient, it will get done. Most of the officials at the airport speak English and you should be able to communicate with them without difficulty. If you keep smiling, you will find most Egyptian officials pleasant and helpful.

Before you leave the plane, your stewardess will hand out Egyptian entry forms to be filled in and presented to airport officials on arrival. You proceed first to health and security officials. An individual traveler who is not in a tour group and does not have a visa must change $150 or £75 into Egyptian currency before completing the formalities. Those who do not have a tourist visa can easily obtain one at the airport. The fee is L.E. 5 and must be paid in Egyptian currency. (Hence, change your money first, get visa second. There is usually a line for both.)

From the security entrance area, visitors proceed into the large main hall of the terminal to claim luggage. Customs inspection is usually perfunctory. Unless there is a large number of passengers in your group or other plane-loads ahead of you, entry formalities and customs normally do not take a long time.

In the luggage claim area there are porters to help with your bags.

Be sure to keep your customs declaration form (Form D) in a safe place. You will need this form or your buying invoices from a bank upon departure from the country in order to exchange your Egyptian currency back into dollars. If you want to re-exchange your leftover Egyptian currency, there is a bank near the airline check-in counters and before entering the security departure point.

There are a few duty free shops for basic items such as perfume, cigarettes and liquor, and a small gift shop and snack bar in the departure lounge. Major airlines, tourist agencies and the government tourist bureau have offices in the arrival building.

At no time is it more practical to be part of a tour group in Egypt than on arrival and departure. Formalities and transfers from the airport or port into town are handled for you by a local travel agent. It can save you a great deal of wear and tear.

Transportation from Cairo Airport. A taxi stand is located immediately in front of the airport building. Getting a taxi is often chaotic, as there appears to be no system for deciding who takes which taxi, but be patient; eventually it gets sorted out.

Even if you are not traveling in a group you should ask your travel agent to arrange for your transfer from the airport to the hotel. It saves the hassle of getting a taxi when you are tired after a long transatlantic flight.

Limo Misr has a fleet of Mercedes cars on radio call. Its airport office is located at the main exit door of the terminal building and a dispatcher is on duty outside the main door where cars are stationed. The price is L.E. 7 to the Nile Hilton and hotels in this area and range up to L.E. 10 to the Mena House and Jolie Ville near the Pyramids. You will always pay more for a "limousine" which generally means nothing more than a standard size, new, clean car—not an oversized one. For example, the regular taxi from the airport to the nearby Heliopolis Sheraton is L.E. 2; the limo L.E. 3. You might easily be charged L.E. 5 if the driver thinks he can get away with it.

You should make a point of collecting small change in Egyptian currency and having it handy at all times. Egypt is a poor, overpopulated country where there are always lots of people around doing things for you—whether you want them to or not. You will need to hand out tips, or *baksheesh,* as it is known in Arabic, all the time. Never give a lot. Rather, give a little, but give it often.

Taxis in the cities are metered, but we haven't found one with a meter that works in five years. Small wonder because the rate is so cheap, no one could afford to drive a taxi if they relied on it. The rate is 12 pts. (15¢) for the first kilometer (1 kilometer = .6 miles); 1 pt. for each additional 200 meters. The drive from the airport to downtown Cairo is about 12 miles and the taxi fare should cost about L.E. 2 on the meter, but, depending on your destination, expect to pay between L.E. 5 to 10, which is a reasonable amount considering the distance. Most important, settle the price *before* you get into the taxi and you can avoid an argument later.

If you arrive by day, the drive through the suburbs of Heliopolis, Abbassiya, and along the Corniche Road by the Nile is a pleasant introduction to the city. When traffic is light, the ride takes about 30 to 45 minutes, but from 8:00 A.M. to 4:00 P.M., when traffic is heaviest, allow an hour or more.

LANDING AT THE PORT. In Alexandria, entrance formalities will be completed on board ship prior to embarkation. Passengers walk directly from the ship into the port building, past the offices of the steamship companies, travel agencies and government tourist office. The entrance corridor also has a post office, telephone service and bank. A few feet away is the customs room where luggage is inspected.

After formalities are completed, visitors who are making the excursion to Cairo proceed to the main entrance of the port building to board chartered buses. Passengers on their own proceed by taxi to downtown Alexandria or the railway station. Taxi fare should be about L.E. 2. From a downtown hotel, a taxi to the railway station costs about L.E. 2; from downtown or rail station to Montazeh Sheraton, L.E. 3. A tour of Alexandria may be arranged with a travel agent at the port before proceeding to Cairo.

Several express trains run daily between Alexandria and Cairo. The three-hour trip through the Delta region is very pleasant and gives one a delightful preview of the Egyptian countryside. At the railway station in Cairo, visitors are usually met by a hotel or travel agency representative. If not, you may entrust your luggage to a station porter wearing a number. He will help you get a taxi. Just outside the Cairo station, you will see the first of many colossal statues of Ramses II, the builder of Abu Simbel and many other great monuments in Egypt.

The trip from the station to a downtown hotel takes about 15 minutes and costs L.E. 2.

CUSTOMS. *Personal effects,* including furs and jewelry, are exempt from import duties provided they are for personal use and will be taken with the visitor upon departure from Egypt. These include new and used clothing and other articles reasonably required by a tourist, such as cameras and film, radio, typewriter, 200 cigarettes or 50 cigars, one liter of alcoholic beverage, and reasonable quantities of foodstuffs, perfume and medicine intended for personal use. Portable televisions are subject to duty. You may be asked to list cameras on the customs declaration form, especially if you are carrying more than one. Valuable personal jewelry, although exempt from duty, must be declared on Form D on arrival.

Commercial Articles: Duty must be deposited on articles of commercial value and will be refunded upon departure.

Firearms: Importing firearms into Egypt is prohibited. Customs authorities may grant tourists temporary licenses for firearms and hunting equipment provided an application has been submitted to the Minister of Interior, Cairo. The application must include the tourist's full name, nationality, passport number, period of stay in Egypt, and a full description of the weapons for which licensing is required. Two photos and an official receipt specifying that covering fees have been paid should be attached to the application. Under no circumstances may you dispose of firearms thus licensed during your stay.

If the necessary documents are not obtained, the arms will be taken by customs officials on your arrival and returned to you when you leave Egypt. On arrival at Cairo airport anyone in possession of a gun must declare the serial number and kind of gun in his possession at the customs office to facilitate departure formalities.

Animals: Animals need a veterinary certificate stating that the pet is in good health, as well as a current rabies inoculation certificate. A small government tax is levied on all dogs brought into or bought in Egypt. On payment of the tax, a small identification tag is issued which should be attached to the dog's collar where it can be spotted easily.

REGISTERING UPON ARRIVAL. Foreigners must register with the proper authorities within seven days of their arrival in Egypt, the day of entry being excluded from this period. Those staying in a hotel are saved the bother as the hotel does it for them. You will be asked to surrender your passport for 24 hours in order to complete these formalities. If you are staying only a very brief time in the hotel, be sure to alert the desk clerk so that your passport will be returned in time for your departure.

If you are staying with a friend in a private home, registering with authorities will be your responsibility or that of your host. It can be done at the *Passport Office,* Al Mogammaa Building, El Tahrir Square, Cairo, or 136 El Saraya Street, Alexandria. Those who register late are fined L.E.20.

$P£ **CURRENCY REGULATIONS AND EXCHANGE RATES.** The unit of currency is the Egyptian pound (L.E.). It is divided into 100 piasters. Each piaster is subdivided into 10 milliemes. Pounds can be written in the following way: L.E. 1 or L.E. 1.000 or 100 pt. (i.e. one hundred piasters). The following banknotes and coins are in circulation:

Banknotes: 1, 5, 10, 20, 50, 100 pounds (L.E.); 5, 10, 25, 50 piasters.

Coins: Coins bear the Salah-ed-Din Eagle or the Sphinx on one side and the value and date of issue on the other.

Silver: 5, 10, 25, 50 piasters.

Brass: 5, 10, 20 piasters.

Coins of several different shapes and sizes for the same denominations are in circulation, and often their values are written in Arabic characters only. These coins can be confusing, so ask your hotel desk or bank clerk or your guide to explain the different coins to you early in your stay. Some old coins are still in circulation and are becoming collectors' items. Memorial silver pieces for 25 and 50 piasters that have been issued on special occasions are also in circulation.

Exchange Rates and Facilities: Visitors to Egypt are obliged to convert currency at authorized exchanges only, found in all major hotels and at the American Embassy on Latin America Street, Garden City. At Cairo airport, exchange facilities are available 24 hours daily; at ports, the bank opens upon arrival of ships. At the official rate, L.E. 1 = $1.23. Or, there are 82 piasters in one U.S. dollar. For the reader's convenience, a Currency Conversion Table at the official rate appears on the following page.

Visitors who arrive in Egypt without a visa and are not members of an organized tour and those whose stay will exceed 48 hours must exchange $150 or £75 upon arrival at the airport or port.

A new law requires foreigners to settle hotel bills with evidence of foreign currencies being exchanged into Egyptian pounds at authorized banks, or with major credit cards.

Despite the government's effort to curb it, a black market where $1 buys L.E. 1 is flourishing. You will be approached frequently near hotels and other tourist locations with offers to exchange dollars or traveler's checks. With the potential savings of 30% it is hard to resist, but you should realize that your actions are entirely illegal. You run the risk of breaking the currency laws, and in Egypt that can mean big trouble.

Currency Regulations: Tourists are allowed to bring in up to L.E. 20 in Egyptian currency. There is no limit to the amount of foreign currency in the form of banknotes, letters of credit and traveler's checks that tourists may bring into Egypt. All currency must be declared on Currency Declaration Form D, given to visitors upon arrival at ports and airports.

Any amount of foreign currency so declared may be exchanged for Egyptian currency at authorized banks or their representatives and should be recorded on Form D or the bank's exchange receipt. Upon departure, tourists may take out the balance of foreign currency declared on Form D or on the bank receipts after deducting the amount officially exchanged and used. Egyptian currency cannot be taken out of the country, but it can be

CURRENCY CONVERSION TABLE*

EGYPTIAN POUNDS	U.S.	PIASTERS	U.S.
L.E. 1	$ 1.23	1	$ .012
5	6.15	2	.024
10	12.30	3	.036
20	24.60	4	.048
30	36.90	5	.062
40	49.20	6	.072
50	61.50	7	.084
60	73.80	8	.096
70	86.10	9	.108
80	98.40	10	.120
90	110.70	20	.240
		30	.360
		40	.480
		50	.600
		60	.720
		70	.840
		80	.960
		90	1.08

*Rates are approximate and subject to change.

reexchanged for the currency with which it was bought. In this case you must show the buying invoice issued by the bank.

To repeat, keep track of your Form D and your bank receipts. You will need to submit them to customs authorities upon departure in order to reconvert any unused Egyptian currency. The bank windows at the airport for reexchanging money are located at the back of the main hall *before* entering the departure lounge.

According to regulations, foreigners who, on arrival, exchange $150 or £75 are, on departure, permitted to reexchange the balance into foreign currency after deducting $25 or £20 for every night spent in Egypt. Be sure to have ALL your currency buying invoices on hand to show the bank teller. One invoice is not enough unless it was for an amount large enough to prove that you spent a minimum of L.E. 20 per day for each day of your stay in Egypt. There is no point in arguing with the teller; if you do not have the proper documentation, he will stick to the letter of the law and will not budge.

Credit Cards and Personal Checks: Egyptian merchants are becoming more accustomed to the use of credit cards but their use is still limited to deluxe and first class hotels and restaurants and to stores that deal with tourists.

Because Egypt's currency exchange regulations are so stringently controlled by the government, it is difficult, if not impossible, to cash a personal check drawn on a foreign bank. The identification required will depend on the bank's policy. To be on the safe side, carry enough traveler's checks or a letter of credit, and exchange them only at banks or their authorized representatives.

TIPPING. In most restaurants and hotels, droves of men hover about you to give you service. If you have been served well, a little *baksheesh* is appreciated. 25 piasters (30 cents) will go a long way, and you will be handing out plenty before the trip ends. Carry a change purse for coins and always ask for change in small denominations when paying a bill. Many people tip as they go, assuming this alleviates the necessity for tipping at the end of their visit. On the contrary, your departure, especially from a hotel, is awaited. You will swear you never saw most of the people before—and you probably haven't. For the occasion, be ready with a handful of piasters, distribute them with largesse, and hope the right ones are in the crowd. As a rule of thumb, remember your TOTAL tip should not exceed 10% of your bill *before* the tax is added. Hotel bills have 12% service, 5% government tax and 2% city tax added to the total amount of your bill.

Staying in Egypt

TOURIST FACILITIES. *Tourist police* are stationed at major points of entry and sightseeing. They wear either a white or black uniform, depending on the time of the year, and a blue badge which says Tourist Police—in Arabic!

Tourist Police:

Head Office, 5 Street Adly	Tel: 923000
Airport, Cairo International Airport	966471
Khan el Khalil, Khan el Khalil	904827
Main Railway Station, Midan Ramses	752555
Pyramids Zone, Pyramids Road (near Mena House)	850259

Tourist guides are available for hire by the day through hotels, travel agencies and the tourist information offices for about L.E. 22 and up per day. Guides are licensed by the Ministry of Tourism and are required to pass examinations on the history and antiquities of Egypt. This, of course, does not mean that you will not be approached by those who are not so licensed and qualified. If you think you are being hustled, enlist the aid of your hotel concierge or the nearest policeman to deal with the situation.

Egypt is one of the oldest tourist countries in the world—and so are some of the guides, known here as *dragomen*. Except for the older men, the dragomen no longer wear the once characteristic turban and sweeping robes. Most dragomen, especially at sites of antiquity, are colorful, if not always accurate and inclined to embellish facts to make a good story. They are being replaced by younger, better educated guides who have trained for the job.

No matter how much a guide knows or tells you, however, there is no substitute for reading in advance. The meaning and pleasure of everything you see will be enhanced so much that you owe it to yourself. (A Suggested Reading List is included in the *Background* section, later in this book.)

For those who visit Egypt on their own and not as part of a tour group, the *Government Tourist Office* can be helpful. These are the major locations of the Tourist Information Offices:

Cairo: Head Office: 5 Adly Street	Tel: 923000
Cairo: Pyramids Office: Pyramids Road	850259
Cairo: International Airport Office	966471
Alexandria: Saad Zaghloul Square	25985
Alexandria: Port	25977
Port Said: Palestine Street	3100
Luxor: The Tourist Bazaar	2215
Aswan: The Tourist Bazaar	3297

TIME. Greenwich mean time plus 2 hours, or 7 hours earlier than Eastern Standard Time; 6 hours during summer daylight savings time.

WEIGHTS AND MEASURES. Metric system: (1 kilogram = 2.2 lbs.); one kilometer = .6 of one mile.

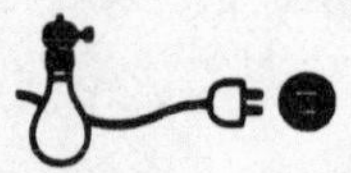

ELECTRIC CURRENT. 220 AC, 50 cycles in Cairo and Alexandria; 110 AC, 50 cycles in Heliopolis and Maadi. Wall plugs are the round two-prong European type. Adapter plugs for American products should be brought with you. American appliances need transformers. Locally made transformers are sturdy and reliable.

LANGUAGES. Arabic is the national language of Egypt. In large towns and major tourist centers you will find English-, French-, German- and Italian-speaking personnel among the staff in hotels and stores. Educated Egyptians almost always speak fluent English and French.

BUSINESS HOURS. *Banks:* Daily—8:30 A.M. to 1:30 P.M., closed Friday. Sunday—10:00 A.M. to 12:00 noon. Some banks are open in the afternoon from 4:00–8:00 P.M. Some close Saturdays and Sundays. All major hotels have exchange facilities which are usually open 24 hrs. daily.

Commercial Offices: Summer—8:00 A.M. to 2:00 P.M. Winter—9:00 A.M. to 1:00 P.M. and 4:30 or 5:00 P.M. to 7:00 P.M. Closed Thursday afternoon and Friday.

Government Offices: Daily: 8:00 A.M. to 2:00 P.M.; closed Friday and national holidays.

Stores: 9:00 A.M. to 1:00 P.M. and 4:30 to 7:30 or 8:00 P.M. summer; 10 A.M. to 5 or 6 P.M. winter.; most shops in the Khan el Khalili bazaar stay open until about 9:00 P.M. Many close on Sunday. Check with your hotel for store hours. The hours keep changing from season to season, and past efforts to standardize them have bogged down.

POST, CABLES, TELEPHONE, TELEX. Post: Airmail letters from New York to Cairo take two weeks for delivery. Surface mail from the U.S. takes three months or longer. The Central Post Office, Ataba Square, is open 24 hours daily. All other post offices are open from 8:30 A.M. to 3:00 P.M. daily except Fridays. Front desk clerks in hotels have stamps and will mail ordinary letters and postcards for hotel guests.

Letters sent to addresses within Egypt cost 6 piasters. Airmail to other countries is 23.5 piasters; postcards are 18.5 piasters.

Letters to tourists with no fixed address in Egypt may be sent in care of "Poste Restante," but the addressee must personally pick up mail from the Central Post Office. (We have never tried it.) As an alternative, Americans may recieve mail at the Consular Section of the U.S. Embassy, 5 Sharia America Latina, Cairo, and at American Express, Sharia Kasr el Nil, Cairo.

Packages require export licenses, which may be obtained from the Central Post Office. Shops catering to tourists will send packages for a fee that includes the license and packaging.

Parcels sent by surface mail from the United States take three to six months to reach the addresses in Egypt, or several weeks by air, and are subject to customs duty.

Telegraph: Cables and telegrams (in English) can be sent from hotels or the Central Telegraph Office at Midan El Tahrir, Sharia Adly and its offices, Zamalek, Dokki and Maadi. Telegrams must be written in block letters, and the sender's first and last name included. The Central Office is open 24 hours daily.

Full rate to New York is approximately 36 pt. per word. Night Letter (LT) is 26 pt. per word (LT, the address and signature count as words, with a limit of 21 words; additional words are charged at a higher rate per word). Full rate to London is about 15 pt. per word. Night Letters cannot be sent to England. Telegraph service within Egypt is also available.

Sending cables to Cairo from the U.S. has been unreliable lately; they may not get delivered. If messages are important, it is better to phone.

Telephone: Cairo, Alexandria and Port Said have dial systems. In other towns telephone service is available through local operators. Public phone booths are located at railroad stations and main squares throughout both cities, and at several large hotels, such as the Sheraton and Holiday Inn. A local call in Cairo costs 10 pt. For Cairo Information, dial 125. Shops usually will let you use the phone for a quick call.

The phone system in Cairo is overloaded and inadequate to handle the increased demand. The system functions slowly and is very erratic. If you make a habit of dialing very slowly and carefully, you may avoid getting wrong numbers. Try to keep your calls to a minimum; otherwise you can waste a great deal of valuable time. Sometimes it is faster to contact someone in person by taxi than by phone. But take heart; telephone service has actually improved over the past year, although it still has a long way to go.

Long distance service is available to the United States, Britain and most of the world. The cost to U.S. east coast is L.E. 7.78 station-to-station for three minutes, almost double for person-to-person. Collect calls cannot be made from Egypt. Arrangements for calls should be made a day in advance. The hotel switchboard operator will provide specific information, or you may dial the overseas operator: 903120. To place a call outside a hotel on your own is difficult, and we would not advise it. The most recent improvement has been the availability of direct dial to the U.S. from certain areas of the city and from certain private and business phones, where calls go through in minutes.

Telex: Facilities are available at the Nile Hilton, Sheraton and Meridien Hotels for hotel guests and at certain private offices. The Executive Service Centers at the Hilton and Meridien hotels offers telex service to outside customers at a 50 percent service charge over the cost of the telex. Meridien rates (based on Egyptian Telecommunication tariff) to the U.S. are L.E. 2.600 per minute. Europe is the same.

PHOTOGRAPHY AND EQUIPMENT. Egypt is a paradise for photographers, but remember that the sun is deceivingly bright, especially at sites of antiquity. You are allowed to take pictures inside most of the tombs and temples, and for this you will need a flash.

You are not allowed to take pictures of military zones, bridges and public works installation or at certain strategic places, such as the Aswan Dam. Your guide will show you where you can take photographs at the Dam site. You are also not to photograph police and military personnel.

To photograph in the Egyptian Antiquities and Coptic museums and inside tombs, one needs special permission, which is usually extended to professional photographers only. Inquiries should be made through the press office at the Ministry of Culture and Information as soon as you arrive in Cairo. Otherwise, you may photograph in the temples and historic sites (but not in tombs) and in museums without using a flash. To use a flash, one must pay a fee of L.E. 25.

Bring ALL film and photographic equipment with you. These items are very expensive in Egypt and selections are limited. For example, black & white film is L.E. 4; Ektachrome, L.E. 7; Agfacolor, L.E. 9; Kodak 64, L.E.15; Instamatic, L.E.13.

Slides of important sites are on sale at leading hotels and gift shops and at sites of antiquities and museums. The quality of the colors varies considerably from one vendor to another. A package of 6 slides costs about L.E. 3.

Keep your camera, lens, film and other photographic equipment in plastic bags. Especially at sites of antiquity, there is a very fine sand dust in the air which can seep into one's camera case.

Serious amateur photographers should carry a light meter, because unless you are familiar with desert conditions, you will be likely to overexpose film. If ever in doubt, use one stop under a normal setting. There is an enormous amount of reflected light, especially during midday. On black and white film, you will be happy with the results of a yellow filter. Tri-X or other film with a high ASA reading is terrific for inside temples but too fast for normal outside shots in the bright sun at antiquity sites. As for color, wonderful results can be had with low ASA film such as Kodachrome II because lighting conditions are ideal. Except that your photographs will have shadows, the best times of day for picture taking are early morning and late afternoon, when colors are deeper and sharper, and the color of the antique stone is mellow.

Black and white film can be developed in one or two days in Cairo. Ektachrome and Agfacolor take 10 days. Kodak 25 slides cannot be processed here. Unless you have some special need to have your used film developed quickly, you should plan to develop film on your return home.

The Nile Hilton photo shop is open from 10:00 A.M. to 1:00 P.M. and 5:00–8:00 P.M. Monday through Saturday; Sunday to 1:00 P.M. The shop develops film, and should you need passport-size photos, these can be made in a hurry for a reasonable price. There are also good photo shops in the Meridien and Sheraton Hotels and many in the downtown shopping area around Kasr et Nil and Sharia Sharif.

HEALTH PRECAUTIONS. *Food:* In leading hotels and restaurants, food is usually clean and well prepared; nonetheless, reasonable caution should be exercised. Eat only food which has been cooked and fruits and vegetables which can be peeled, unless you are well traveled and know what your system can adjust to quickly.

Do not be alarmed if, after a day or two, you get the local version of *turista,* which in Egypt is commonly known as gyppie tummy. A doctor or pharmacist in Cairo or Alexandria will most likely prescribe Sulphur Guanidine or Entero-Vioform, but our experience has been that nothing is better than Lomotil, obtainable from the same sources. The most important thing to remember is to take the medicine the moment you feel something coming on. Do not try to be a hero or think that if you ignore it it will go away. Call for a doctor if you run a fever. If you take medicine immediately, the upset should not be serious. As a further precaution, always cover up when you sleep. There is a marked difference between inside and outdoors in the daytime, and temperatures drop considerably at night. Sometimes a chill can bring on or aggravate stomach upsets. Also, drink plenty of liquids to avoid dehydration when you have an upset stomach. Try to avoid ice water.

Water: Drinking water in Cairo and Alexandria is safe in leading hotels. If you have an easily troubled stomach, it is a good idea to drink only bottled water, which is available in hotels and restaurants throughout Egypt.

Getting Around in Egypt

HOW TO GET AROUND. For supercharged Americans or Europeans, Egypt is often an exercise in patience. Public transportation in particular can be a trying experience. There was a time when the use of public buses could be recommended for experienced travelers, provided they did not use them during rush hours. These days one would have to be a little masochistic to get on a city bus. They are packed solid.

As a consequence visitors must rely on taxis, and although they are not expensive, there are not enough of them in Cairo to meet the demand. During the rush hour it is almost impossible to find one. If you become stranded, the wisest course is to walk to the nearest hotel. Taxis are more likely to show up there to drop off passengers. Also, do not hesitate to hail one which already has a passenger. Most Egyptians are very willing to share. *Limo Misr,* a radio-taxi service, offers 24 hr., citywide cabs at fixed rates. Phone: 831358, 835174. One may also hire one of the Limo Misr cars with driver by the day.

A taxi ride in Egypt could be one of the most eventful experiences of your life. Egypt is a flat country and most of the roads are straight as an arrow, so it takes a bit of doing to make a simple car ride memorable. Yet, the traffic jams which sometimes develop are unbelievable, and they materialize out of nowhere. With a healthy sense of humor and a great deal of patience, you will be able to come through the ordeal intact. Otherwise, you could easily be reduced to tears. Whatever happens, logic is your least useful tool. Somehow, and only Allah knows how, after a short time and a great deal of horn blowing and gesticulating, the traffic will flow again.

Taxis: In Cairo taxis are painted dark blue and white, and in Alexandria, black and orange. The fare is registered on a meter on the driver's right side. The flag fall charge is 12 pt. (15¢) for the first kilometer and 1 pt. for each additional one-fifth kilometer. Most taxis are made by the local Fiat assembly plant. The car is called a Nasr.

Taxi drivers might speak a smattering of English, but do not count on their understanding anything but Arabic. They seldom know the names of any but the major streets. Since street names seem to change with the political winds—one might find them a better barometer than the newspapers—it is possible to sympathize with taxi drivers for not being able to keep up with the trend.

If you do not know the direction to your destination, ask your hotel concierge or doorman to write the address in Arabic on a piece of paper and to instruct the taxi driver. If you want to direct him yourself, you should learn these words: *doughri* or *ala toul* (straight ahead), *yameen* (right), *shamal* (left), '*andak* (stop).

The average taxi ride in downtown is about L.E. 2. There is no extra charge for night service, but taxi drivers might want to charge more. Also, because the official taxi fares are too cheap, cab drivers have taken to the age old trick of saying the meter does not work. In this case, try to determine the price in advance or be prepared to be generous. Even on the rare occasions when a meter works, drivers expect to be paid triple the meter reading—and still the price would be a bargain.

As an aid to tourists, when one takes a taxi from a hotel or major tourist attraction a tourist policeman records the date, time, destination and taxi number. Should you have any problems with a taxi driver, he can be traced. Another benefit is that through the records of the tourist police, it is sometimes possible to recover an item left in a taxi.

Car Rentals: Renting a car in Egypt is one of the true bargains left. *Hertz* rates start at about L.E. 8.90 per day for a 4-seater Fiat plus 8 pts. per kilometer. For another L.E. 7, you can have an English-speaking driver for 10 hrs. daily. From experience, we can recommend the company and its drivers, and in Cairo traffic, the drivers are worth every piaster. Be generous with your tip at the conclusion; drivers make so little one wonders how they manage to live. Hertz has an office at the airport and at several hotels. Its headquarters is 15 Kamel el Shennawi St., Garden City (near the British Embassy). Phone: 22948. Reservations can be made through the company's offices in the U.S. *Avis, Econ-Cars* and other chains are also represented.

Horse Carriages: These are tourist attractions rather than a means of transportation. They are seen nowadays in Alexandria, Luxor and small villages, but very seldom in Cairo. The fare should be agreed upon before engaging the carriage and generally should not be more than L.E. 1 for a short ride.

TRAINS. A network of trains connects Cairo with the major towns of the Delta and with the important sites of antiquity in Upper Egypt. There are three classes on Egyptian trains. The third class should not be used by visitors. By western standards, first class travel by train is comfortable and cheap and the air conditioning systems, winter or summer, are good. Second class is adequate for short trips to Alexandria, but cars are not air-conditioned. Reservations must be made in advance at the Cairo Railway station at Midan Ramsis, Alexandria Railway station in the central part of town, or through a travel agency. Demand is greater than supply. You must book several days in advance.

On one's first trip to Egypt, first class travel by express trains is recommended, especially for the trip between Cairo and Alexandria; it is a pleasant introduction to the Egyptian countryside and way of life. First class Cairo–Alexandria passengers may reserve in advance seats in air-conditioned cars. The train ride between Cairo and Alexandria is very comfortable and enjoyable. Coffee and other beverages, sandwiches and cakes are served at a small cost. Trains are very punctual. Rail travelers to Alexandria must reconfirm their return passage. The train station in any major city is located in the center of town.

One or more sleeping cars are attached to the express night train from Cairo to Luxor and Aswan. Compartments are for two passengers.

The train to Luxor and Aswan rides on the edge of the desert all the way. Fine sand dust collects in compartments of even the newest and most modern trains. For the trip wear something comfortable and easy to wash, and pack cameras and cosmetics in plastic bags.

Wagon-Lits operates the new sleeping cars on the Cairo–Luxor/Aswan route. They are a great improvement over the old ones in comfort and cleanliness, but it's not the Ritz! The dinner and breakfast, included in the price of the sleeper, is a tourist-class airline meal. Bottled water, coffee and all other drinks are extra. These plus all the tips you need to hand out add another L.E. 5 to 10 to the journey. Tel. 985-764; 981-608.

The Railway Authority offers some group reductions, and for students it gives discounts of about 50% of the regular fare. Inquire at the Tourist Administration for specific information. In Cairo information about train service may be obtained by calling the Ramses Station, 753555.

Railway Fares (one way)

		Coach	*Sleeper (per person sharing double)*
Cairo–Alexandria	1st class	L.E. 3.80	
(travel time about 3 hours)	2nd class	2.00	
Cairo–Luxor	1st class	8.96	L.E. 33.73
(travel time about 12 hours)	2nd class	4.89	
Cairo–Aswan	1st class	11.27	33.73
(travel time about 15 hours)	2nd class	6.35	

Individual travelers (as opposed to groups) cannot get confirmation on a Luxor–Aswan ticket in Cairo, but they can get confirmation on an

Aswan–Cairo ticket. Therefore it is better to travel all the way to Aswan first, and then come back to Luxor. A compartment for one person is L.E. 55.

Train Schedule. First and second class air-conditioned trains. (Train schedules are usually consistent and reliable, but travelers should reconfirm departure times given here before finalizing an itinerary. Information: 741-319.)

LOWER EGYPT

Cairo Depart	*Alexandria* Arrive	*Alexandria* Depart	*Cairo* Arrive
8:00	10:35	7:50	10:25
8:55	11:40	9:20	12:05
9:30	12:15	14:15	16:50
11:20	2:00	18:25	21:05
12:20	15:00	19:25	22:15
14:00	16:35		
15:50	18:20		
17:50	20:20		
19:00	21:40		
20:00	22:30		

UPPER EGYPT

Cairo Depart	*Luxor* Arrive	*Aswan* Arrive
7:30	18:14	23:20
19:00	6:00	10:00
19:35	7:30	

Aswan Depart	*Luxor* Arrive	*Cairo* Arrive
14:35	19:30	06:40
18:10	22:00	09:45

TO SUDAN

Depart	*Arrive*
Cairo 20:00 Sun/Wed train	Aswan High Dam 13:00 Mon/Thu
Aswan High Dam 16:00 Mon/Thu boat	Wadi Halfa 08:00 Wed/Sat
Wadi Halfa 14:00 Wed/Sat train	Khartoum 17:00 Thu/Sat

DISTANCE BETWEEN CAIRO AND OTHER CITIES

From Cairo to:	*Kms. (Miles) by road*	*Kms. by rail*
El Alamein	304 (182)	326
Alexandria (Via the Delta Highway)	225 (135)	208
Alexandria (Via the desert road)	221 (132)	
Assiut	380 (228)	375
Aswan	890 (534)	879
Baliana (Abydos)	556 (304)	518
Delta Barrages	25 (15)	
Damietta	191 (114)	205
Edfu	785 (470)	776
Ein Sukhna	189 (113)	
Esna	732 (429)	724
Fayyum	103 (62)	130
Helwan	32 (19)	
Ismailia (Via Bilbeis)	140 (84)	159
Kharga Oasis	600 (359)	737
Kom Ombo	835 (560)	834
Luxor	676 (406)	671
Maadi	14 (8)	
Mallawi (Tell-al-Amarna)	(173)	
Mersa Matruh	490 (294)	510
Minia	243 (146)	247
Port Said	220 (132)	237
Rosetta	263 (157)	269
Sallum	714 (428)	759

AIR TRAVEL. *EgyptAir* operates between the major cities, with regular daily flights from Cairo to Luxor/ Aswan and Abu Simbel, and flights several times weekly to Hurghada and New Valley. Air travel is recommended for anyone whose time is limited. Fares are reasonable. The carrier can also arrange combined air-and-hotel tickets to Luxor, Aswan and a day tour to Abu Simbel. In fact, the tour to Abu Simbel by air offered by all travel agencies in Egypt, the U.S., Europe, etc. is the same one and is a monopoly of the airlines.

EgyptAir Offices: Cairo: Midan Opera, 9 Sharia Talaat Harb; Nile Hilton Hotel, 6 Sharia Adly.

Alexandria: Midan Saad Zaghloul.

Port Said: Sharia al Gumhruia.

Airfares (subject to change)	*Round Trip*
Cairo to	*L.E.*
Abu Simbel	134.70
Alexandria	27.60
Assuit	61.80
Aswan	95.10
Hurgada	73.60
Luxor	67.70
New Valley	73.60
Luxor to	
Abu Simbel	67.70
Hurgada	28.00
New Valley	56.70
Aswan to	
Abu Simbel	40.40

Flights between Cairo and Upper Egypt

(Schedules are subject to change. Be sure to check locally and *always reconfirm your reservations*.)

05:00	Cairo–Aswan–Abu Simbel	08:50	Aswan–Luxor–Cairo
06:30	Cairo–Luxor–Aswan	15:20	Aswan–Luxor–Cairo
13:00	Cairo–Luxor–Aswan	16:00	Abu Simbel–Cairo

The number of flights in and out of Cairo is not adequate for the demand. This is as true on international flights as it is on domestic ones so be sure to reconfirm your reservations to onward destinations within Egypt or to other countries as soon as you arrive in Cairo. Flights to and from Upper Egypt are constantly overbooked, but they do work on a first-come, first-served basis, so it pays to get to the airport early. If you foresee having to purchase a ticket in Cairo, do it as soon as possible. International tickets must be purchased in Egyptian currency at the official rate of exchange. You may use an American Express credit card.

If you cannot get a reservation and you must travel, you can go to the airport and stand by. There are frequently no-show seats available at the last minute.

Check arrival and departure times before leaving for the airport, as flights may be delayed. This is especially true when you are meeting incoming flights.

Air Sinai provides regular service to Sharm el Sheikh, St. Catherine's Monastery, Al-Areesh in the Sinai Peninsula, Hurgada on the Red Sea, and Tel Aviv. Its main office is located in the new wing of the Nile Hilton Hotel. Phone: 760948. Round trip to Cairo/St. Catherine's is L.E. 102. In the U.S., Canada and U.K., information is available from *Egypt/Air*.

Airport Information Office: 873957; Arrival and Departure Times: 749786; 749370.

You should be at the airport a minimum of one or two hours before flight time. The trip from town to the airport in Cairo is about 30 minutes to an hour depending on traffic, which is heaviest from 8:00 A.M. to 2:00 P.M.

NILE STEAMERS. A voyage up the Nile by steamer is one of the most delightful trips in Egypt, and now with 56 boats—a six-fold increase within the past decade—supply has matched demand. Most of the new vessels are in the four- and five-star categories and offer three- to five-night cruises between Luxor and Aswan, plus Abydos and Denderah; or seven- and 11-night excursions that travel to Middle Egypt or sail between Cairo and Luxor/Aswan.

Prices range from $70 to $120 per person per day for the four-star; $150 to $200 per person per day for the five-star, during the high season months of October through April; and $50 to $70 for four-star and $100 to $120 for five-star from May to September. Generally, prices include all meals and sightseeing in the company of a trained guide or Egyptologist.

A cruise on the Nile differs from ocean cruising in several ways. Nile steamers, compared to ocean-going cruise ships, are small and cozy like a yacht and have informal and comfortable atmospheres. Some ships accommodate as few as 20 passengers, while the largest take up to 152 people.

Staterooms, slightly smaller than those of standard cruise ships, are comparable in size to cabins on ships that sail the Greek islands. They are well-appointed and comfortable. Most are fitted with twin lower beds; some have wall pull-down bunks for a third person, dressing table or night-stand, closet, and private bath with shower. Ships with suites often have full bath with tub. Four- and five-star ships are fully air conditioned.

Small ship size limits the recreational and entertainment facilities, but these are not important considerations on a Nile cruise where the attractions are the antiquities and the scenic countryside. On the other hand, ships holding 80 or more passengers have lounges for reading and relaxing, bar, sundeck, swimming pool, pleasant dining room with full table service and evening entertainment. Laundry services and hair salon are also available.

Nile cruises begin in one of three places—Cairo, Luxor, or Aswan. More and more companies are offering long cruises throughout the year because they are increasingly popular and because the new ships are air conditioned. A likely trend is cruises from Cairo to mid-points along the Nile, such as Minya, rather than from Cairo all the way to Luxor.

Passengers who begin their cruise in Upper Egypt usually travel to Luxor or Aswan by plane or train. In Luxor, a modern town next to the ancient site of Thebes, the ships dock on the east bank of the river near the Etap and Winter Palace hotels, within walking distance of Luxor Temple and the Luxor Museum, and a short carriage ride from Karnak Temple, the most colossal ancient monument in the world.

Sightseeing includes a full day on the West Bank of the Nile, in the Valley of the Kings, where the tombs of Tutankhamun and other pharoahs were found; the Valley of the Queens; the Tombs of the Nobles, which contain some of the most important art of ancient Egypt; and other great temples and monuments.

From Luxor, many cruises sail downstream (north) to visit the Temples of Denderah; others take in only the sites between Luxor and Aswan. Abydos is one of the oldest sites of worship in the world and, because of its art, is considered the most important temple in Egypt. Tours beyond Abydos are available on longer cruises which stop at Tel al Amarna, the capital of Pharoah Akhenaton and his beautiful wife, Nefertiti; at Minya, the largest town of central Egypt; and at Beni Hassan, site of 12th century tombs—unusual tomb drawings show ancient Egyptians practicing judo and playing ball games that appear to be similar to those we play today.

From Luxor, ships also sail upstream (south) to Aswan, and stop for sightseeing at Esna, Edfu and Kom Ombo—all sites of temples dating from the Ptolemic and Greek periods. If the cruise begins in Aswan, the same itinerary is followed in reverse order, sailing downstream to Luxor.

Aswan was the capital of Nubia and an important trading place in ancient times. Today, it is primarily a winter resort and the administrative center for the High Dam and the surrounding region. Aswan is dotted with antiquities, most importantly the Temple of Philae, which is located on an island in the middle of the river.

Egypt without the Nile River seems inconceivable. One's first view of the river snaking its way through the desert is a dramatic illustration of its importance throughout Egypt's history. Beyond the ribbon of green—the land irrigated by the Nile—the desert begins and stretches endlessly into the horizon on both sides.

The Nile flows so gently that ships glide almost imperceptably. The banks of the river are never more than a short distance away, and passengers can enjoy a close view of rural life in Upper Egypt. Life on the land bridges centuries. Cruise passengers see scenes along the river banks and in the green fields that replicate ancient drawings on the walls of the temples and tombs. The sense of endless time and tranquility is almost overwhelming, particularly in contrast to the roar and clamor of Cairo.

The following is a listing of companies and their operating Nile steamers:

Abercombie & Kent, 1000 Oak Brook Rd., Oak Brook, IL. 60521. Operates *Abu Simbel,* 10 cabins and *Aswan,* 10 cabins.

Club Med, 40 W. 57th St., NYC 10019. Operates *Seti First,* 53 cabins and *The Prince du Nil,* 25 cabins.

Eastmar Travel, 13 Kasr el Nil St., Cairo Tel. 753147. Operates *Memphis,* 21 cabins; *Nefertari,* 42 cabins; *Neptune,* 58 cabins; and *Nile Star,* 40 cabins.

Cairo Hotel & Nile Cruise Co., 23 bis, Ismail Mohamed St., Zamalek, Tel. 651511. Operates *El Nesr,* 45 cabins and *Horus,* 45 cabins.

Gayed Company for Floating Hotels, 17 Mahmoud Bassioony St., Cairo Tel. 743466. Operates *El Salam,* 40 cabins.

Nile Hilton, Cornish St., Cairo Tel. 740880. Operates *Isis,* 48 cabins and *Osiris,* 48 cabins.

Jolly Travel, 8 Talaat Harb St., Cairo Tel. 759789. Operates *Alexander the Great.*

Middle East Floating Hotels Co., 14-B, Dr. Taha Hussein St. Zamalek, Tel. 800643. Operates *Arabia,* 41 cabins.

President/Concorde Hotels Co., 13 Maraashly St., Zamalek, Tel. 800517. Operates *Nile Concorde,* 20 cabins; *Nile Emperor,* 80 cabins; *Nile President,* 64 cabins; and *Nile Princess,* 31 cabins.

Pyramids Tours, 1 Talaat Harb Sq., Cairo Tel. 758655. *El Karnak,* 22 cabins; *Pyramids,* 22 cabins; *Queen Cleopatra,* 18 cabins; *Queen Nefertiti,* 22 cabins; *Ramses,* 18 cabins; and *Tutankhamon,* 18 cabins.

Sheraton Hotels, 48-b, Guiza St., Orman Bldg., Cairo Tel. 987200. Operates *Ani,* 76 cabins; *Aton,* 76 cabins; *Hotep,* 76 cabins; and *Tut,* 76 cabins.

Sphinx Tours, 2 Behler St., Cairo Tel. 754088. Operates *Nile Queen; Nile Sphinx,* 50 cabins; *Reve Vacance,* 20 cabins; and *Sphinx,* 25 cabins.

Sunnyland/Gabry Tours, 1 Talaat Harb Sq., Cairo Tel. 746268. Operates *Nile Explorer,* 20 cabins.

Trans Egypt Travel, 21 Aziz Abbas St., Zamalek. Tel. 744313. Operates *Neptune,* 58 cabins and *Triton,* 47 cabins.

Cairo Marriott Hotel, Sharia el Gezira, Zamalek. Operates *Flower of the Nile.*

Oberoi Hotel is scheduled to launch two ships this year.

VISITING UPPER EGYPT. For the full excursion to Upper Egypt, a prearranged trip may be bought in Cairo. The package includes round trip train, plane and/or steamer fare, food, hotel accommodation and guides. If you are a seasoned traveler, you may prefer to go on your own and pay each item separately as your needs require. The latter plan is more costly, but it enables you to remain in places of your choosing and to travel at your own pace. We can not stress strongly enough, however, that for most people on a first trip to Egypt, a prearranged tour organized through a *reliable travel agent* is practical and more satisfactory.

The latest touring development for visiting Upper Egypt is the all motorcoach tour which is being sold locally and in the European market. It provides for travel of about 200 miles per day from Cairo to Minya, Assuit, Luxor and Aswan, with stops along the way at sites of antiquity which are otherwise inaccessible. The 40-passenger luxury coaches are air-conditioned and comfortable.

In planning your itinerary you should investigate the new alternatives that offer the possibility of more extensive and less costly modes of travel if you tend to travel on your own.

For the onward journey from Egypt to Sudan, boat passage to Sudan via Lake Nasser must be booked in Cairo and paid for in Egyptian pounds exchanged at the official rate. It is also possible to drive from Cairo to Aswan by car, ship the car to Wadi Halfa, and then either drive or send the car by train to Khartoum. All visas and permits must be obtained before leaving Cairo.

From Aswan, one can also go to Wadi Halfa by third-class steamer. Such a trip would not be recommended for any but the hardiest and most rugged traveler. You must bring your own food as meals are not included.

Intra-City Bus Service. Travel between Cairo and Alexandria and other major cities by deluxe, air-conditioned motorcoach is comfortable and cheap. Tickets may be purchased at a small office at Midan el Tahrir, from where buses leave. Round trip to Alexandria from Cairo in one of these air-conditioned buses is L.E. 7.

Misr Travel and other well-established travel agencies have new air-conditioned luxury motorcoaches which are available for local as well as long distance travel, including excursions to Upper Egypt and can be chartered for groups.

A new service from Cairo to St. Catherine's Monastery is available from *Shark el Delta Line,* Kolai Terminal on Fri., Sun., and Tues. at 9 A.M. and returning the following days at 6 A.M. Fare is L.E. 6, one-way.

For motorcoach service to Upper Egypt see later in this book.

Intra-City Taxi Service. Peugeot taxis, leaving from in front of the Ramses Railroad Station and Tahrir Square, are an economical way to travel around Egypt. The taxis are stationwagons and usually hold up to seven passengers, plus the driver. One way to Alexandria per person is L.E. 5; to Ismailia, L.E. 4; to Suez, L.E. 4; to Port Said, L.E. 5.

MOTORING IN EGYPT. The *Automobile Club of Egypt,* 10 Sharia, Kasr el Nil, can be helpful in supplying information on driving to the different regions of the country. Incidentally, the club has one of the best restaurants in town. It is for members only, but if you write ahead to the secretary, you will be welcomed as a visitor. Phone: 743355.

The *Touring Club of Egypt,* 8 Sharia, Kasr el Nil, is next door to the Automobile Club.

A tourist entering Egypt with a car registered in a foreign country is exempt from local customs duties for a period of 90 days under the following regulations:

a. the owner must hold a triptych or *carnet de passage en douane* from a recognized automobile club (i.e., AAA); otherwise he must pay a deposit which will be refunded upon departure;
b. the owner must have an international driving license valid for the 90 day period;
c. the car must have an international motor vehicle license;
d. customs officials must verify that the owner has no fixed residence in Egypt.

At the customs house the car owner is given a label for a 90-day tax exemption to post on the car's front window. If the stamp is not displayed, you may be stopped by police. If the car remains in Egypt after 90 days, the owner must pay L.E. 6 per year from the date of expiration and will be subject to road tax.

There is an excellent project circulating in the government bureaucracy to expand tourist facilities, roads, gasoline and service centers, motels, etc., throughout the country to make touring by car and camper readily available. The plan will take a decade to implement in its entirety but parts of it are already underway—spurred on by an increasing demand from Europeans for this type of tourism.

Importing Other Vehicles: Under a triptych, motor bicycles, scooters, motorcycles, small aircraft, minibuses with up to nine seats, boats, luggage and caravan trailers, commercial passenger buses and taxis may be imported temporarily.

Vehicles to be used for demonstration or exhibition purposes may be imported for 90 days against a deposit on the customs duty and taxes.

Nonmotorized bicycles may be temporarily imported duty free as personal effects without customs documents.

Length of Stay: Vehicles temporarily imported by tourists may remain in Egypt for up to three months, or for as long as the triptych is valid, whichever is the shorter period. During the 90 day period there is no limit on the number of times one may enter Egypt, provided your visa is valid.

Tourists who want to keep a vehicle in Egypt for a longer period may apply to the Automobile Club of Egypt, which will forward the request for extension to the proper authorities, provided the visa is extended. You should contact the Automobile Club at least one month before the document is due to expire.

If you are planning an extended visit in Egypt, a car will add tremendously to the pleasure of your visit.

Private cars for use during a long-term stay may also be imported into Egypt duty free on condition that they are exported from the country when the owner leaves. Otherwise he must pay steep customs duties. If, however, one intends to pay the duties and sell the car in Egypt, check first with the American Embassy on importation regulations. They change rather frequently. At present cars manufactured by Ford and Willis-Jeep must be re-exported, as well as cars with right-hand drive, diesel engines, and four-wheel drive.

Insurance: By law all car owners must carry third party personal liability insurance. Good insurance coverage is advisable and is available at reasonable prices. Rates vary according to the engine size, horsepower and value of the car.

License: If you remain in Egypt longer than 90 days, an Egyptian driver's license is necessary and is issued upon presentation of three photos, certificate of medical examination, U.S. or international driver's license, and payment of a small fee.

Those who do not have a valid international driver's license will be required to take a driving test. A driver's license must be obtained before the license plate can be issued. Bring a valid U.S. or international driver's license to save yourself a great deal of time and endless trouble.

Rule of the Road: Traffic moves to the right. Do not plan to drive at night except in major cities.

Garage and Repairs: New cars will minimize the problem of repair and spare parts. Small cars are more practical to operate.

Spare parts are not readily available because of import restrictions, and are very expensive when they are. Those planning a long stay or a great deal of driving should bring spare parts for their cars, especially those most subject to wear, such as gaskets, fan belts, spark plugs (ignition points), fuel lines, pumps and filters, head and tail lights. Egypt has a local tire industry and Fiat assembly plant.

General Motors, Mercedes, Fiat, Opel, Peugeot, Volkswagen, Toyota and Mazda, etc., maintain agencies with their own repair shops. Most garages have good mechanics, and body work and paint jobs are inexpensive by U.S. standards.

Gasoline and Service Stations: In Cairo and Alexandria, petrol and service stations are plentiful, but outside of main towns they are scarce. Before starting on a long trip, be sure to get all the pertinent information you might need about road conditions and location of petrol stations from the Automobile Club or Tourist Administration.

Gasoline is called benzene and is sold by the liter. The medium grade costs 11 piasters; super costs 13 piasters (approximately 65¢ per U.S. gallon). Because of the low octane ratings of gasoline in Egypt, the super grade (similar to our regular) should be used. Imported cars need to have their engines adjusted to the local octane rating. Car engines and mechanisms function well, but should be cleaned frequently because of the ever present sand dust in the air and impurities in the gasoline.

Security Regulations: Travel in the area near the Libyan border is restricted by the government for military reasons. Permits for travel in other security areas can be obtained from the Travel Permits Department of the Ministry of Interior, corner of Sharia Sheikh Rihan and Sharia Nubar (two blocks east of the American University).

Travel to Israel from Egypt by land is possible by private car as well as by motorcoach. Allow two to three hours for customs formalities at the border. Excursions can be purchased through local travel agencies in Cairo or from agents in the U.S. (See page 9.)

Inquire about regulations from the Automobile Club before starting out on a trip, and always carry your passport with you.

A chart of distances from Cairo to major towns throughout Egypt appears earlier in this section. A brief description of major roads follows.

Tourist Roads of Lower Egypt: Alexandria–Cairo (220 kms.–136 miles), paved desert road. 109 kms. (68 miles) along the paved desert road another road leads to Wadi Natrun, the famous valley where several ancient Coptic monasteries are located. Just before reaching Cairo the road passes the Pyramids of Giza.

Alexandria–Cairo (221 kms.–138 miles), a direct road which links Cairo to Alexandria, passes through the Delta region by way of its main towns and through nearly all the *Muhafezat* (governorates) of Lower Egypt.

Port Said–Ismailia–Cairo (240 kms.–150 miles), the best four-lane divided highway in Egypt, leaves from Cairo alongside the airport. The canal road between Ismailia and Cairo parallels the desert road to the north and passes through El Qassasin, El Tell El Kebir and Bilbeis.

Port Said–Ismailia–Suez (170 kms.–106 miles) runs parallel to the Suez Canal.

Suez–Cairo (134 kms.–84 miles), a desert road linking the Red Sea to the Nile, follows the historic pilgrimage and trade route.

Cairo–Fayum (70 kms.–44 miles) is a good two-lane highway and an interesting and pleasant drive through the countryside.

Coastal road Alexandria–Sallum (508 kms.–317 miles) forms part of the eastern international road in North Africa from Alexandria to Morocco (5,250 kms.–3,262 miles). It is an asphalt road along a fertile region near the Mediterranean coast and passes through El Alamein and Mersa Matruh.

Western desert road Mersa Matruh–Siwa Oasis (302 kms.–188 miles) goes through Mersa El Assatil, and was used by Alexander the Great when he visited the Amun Temple at the Siwa Oasis. The first 60 and the last 24 miles are paved; the middle (104 miles) is desert road.

Tourist Roads of Upper Egypt: Cairo–Aswan (approximately 900 kms.–560 miles) is paved throughout and forms part of the international route from Cairo to Cape Town. It passes a large number of antiquity sites and links Egypt to Sudan along the Nile via Shellal to Wadi Halfa, covering a distance of 480 kms. (300 miles). The drive from Abydos to Luxor takes under three hours and from Luxor to Aswan about four hours.

Assiut–El Dakhla and El Kharga Oasis: the road from Assiut to El Kharga (137 miles) and from El Kharga to El Dakhla (118 miles) is paved.

The oases are scattered with historical monuments of the 18th Egyptian Dynasty and Roman and Coptic monuments.

The Red Sea resort of Hurghada may be reached from Cairo through El Saff, across the desert to Zafarana, and south to Ras Ghareb and Hurghada; from Suez, straight south through Ein Sukhna to Hurghada; from Qena, to Safaga to Hurghada; from Edfu, to Mersa Alam and Hurghada. In Sinai, there are roads to St. Catherine's Monastery, Sharm el Sheikh and Ras Muhammad; El Arish and Rufa.

Leaving Egypt

EXPORTING GIFTS. On departure, visitors may take out gifts and souvenirs made in Egypt provided the goods were bought with the currency properly exchanged on Form D. Gifts and souvenirs up to L.E. 35 may also be sent from Egypt through a local travel agent and through reliable shops that sell handicrafts, provided they are not for commercial use.

Antiques cannot be exported. The government has become very strict about their sale or purchase.

CUSTOMS GOING HOME. If you propose to take on your holiday any *foreign-made* articles, such as cameras, binoculars, expensive time-pieces, and the like, register them at the airport or local custom houses in major cities before departure. The registration is valid once and for all. Otherwise, on returning home, you may be charged duty.

AMERICANS who are out of the United States at least 48 hours and have claimed no exemption during the previous 30 days are entitled to bring in duty-free up to $400 worth of articles for bona fide gifts or for their own personal use. The value of each item is determined by the price actually paid (so save your receipts). Every member of a family is entitled to this same exemption, regardless of age, and the allowance can be pooled. Handicrafts from the developing world, which includes Egypt, are exempt from customs duty.

Do not bring home foreign meats, fruits, plants, soil or other agricultural items when you return to the U.S. To do so will delay you at the port of entry. It is illegal to bring in foreign agricultural items without permission because they can spread destructive plant or animal pests and diseases. For more information, write to: Quarantines, U.S. Department of Agriculture, Federal Building, Hyattsville, MD. 20782.

Not more than 100 cigars may be imported duty-free per person, nor more than a quart of wine or liquor (none at all if your passport indicates you are from a "dry" state, or if you are under 21 years of age).

Antiques are defined, for customs purposes, as articles manufactured over 100 years ago and are admitted duty-free. If there's any question of age, you may be asked to supply proof.

Small gifts may be mailed to friends, but not more than one package to any one address and none to your own home. Notation on the package should be "Gift, value less than $25." Tobacco, liquor and perfume are not permitted to be mailed.

To facilitate the actual customs examination, it's convenient to pack all your purchases in one suitcase.

Purchases intended for your duty-free quota must accompany your personal baggage.

CANADA. Residents of Canada may claim an exemption of $150 a year plus an allowance of 40 ounces of liquor, 50 cigars, 200 cigarettes and two lbs. of tobacco. Personal gifts should be mailed as "Unsolicited Gift—Value under $15." For details, ask for the Canada Customs Brochure "I Declare."

GREAT BRITAIN. There is now a two-tier allowance for duty-free goods brought into the U.K., due to Britain's Common Market membership. The Customs and Excise Board warn that it is not advisable to mix the two allowances.

If you return from an EEC country (Belgium, Denmark, France, W. Germany, Holland, Italy, Luxembourg) and goods were bought in one of those countries, duty-free allowances are:

300 cigarettes (or 150 cigarillos, or 75 cigars, or 400 gr. tobacco); 1.5 liters of strong spirits (or 3 liters of other spirits or fortified wines) plus three liters of still table wine; 75 gr. perfume and .375 liter toilet water; gifts to a value of £50.

If you return from a country outside the EEC *or if the goods were bought in a duty-free shop on ship, plane or airport,* the allowances are less:

200 cigarettes (or 100 cigarillos, or 50 cigars or 250 gr. tobacco); 1 liter of strong spirits (or 2 liters of other spirits or fortified wines) plus 2 liters of still table wine; 50 gr. perfume and .26 liter toilet water; gifts to a value of £10.

BY WAY OF BACKGROUND

Re, the Sun-God

BY WAY OF BACKGROUND

Egypt is *Masr* in Arabic. It occupies the northeastern corner of Africa and is connected to Asia by the Sinai peninsula.

Egypt is bordered by Libya on the west, Sudan on the south, Saudi Arabia on the southeast, Israel on the east and the Mediterranean Sea on the north. Specifically its coordinates are 24° and 36° east Greenwich; 22° and 31° north.

Egypt's territory covers 386,000 square miles, but less than four percent is inhabited, cultivated land; the rest is desert. The Nile, like an elongated oasis, cuts Egypt from south to north for a distance of almost 900 miles from Wadi Halfa on the Sudan border to Cairo. There the river divides into two main branches, each 150 miles long. The Rosetta branch on the west and the Damietta on the east form the great Delta, the graphic name given it by the Greeks because it has the shape of a triangle.

Cairo stands at the apex of the Delta—a significant position for the capital throughout its long history. The area north of Cairo to the Mediterranean is known as Lower Egypt. The Nile Valley stretching south from Cairo to Sudan is referred to as Upper

Egypt. In antiquity the area south of the first cataract near Aswan to the northern territory of the Sudan was known as Nubia.

Physical Features

Egypt is divided into three major regions:

I. The Nile Valley

In Upper Egypt south of Aswan, the Nile Valley is desert. Limestone cliffs on both sides of the valley reach 3,000 feet above sea level in the east and 2,400 feet in the west. The area is an extension of the Sahara and is the most arid and least fertile part of the country. From Aswan north to Cairo the Nile runs through a valley that varies in width from one to six miles and reaches its widest span of nine miles at Kom Ombo. On both sides of the valley, rock hills rise to 900 feet above sea level.

In Lower Egypt beginning nineteen miles north of Cairo, the Nile forks into two branches between which lies the Delta, said to be the most fertile land in the world. East of the Delta, the Suez Canal zone extends north from the Gulf of Suez at the head of the Red Sea to Port Said on the Mediterranean Sea. The Suez Canal links the Red Sea at Suez with the Mediterranean at Port Said. Ismailia, also in the Canal zone, is connected by a canal to Cairo.

The heavy fighting in the 1967 war all but destroyed these three towns. At the start of the war the people living here fled to Cairo and Alexandria—almost doubling those cities' population overnight. Following the reopening of the Suez Canal in June 1975, the former inhabitants returned to their towns as reconstruction and new housing were completed. Because of the country's enormous population growth in the last decade, the canal cities already are more populated than before the war.

II. The Eastern Desert (Arabian Desert)

From the Nile Valley stretching to Sinai and the Red Sea are desert and limestone mountains. The southern portion of the Eastern Desert along the west coast of the Red Sea is a sterile area characterized by a range of barren mountains 6,000 feet high. It is rich in minerals and stone. The north portion, Sinai, is the gateway to Egypt from the east. It is triangular in shape and stretches for 240 miles from north to south and 120 miles from east to west. The northern and southern parts have water from rainfall but in the central part water is scarce.

III. The Western Desert (Libyan Desert)

The area extending west of the Nile Valley to the Libyan border and from the Mediterranean coast in the north to the Sudan in the south represents two-thirds of the total area of Egypt. Its average altitude is 1,500 feet.

This land mass is divided into frontier districts centered about its fertile oases. In the northern portion lies the Northern Plateau, the region of the Great Depressions, Siwa Oasis, Qattara Depression, Wadi el Natroun and the Baharia Oasis. In the south are Farafra, Dakhla and Kharga Oases. Fayum, one of the largest oases, is linked to the Nile by a 90-mile irrigation arm and is considered part of the Nile Valley.

The Western Desert is scheduled to have some of the most far-reaching and imaginative development of any area of the world. Already the area is being widely prospected for oil, and plans call for massive reclamation of the land from the desert by tapping underground water reserves. To date, $60 million have gone into research and much more will need to be spent before the effort can be meaningful. An 18-month study of the Western Desert by an American team, released in autumn 1977, shows an underground lake containing an estimated 2.5 billion acre-feet of water and extending 500 miles. It, of course, needs to be developed so that new lands can be brought under cultivation, but at least Egypt's future has been brightened by the discovery.

The physical isolation of Egypt, hemmed in as it is by desert and sea, had a profound influence on the course of its history. By being set apart from the other civilizations of the ancient world that rose in the Mesopotamian Valley and advanced to the Eastern Mediterranean, Egypt developed a distinctive culture, which persists to this day. Today, for example, despite modern influences and rapid communications, Egyptian art is distinctive and springs from its native traditions in a way unlike any other Middle Eastern culture.

Population

Approximately 45 million people make up Egypt's population, of which 95 percent live along the fertile banks of the Nile. The density, which averages almost 5,000 people per square mile in the cultivated areas, is one of the highest in the world and dramatically illustrates the meaning of the Nile to Egypt.

Today, the population in Cairo is estimated to be 10 million; Alexandria's is about four million. These numbers were greatly swollen by the people who fled from the Suez area during the 1967 war. Other large cities are Minya, Assiut, Sohag, Nag Hammadi, Qena and Aswan in Upper Egypt; Tanta, Zagazig, Damanhour and Mansourah in the Delta.

The people are grouped into four main categories:

The *fellahin,* who are peasant-farmers living in the villages along the Nile and in the Delta. They are the bulk and national strength of the country. A shift of population from the countryside to the cities in the past three decades has created an estimated proportion of 65 percent rural and 35 percent urban.

The Copts, who might be considered the most direct descendants of the ancient Egyptians. They are both urban and rural.

The Bedouins, who are nomadic Arabs and probably account for less than two percent.

The European, Turkish and Levantine minorities who are no longer as important in the life of Egypt as they were in the hundred years before the 1952 revolution, when they dominated the commerce and politics of the country.

Religion

Islam is the major religion in Egypt. Approximately 85 percent of the population are Sunni (orthodox) Moslems.

Christians make up an estimated 14 percent. Most belong to the Coptic Church, the Monophysitic branch of Christianity, which split from the general church at the Council of Chalcedon in A.D. 451. Others belong to various sects of European and Eastern churches. The number of Jews is very small.

Language

Arabic is the official language of the country. Most educated Egyptians speak at least one or two other languages, usually English and French.

Government

Egypt is a republic with a unicameral legislature, the National Assembly, elected by universal suffrage every six years. The 360-member National Assembly selects a president whose nomination is submitted to public referendum. The president appoints the Council of Ministers.

Administration

Egypt is divided into 25 governorates, five of which are towns—Cairo, Alexandria, Port Said, Suez, Ismailia. The eight of the Delta are Behira, Damietta, Kafr el Sheikh, Garbia, Dakhlia, Sharkia, Tahrir and Qalyubia. Another eight are in Upper Egypt—Fayoum, Beni Suef, Giza, Minya, Assiut, Sohag, Qena, Aswan; and four are frontier areas, Red Sea, New Valley, Matruh and Sinai.

The governorate ordinarily is made up of a city and its suburbs or part of a territory composed of a chief town and main district. Each governorate (*muhafezate*) has a governor (*muhafez*) and a governor's council.

Economy

From ancient times Egypt's economy was based on the Nile. Controlling its flow and benefiting from its annual flood was the major preoccupation of the people. The task was accomplished by diverting the waters and the fertile soil carried by the river into basins from which the farmlands were irrigated.

As the engineers became more sophisticated, they learned to store the Nile waters in great reservoirs in the Sudan and at Aswan in Upper Egypt, and they built a series of dams and barrages along the river to divert water throughout the year into the network of irrigation canals. In order to bring more and more land under cultivation, the level of the dams was raised. This system served about 80 percent of the cultivated area and made possible two or three crops a year. Finally, with the building of the new High Dam at Aswan, the Nile waters were brought under year-round control.

Egypt's main crop is long-staple cotton, some of the world's finest. The bulk is raised in Lower Egypt, and from the time it was introduced into Egypt by Mohammed Ali early in the 19th century, it traditionally accounted for 80 percent of all exports. Following efforts at diversification and industrialization, this one-crop dependency is changing. Until recently Egypt grew enough wheat to meet its domestic requirements, as well as a wide variety of fruits and vegetables. Unlike most of the Middle East where a basic staple is rice, Egypt's is *fool*, the fava bean.

Egypt's industry is centered primarily in Alexandria, Cairo, several Delta cities and Assiut. Before the revolution of 1952, it was devoted mostly to textiles, and there was a small consumer goods and food processing industry.

Efforts at expansion and diversification were started in the 1960's, and now Egypt produces the bulk of its domestic requirements for consumer goods and has built the foundations for its industrial development. Negotiations are under way with many leading American companies to open plants here, and it is likely that such development will accelerate over the next decade if the present favorable investment climate continues.

Prior to the 1967 war, transit fees from the Suez Canal accounted for approximately one-half of Egypt's foreign exchange. After its closure in 1967 and the loss of revenues, coupled with years of war or threat of war, Egypt's economy was badly drained.

Following the October war of 1973 and the reopening of the Suez Canal in 1975, Egypt's economy appears to have gained a new lease on life. However, it needs a massive infusion of capital, which the government hopes to attract through a series of new laws providing incentives and tax benefits to foreign investors. During his eleven years as president, Anwar Sadat traveled far and wide to promote his country and encourage investment to help in developing Egypt's industrial capacity. One of the most talked about projects is the creation of a free zone in the Canal area which is envisioned as someday rivaling Singapore and Hong Kong.

Another source of income, greatly expanded in the past few years, has been tourism. Egypt welcomed approximately 1.3 million visitors in 1982. From a base of 18,000 hotel beds in 1976, Egypt has increased capacity to 44,000 beds and added an estimated 50,000 new jobs in the tourism sector.

Taboos and Customs

Although there is a western facade among modern, young and educated Egyptians, Egypt is the East. You will find all the modern conveniences to make your visit comfortable, but do not expect Egypt to be like home. Its way of life is different from ours. The difference is its fascination and the reason to journey 5,000 miles to see it.

If you are disturbed by poverty, remember that Egyptians are bitterly aware of their low standard of living, and against some of the worst odds in the world, they are working hard to improve it.

From the time Cambyses stormed into Egypt in 525 B.C. until the revolution of 1952, someone other than the Egyptians ran Egypt.

Throughout history it has been a prize of conquest and, depending on how well it was organized and ruled, Egypt had the potential of making its rulers incredibly wealthy.

But that has passed. Now, Egypt is run by Egyptians. They are intensely proud of their country and want to move on as rapidly as possible to develop it into a modern nation, although their efforts are often frustrated by a stupefying bureaucracy and a legacy of traditions which sometimes run counter to modern society. During your visit you will be reminded frequently of the difficulties in transforming a nation whose patterns are 7,000 years old.

Most Egyptians are Moslems, in which they take a pride second only to their being Egyptians. This does not mean, however, that they stop whatever they are doing five times a day, face Mecca and begin their prayers. On the contrary, most Egyptians you are likely to meet are urbanized and have altered their religious habits to cope with 20th century city life. Yet many in the city and most in the villages observe Moslem traditions of prayer when they can and abstain from alcoholic beverages. Even the most sophisticated and urban Moslems seldom eat pork, although pork is available in Cairo.

Islam is one of the most pervasive religions in the world and its hold on Egypt is unquestionable. As the seat of Islam's oldest and most important institution of learning, Al Azhar, Egypt has been a focal point for Islam for centuries. This, as much as any other factor, has given Egypt her bond with the other Arab countries and her leadership in the Moslem world. When one considers that there are almost 700 million Moslems spread out across the world, the scope of leadership is significant and perhaps explains why Egypt often has been able to exert more influence than her size might appear to warrant.

Most Westerners, unless they have studied Islam, have many false notions about it. Orthodox Moslems do pray five times a day and the ritual of prayer prescribed by the Koran can be observed in the mosques at prayer time, or even on a sidewalk or side street or in the fields. Moslems are not self-conscious about saying their prayers in front of others.

Women's Role

Modest dress, not veiling, is prescribed for women in the Koran, the holy book of the Moslems. A veiled Egyptian woman is an unusual sight in Cairo now, but even when the custom was prevalent, the style in Egypt was a fishnet affair and was never the heavy hood-like covering of North Africa or Arabia. Occasionally, you might see a woman from the village in a semiveiled costume, but the veiled women you see nowadays in Cairo and Alexandria are likely to be those who visit Egypt frequently from the Arabian Peninsula and from other North African countries where veiling is still practiced.

Visitors should be aware that a conservative revival is enjoying a certain amount of popularity currently and is manifested by a surprisingly large number of young women wearing long dresses and covering their heads (but not their faces) on Cairo streets. It is hard to assess its true depth at the present time.

While the Koran allows men to have four wives, it also requires them to treat them equally. These days, most men find that very difficult to do. Economics, if nothing else, is putting an end to polygamy. The Egyptian women, especially the younger generation, are emancipated, although Women's Lib might not think so.

The struggle for women's rights began in the 1930's during the British occupation, when women were active in the nationalist movement. It continued its militancy up to and through the early part of the 1952 Revolution, and then it subsided. Most of these early fighters are now quite elderly, and the new generation of women has not taken up the challenge in quite the same way. Instead, the younger generation of liberated women seem to be pressing ahead with education, entering the job market at every level and becoming economic assets to their families.

Women have been active in most professions for several decades and they have held high government positions, including cabinet posts and seats in the National Assembly, where at present there are nine. The head of the nation's television is a woman—certainly one of the country's most influential positions. Although the changes in this century have been profound, one would have to say that in the past decade the changes in the role of women have been radical. To find, as one does now, young girls from the villages working as waitresses in the hotels in Aswan, or as barmaids in Cairo—with family concurrence—would have been unthinkable a few years ago.

Women Traveling Alone

Unless you are a seasoned traveler, your first trip to Egypt will be more fun and less costly if you join a group—especially for the trip to Luxor, Aswan and other sites in Upper Egypt. It is easy for an individual to join such groups, as leading travel agencies in

Cairo and Alexandria have groups leaving daily for major sites of interest.

On the other hand, if you do not like to travel with anyone else, you need not hesitate. There are so many tourists roaming all over the country that Egyptians, even in the most remote places, are accustomed to foreign women on their own.

It is only fair to add, however, that if you do travel alone, your behavior should be circumspect and your dress modest. For example, bareback dresses and shorts should be kept for the beach, and wearing of very short skirts and low-cut dresses and blouses should be avoided on city streets. Egypt is a Moslem country, and while not as conservative as some, discretion is advisable. It is especially important for women entering a mosque to be respectably dressed. Egyptian men have a habit of staring, but they will not bother you unless you give the impression you want to be approached.

Egypt has one of the lowest crime rates in the world. There is some petty theft around hotels and sightseeing locales, but it is trivial compared to crime in large American cities. Crimes of violence, outside of family feuds and vendettas, are almost unknown.

An Egyptian Welcome

In spite of the history of on-again, off-again relations between the United States and Egypt, you will find that Egyptians really like Americans and they are eager to tell you so. The visit by the American president to Egypt in 1974 was the first step in reconciling the relationship, which had been broken since 1967. The visit in 1975 of the Egyptian president to the United States began a new chapter in the relations between the two countries and was further strengthened by his repeat visits. The courage of President Sadat's visit to Jerusalem in 1978 and his subsequent efforts for peace won him admiration around the world, as the outpour of emotion showed upon his tragic death in October of 1981. Sadat frequently has been at the head of the list of world leaders most admired by Americans.

Relations between Egypt and Western Europe, strained since the 1956 invasion and 1967 War, have improved even more dramatically. British visitors will often find, as they do in India, that the past is remembered more often for its beneficial aspects, and anti-colonial bitterness has faded as Egyptian independence has flowered.

Egyptians are good-natured, friendly and accommodating to

visitors, but they are more reserved when dealing with foreigners than Americans. Top-level educated and urban Egyptians are worldly and sophisticated, but the majority of Egyptians living along the banks of the Nile have never ventured beyond their village and their way of life, except for radio and television, has changed little for thousands of years.

Egyptians are "body" people. They slap, hug, kiss, push, shove, touch each other a great deal. They love their children and are openly warm, affectionate and indulgent with them. At the same time, they demand respect, loyalty and obedience from them. Important decisions such as marriage, divorce, careers and travel are still family matters, and the opinion of the family is often the most important deciding factor.

Throughout the Mediterranean world, and more especially in Egypt, there is a total unconcern for time, which is frustrating and irritating for Westerners. Yet, it is precisely the Egyptians' relaxed manner that accounts for a great deal of their charm. They are extremely patient. They cannot be hurried—don't bother to try. Instead, anticipate your needs much further in advance than you might at home and don't be timid about repeating them frequently.

Bukra means tomorrow. It is an expression used constantly in Egypt. It is the tomorrow of the future. It has no time limit. *Bukra fil mishmish*—tomorrow when the apricots bloom—is a special Egyptian tomorrow stretching to infinity.

So relax! You will enjoy your visit many times more if you adjust to rather than fight the system.

Suggested Reading List

Background Reading: Abu-Lughob, Janet. *Cairo: 1001 Years of the City Victorious*. Princeton University Press, 1971. This well-illustrated book traces the history of the city and its many historic monuments.

Al Sadat, Anwar. *In Search of Identity*. Harper and Row, New York, 1978. An autobiography of Egypt's second president.

Aldridge, James. *Cairo*. Little, Brown & Company, Boston, 1969. Of all the books on Egypt, none is better written, more informative and more useful for a visitor to read before a visit. Using the vehicle of the tale of a city that is over 1,000 years old, the author tells the history of Egypt. Through his extensive research, he was able to include many details often overlooked by writers on Egypt and he writes with an understanding seldom found.

Billard, J. B. *Ancient Egypt*. National Geographic Society,

1978. Chapters are written by scholars and recognized specialists, and profusely illustrated with photographs from the Society's superb collection.

Carter, Howard. *The Tomb of Tutankhamen*. E. P. Dutton, New York, 1972. The story of the discovery by the man who made it. Beautiful color plates as well as black-and-white photographs.

Casson, Lionel. *Ancient Egypt*. Time-Life Books, New York, 1965. Excellent summary of ancient Egypt's history, culture and religion. Strongly recommended as an introduction or as a refresher.

Ceram, C. W. *Gods, Graves and Scholars: The Story of Archaeology*. Knopf, New York, 1952. This book was written for the layman, and is one of the best books ever written on archeology. Informative and easy to read. Now available in paperback. It is especially good for the chapter on Howard Carter's discovery of the tomb of Tutankhamun.

Creswell, K. A. C. *A Short Account of Early Muslim Architecture*. Pelican, London, 1958; Verry, 1972. The leading authority on Islamic art and architecture. The book is available in paperback.

David, A. Rosalie. *The Making of the Past: The Egyptian Kingdoms*. E. P. Dutton, 1975. Excellent detailed descriptions, drawings and diagrams of the major antiquities, to be studied in advance of one's visit and upon return.

Fagan, Brian M. *The Rape of the Nile: Tomb Robbers, Tourists and Archaeologists in Egypt*. Scribner's Sons, New York, 1975. This book will give you an appreciation of the history of the antiquities of Egypt, which is more tragic and more glorious than any fiction. Better read before you go, but this is good reading upon return. Richly illustrated, succinctly written, it offers another dimension to the understanding of Egypt.

Huxley, Julian. *From An Antique Land: Ancient and Modern in the Middle East*. Crown, New York, 1954. For a general book on the area, it is informative and nicely illustrated. The author's observations on the Pyramids of Giza are especially good.

Moorehead, Alan. *The White Nile*. Penguin, London, 1963; *The Blue Nile*. London, Four Square, 1964. Available in paperback, and in a handsome hardback edition with good illustrations. Originally based on articles which appeared in the *New Yorker* magazine in 1961–62. The companion volumes are highly recommended for entertaining reading on Egypt and the Nile.

Sitwell, Sacheverell. *Arabesque and Honeycomb*. Robert Hale, London, 1957. If you read Sitwell before going to Egypt, you might never go, but if you overlook the classic colonial bias, you will find interesting vignettes on Cairo, especially on the mosques.

History and Culture: Breasted, James. *History of Egypt from the Earliest Times to the Persian Conquest.* Scribner's Sons, New York. This is the classic work in English on Ancient Egypt by one of the best known and most respected Egyptologists. Although the work of latter scholars has clarified or changed some of Breasted's theories and assumptions, this book is the place for any serious student to begin.

Cromer, E. B. *Modern Egypt.* Macmillan, New York, 1908. Two volumes. For anyone planning to spend some time in Egypt, the work is very important. Cromer was the British High Commissioner in Egypt for over two decades and for all practical purposes ran the country singlehanded.

Guillaume, A. *Islam.* Penguin, 1954. The traveler who reads about Islam, in addition to Egypt, will enjoy his visit to Egypt much more.

Lane, E. W. *Manners and Customs of the Modern Egyptians.* London, 1954. The book was first published in 1835 and has had many subsequent editions. It is considered a classic as social history and is interesting background reading.

Hardy, Edward. *Christian Egypt: Church and People.* Oxford U.P., New York, 1952. One of the few books in English on the subject.

Russell, Dorothea. *Medieval Cairo and the Monasteries of Wadi Natrun.* Weidenfeld and Nicolson, London, 1962.

Wynn, Wilton. *Nasser: A Search for Dignity.* Arlington, New York, 1959. As a young American teacher in Egypt, the author taught many of the leaders who staged the revolution of 1952. For many years he was the Associated Press correspondent in Egypt and is now the senior correspondent for *Time* magazine. Few Americans writing on the modern Middle East are as well acquainted with their subject.

Aids to Sightseeing: Baedeker, K. *Egypt: Handbook for Travelers.* Leipsig, 1885. The book is now a collector's item but it is a classic. A later 1925 edition has recently been reprinted and is available in some Cairo bookstores.

Cowley, Deborah, and Aleya Serour. *Cairo: A Practical Guide.* American U. Press, Cairo, third edition, 1981. Referred to several times in this book. It is the only one of its kind and when updated, is indispensable for someone planning to live in Cairo, especially for the shopping guide, list of doctors, and other such material not readily available elsewhere. It is also the most complete directory of phone numbers available in English.

Guide-Poche Univers. *Egypt.* Editions Marcus, Paris, 1976.

Originally written in French, the book is especially useful for its detailed maps and drawings of antiquity sites and explanations of ancient religion and mythology. It is not, however, accurate in some of its material on Islam.

Devonshire, Mrs. R. L. *Rambles in Cairo*. Les Editions Universitaires d'Egypte, 1947. For detailed descriptions of mosques and Islamic monuments, the book is useful for background details and includes map.

Dodge, Bayard. *The Azhar*. Middle East Institute, 1961. The author traces the history of the ancient mosque and university.

Fakhry, Ahmed. *The Pyramids*. Univ. of Chicago Press, 1975, paperback. A highly readable account of the building of the pyramids by a scholar who spent his life studying them.

Parker, Richard B., and Robin Sabin. *A Practical Guide to Islamic Monuments in Cairo*. American University, Cairo, 1974. By far the best easy-to-read (and carry) guidebook on Islamic Cairo and a must for anyone interested in this aspect of the city. With its maps and detailed information, it makes it possible for someone to sightsee on their own. It also gives readers enough historic background and definition of terms to help them enjoy it. Mr. Parker, a foreign service officer who served a tour of duty in Cairo, was disappointed by the lack of an adequate guidebook to the great Islamic antiquities of Cairo and so wrote one. We can all be grateful. It is available in Cairo bookstores.

THE EGYPTIAN SCENE

Anubis, God of Funerary Rites

EGYPT'S MARVELOUS HISTORY

A 63-Century Epic

Four thousand years before the birth of Christ, a civilization emerged on the green ribbon which cuts across the Sahara wasteland, and in the thirty centuries of its preeminence it reached a stage of development and sophistication that none of its contemporaries surpassed and few to this day have equalled. For example:

—With our vast engineering technology, the building of the pyramids remains a mystery.

—With all the miracles of modern science, we do not know the ancient Egyptians' secret of mummification.

—Papyrus, the first paper (and origin of the word from Greek), enabled the Egyptians to keep prodigious records, unlike their contemporaries who used clumsy clay tablets.

Record keeping played a major role in the Egyptians' ability to organize society and maximize the benefits of the Nile waters, which in turn led to their great prosperity. But what really set the Egyptians apart from all the rest was their ability to sustain their civilization almost without interruption for thirty centuries—a feat no others have achieved. The reason is found in the unusual relationship of Egypt and the Nile River.

The river valley, protected by the desert on both sides, acted as a barrier that discouraged invasion and enabled the people to live in relative security. At the same time, to control the river's annual flood, the villages along the Nile had to cooperate to survive. Cooperation, in turn, meant organization. And it was this organization, more than any other factor, that enabled Egypt to endure.

By the time Herodotus, the great historian of the Greeks, visited Egypt in 450 B.C., it was already an ancient land, since its first fixed date can be placed around the beginning of the fourth millennium B.C. Logic tells us that this civilization would have had to have been even older, since its system of writing did not spring into being full blown.

Who, then, were the Egyptians and where did they come from?

The origins of the Egyptians remain a puzzle to historians to this day. From archeological discoveries we know that in prehistoric times the area of the Nile Valley was green, forested, peopled, and rich in animal life. But over the millennia, the nature of the land was altered so drastically that these earliest inhabitants left or perhaps were forced to leave. The area had become denuded, rainless and barren. Scholars say there is no evidence of a connection between prehistoric man in Egypt and the ancient Egyptians with whom the country's recorded history begins.

Authorities do not agree on the origins of these latter day Egyptians either. Earlier theories held they were African. While most agree there were some African migrations into the Nile Valley, the current belief is that the Egyptians were tribes from the Libyan desert on the one hand and from the Arabian desert on the other. From their language, scholars have concluded that the immigrants were predominantly Semitic in origin and that they probably settled in the Nile Valley prior to 10,000 B.C.

Too many centuries of Nile silt have piled up in the Delta to enable Egyptologists to uncover the remains of the "Red Kingdom"—so named because of the red color of the Nile mud. At least we know that by 4000 B.C. there was a flourishing, sophisticated civilization.

It had already devised a calendar of 360 days which was divided into 12 portions of 30 days each. The difference was made up by having five sacred feast days at the end of each year. This civilization had developed a writing system, a measuring system, and it recorded this information on paper made from the papyrus leaf by a method that we have only recently learned to imitate.

Simultaneously, another kingdom had developed along the Upper Nile as far as the first cataract near Aswan. It was known as the White Kingdom, presumably for the same graphic reason—the land's color was white. Its leader wore a white crown; its emblem was a white flower.

Upper and Lower Egypt United

At some time around 3100 B.C. (some authorities say as early as 3400 B.C.; others as late as 3000 B.C.), a leader whom history has called Menes from Thinis (near Abydos) united the White and Red Kingdoms. As Egyptologists interpret it, he united the crowns of Upper and Lower Egypt—a prerequisite for governing this land of potential wealth that was recognized by every ruler from Menes down to the Romans. The reason for this need was, of course, control of the Nile.

None of the tombs of the rulers prior to Menes has ever been discovered, but archeologists have been able to piece together from funeral mounds of lesser citizens a considerable amount of information on these early Egyptians.

From Menes, however, the historical evidence is abundant, and for this reason we start the story of ancient Egypt with his reign, the first of 30 dynasties that ruled Egypt from 3100 B.C. to the coming of the Romans in 30 B.C.

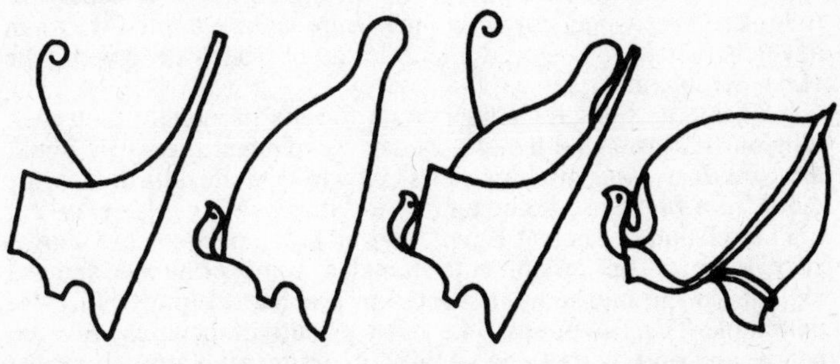

Lower Egypt Red Crown — Upper Egypt White Crown — Double Crown — War Crown

Menes moved to Memphis, where he established the first capital of the united land. The site is located only twenty miles from Cairo.

In the furniture, utensils and jewelry of daily life there is compelling evidence that by Menes' time, Egyptian civilization had already achieved an exquisite mastery of its crafts, as can be seen in the Egyptian Antiquities Museum in Cairo. The refinement and strength of the statues, the fineness of their utensils, the grace and precision of alabaster carved to represent natural objects, the magnificent design and craft of furniture inlaid with ivory and ebony and the skill in the working of gold jewelry and precious stones are only a few of the examples.

Furthermore, an inventory of the land was made at regular intervals. To have been able to produce and maintain such an elaborate bookkeeping system is further evidence of the level of sophistication the Egyptians had reached by this period. We also know that a state religion began to develop, vaguely centered in the person of the king as the unifier of the land.

The union forged by Menes was not a peaceful one in the beginning, as might be supposed. For decades the two sections fought—the south having to subdue the rebellious north. The final reconciliation of the warring states was attributed to the most important god of ancient Egypt, Osiris, god of the nether world, whose role was to judge those passing through the nether world to eternity.

The Gods of Egypt

To understand the civilization of ancient Egypt, it is necessary to look at two aspects of its life that were so intertwined they can never be separated. One is the Nile, as has been described; the other is religion.

No force had greater influence on the life of ancient man than religion. It permeated his life. Religion explained the world about him, his fears and his hopes. Its outward manifestation was the motif from which art, architecture, literature, and science evolved.

The religion of ancient Egypt, of which one needs some knowledge to enjoy the monuments, temples, tomb drawings and the exhibits in the museums, is rooted in prehistory, long before the pharaohs. The Egyptians, like most primitive societies, revered nature and both feared and admired its traits—the strength of the lion, its tenderness toward its young. Throughout its ancient history, animals were associated with the gods in one form or another. They dwelt in the temples and were mummified in the same manner as human beings, although it was not until much later in history that they were worshiped.

In his surroundings—the trees, the birds and beasts—the Egyptian saw his gods. They were creatures like himself, but they possessed strange powers which he did not, such as the flight of a bird, and spirits over which he had no control. Some of these spirits were his friends who would help and protect him; others wanted to harm him. Misfortune, he believed, came from one of the evil spirits around him.

Beyond these local spirits, the Egyptian needed to explain the sky, the earth and the other grand elements of his world. In a land where the sun is powerful and plentiful, it is no surprise that it was given special status. The Egyptians, we presume, perceived that life was dependent on the sun. Over the centuries, worship of the sun was almost universal, although it took different forms in different places, and two or more forms were sometimes blended into one.

The chief center of sun worship was On, a city in the Delta, which the Greeks called Heliopolis. Here, the sun god was known as Re (Ra). The theory held that Re had two barques in which he sailed across the heavens, one for the morning and the other for the afternoon. When he entered the nether world in his barque to return to the east, he brought light and joy with him. The symbol of his presence in the temple at Heliopolis was an obelisk. At Edfu, another center for the worship of the sun, he appeared as a hawk and was named Horus.

The explanation for heaven and earth also varied—some saw a huge cow with her head in the west, the earth stretched between her feet; her belly studded with stars represented the arch of heaven. In another place they saw a female figure bending over the earth, with her feet in the east and her outstretched arms in the west. Both of these representations can be seen frequently in drawings and temple carvings throughout Upper Egypt.

Eventually, local ideas were mixed with myths from other places. Hence, the sun was born every morning as a calf or as a child, depending upon whether one believed the heaven was a cow or a woman. The flight of a bird and the movement of the sun became one, and the sun with outspread wings was one of the most common symbols of ancient Egypt. In a later form, it became a protective goddess as can be seen on many of the exhibits in the Tutankhamun collection.

As society became more sophisticated and the Egyptian less awed by the mysteries of nature, his gods underwent a transformation. Gradually, the three aspects—nature, animal and man—

were fused. By the time of Menes (I Dynasty) the gods had come to be conceived in human form.

One of the earliest deities to undergo this fusion was Hathor, the goddess of love and childbirth. She was given a human body and head but retained an element of her animal manifestation—a pair of cow's horns.

Thoth, god of wisdom and truth, also acquired a human body but kept the head of the ibis. Anubis, who assisted Osiris as judge of the dead and guardian of the tombs, also took on a human body but kept the head of a jackal.

To explain creation, the Egyptians evolved a theory that reasoned: If the sky was a sea upon which the sun and the heavenly lights sailed westward every day, then there had to be a waterway by which they could return. They concluded that there was another Nile beneath the earth. Through its long dark passage the celestial barque sailed at night and reappeared in the east each morning. This other Nile was connected with the earthly Nile at the first cataract—the place where the people who first believed this myth thought the earth ended.

According to James Breasted in his *History of Egypt* (New York, 1909), this concept of the encircling sea was inherited by the Greeks who called the sea Okeanos, or Ocean. "In the beginning only this ocean existed, upon at which there then appeared an egg, or as some said a flower, out of which issued the sun-god. From himself he begat four children, Shu and Tefnut, Keb and Nut. All these, with their father, lay upon the ocean of chaos, when Shu and Tefnut, who represent the atmosphere, thrust themselves between Keb and Nut. They planted their feet upon Keb and raised Nut on high, so that Keb became the earth and Nut the heavens.

"Keb and Nut were the father and mother of the four divinities, Osiris and Isis, Set and Nephthys; together they formed with their primeval father the sun-god, a circle of nine deities, the 'ennead' of which each temple later possessed a local form.

"This correlation of the primitive divinities as father, mother, and son, strongly influenced the theology of later times until each temple possessed an artificially created triad, of purely secondary origin, upon which an 'ennead' was then built up."

Besides these gods of the earth, the sun and the heavens, there were also those who lived in the nether world. As we said earlier, this world was conceived of as a long gloomy passage along which a subterranean river—the other Nile—carried the sun from west to east. Here dwelt the dead, whose king was Osiris. According to the legend, Osiris had succeeded the sun god as king on earth, aided by his faithful sister-wife, Isis.

Isis and Osiris

Osiris had been a good and beloved ruler, but he was craftily misled and slain by his brother Set who was jealous of him. Set cut the body of his brother into a million pieces and scattered them about the land. Where each piece fell, the land was fertile and a green blade grew. Isis in her consternation roamed the earth in search of the pieces of Osiris' body. When, after great tribulation, Isis had regained the body of Osiris, she prepared it for burial with the help of an old god of the nether world, Anubis, the jackal-god, who thereafter became the god of embalmment. The charms Isis spoke over the body of Osiris were so powerful that he was resurrected; and although it was impossible for the departed god to resume his earthly life, he lived on as lord of the nether world.

Isis later gave birth to a son, Horus, whom she secretly reared among the marshes of the Delta to become his father's avenger. When he grew to manhood, the youth pursued Set and in the terrible battle that raged from one end of the earth to the other, both were mutilated. Finally, Set was defeated and Horus was able to assume the earthly throne of his father.

Set went to the tribunal of the gods, where he challenged the birth of Horus and his claim to the throne. But, defended by Thoth, the god of wisdom and truth, Horus was vindicated. Some versions say that it was Osiris himself who was vindicated.

Thereafter, every pharaoh ruled on earth as Horus. When he died, he became Osiris and ruled the underworld. His son, the new pharaoh, ruled on earth as Horus.

The ancient Egyptians believed that upon death all persons had to pass through the nether world for the last judgment by Osiris and 42 assistant judges, one for each of the nomes (provinces) of Egypt.

Death, the Egyptians believed, was a continuation of life, which is why they spent so much time and effort in preparation for it. Upon death, 70 days were needed to prepare the body for embalming, and during that time the body and the "Ka" (one's spirit and alter ego) wandered through the underworld searching for Osiris, who is represented in the tomb drawing with either a white face (death) or a green face (vegetation or rebirth).

The dead person and his Ka had to pass through the judgment hall where he told each of the judges what he had done in life and answered for his sins. The sins were no different than ours today—murder, stealing, lying, deceit, adultery, blasphemy, etc. To test the truth of his plea and to pass judgment on his eternal life, his heart was weighed on a scale of justice with a feather (the symbol of truth) as balance. If the heart (thought to be the seat of intelligence) was as light as a feather, the judgment would be favorable. The standard was high. Those who failed the ordeal were condemned to hunger and thirst in the darkness of the tomb. In this judgment, the Egyptians introduced for the first time in history the idea of future accountability, where man's eternal life depended on the ethical quality of his earthly one.

Although it started in the Delta, Abydos in Upper Egypt became the main center of the Osiris myth and an important place of pilgrimage. An annual series of dramatic presentations in which the main incidents of Osiris' life, death and final triumph were enacted, it drew audiences from all over the land. In some parts of the drama, the ordinary people were allowed to participate with the priests—and the spectacle was undoubtedly magnificent, not unlike the later passion plays of Christianity.

The Osiris cult covers only a few of the gods and their overlapping personalities that populated the region of ancient Egypt. But it gives some idea of the complexity of the role of religion in daily life. It further helps to explain why the Egyptians saw death as a continuation of life and spent so much of their earthly life preparing for the eternal one.

The cult of Osiris is the most basic and consistent theme of Egyptian history from ancient times down through the centuries, including the Christian period to the coming of Islam. The myth of Osiris was easy for people to understand; they could identify with it. Hence, it was easy for a cult to develop around it. Isis became the ideal wife and mother, and Horus, who originally belonged to the sun myth and had nothing to do with Osiris, became the embodiment of the good son and the ultimate triumph of a just cause.

Under the Greeks and later under the Romans, many of the Egyptian gods were merged with those of the Greeks and Romans. Osiris became a form of Zeus; Venus had many of the attributes of Isis and so on. It takes very little imagination to trace Greek and Roman myths from the Osiris legend and to see how many of the stories of Hebraic and Christian literature derived from it.

The concepts of the trinity, the last judgment, redemption, resurrection and many more were later to become cornerstones of the Christian faith and were adopted in modified forms into Islam.

The Three Kingdoms

The dynasty of Menes and the one that followed covered about

400 years, during which Egypt emerged from prehistoric obscurity. From that point its history, beginning with the III Dynasty, is divided into three main periods, each separated by intermediate periods when the country's fortunes were temporarily at a low ebb. Each of the three kingdoms was characterized by great accomplishments:

The Old Kingdom (2700–2200 B.C.) was the period during which the great pyramids were built.

The Middle Kingdom (2200–1800 B.C.) saw Egypt's political and economic strength expand and its art reach a peak.

During the New Kingdom (1600–1100 B.C.) the nation reached its zenith as a political power and acquired history's first empire. After this period, Egypt's days as a great nation were over, although the pharaohs continued to occupy the throne for another eight centuries.

Egypt's political and social structure was formed early and changed little over the centuries. Power was in the hands of a pharaoh cast in the double role of king and god at the pinnacle of the society. And, like the pyramids the pharaohs built, an elite group of officers and priests to whom the pharaohs delegated authority were situated at the top just below the ruler, while the entire structure was supported by a broad base of highly organized workers and peasants.

For four centuries the dynasty begun by Menes continued to consolidate his gains and develop a prosperity which laid the foundation for the first great epoch of Egyptian history. During the next 500 years, from the III to the VI Dynasties, building, government and administration reached levels that were never surpassed in later periods.

For us today, this period can be seen in the masterpieces of the Step Pyramid at Sakkara, the first large structure in stone; the three Pyramids of Giza; and the collection of superb sculpture and artifacts that fills a quarter of the Antiquities Museum in Cairo and a part of collections in museums around the world.

The mere organization of labor involved in quarrying, transporting and assembling this vast amount of material would even today tax the richest nations. The maintenance of a city of a hundred thousand laborers, who were nonproducing and a constant burden on the state, tells us something of the wealth and power of the early pharaohs.

During this period the first known seagoing vessels were built, making possible the expansion of trade north to Phoenicia and south beyond Nubia to Somali. The power of the landed nobility developed into what was history's first feudal system.

By the VI Dynasty Egypt faced several internal difficulties. Spiritually, the omnipotence of the pharaoh was diminished somewhat by the priests; economically, the strain of building and maintaining the pyramids had severely weakened the country. Finally, after the 90-year reign of Pepi II, the country began to come apart. The organization so necessary for controlling the Nile and maximizing its benefits broke down.

After a brief 30 years (VII and VIII Dynasties), which historians describe as one of internal confusion, the seat of power shifted from Memphis to Heracleopolis, about 55 miles south of Memphis in the area of Fayum. Eighteen kings (IX and X Dynasties) were at the helm.

Meanwhile, a powerful family of princes in Thebes, near present-day Luxor, gained strength and ultimately triumphed over the north. They established the XI Dynasty about 2160 B.C., and the center of power moved to the south. From the demise of Memphis to the triumph of Thebes covered about 300 years.

This period, designated by the XI and XII Dynasties (2160–1788 B.C.), is known as the Middle Kingdom, the classical period of Egyptian history during which Egypt was once again united.

The XII Dynasty was founded about 2000 B.C. by another Theban family under Amenemhet II, who consolidated the power of the state by dealing with the powerful landed nobles one by one. His successors moved the capital back to the north and established their rule at Lisht, about 20 miles south of Memphis. They continued to reorganize the domestic affairs of the country, curbing the power of feudal lords and replacing them with governors and advisors from Thebes whom they could trust. It took five kings more than 150 years to supplant their power.

The XII Dynasty kings also expanded the Nile's irrigation system, especially at Fayum. In the artistic field, art, jewelry and literature reached a peak never again equalled for its refinement. The rulers of the XII Dynasty also continued to expand the country's control beyond its borders, and under Amenemhet's grandson, Sesostris III, the Egyptians invaded Syria for the first time. The pharaoh personally led his army, and he became a legend as he extended Egypt's control over 1,000 miles of the Nile. (This period paralleled the Biblical era of Abraham's arrival in the land of Canaan.)

Under Amenemhet III, the nation reached one of its greatest periods of power, productivity and artistic achievement. The Theban rulers also elevated to national prominence an obscure Theban god, Amon, who was to become one of the great forces in ancient history. The image of Amon accompanied the Egyptian army through the ancient world. A thousand years later Alexander the Great would seek his aid in ruling Egypt. The most massive temple of all time—the Temple of Karnak—was erected in his honor. Here, the most spectacular feast of the year was held at the time of the flood to honor him.

Once again a great era was followed by an unstable one under the XIII Dynasty in the 18th century B.C. This is known to historians as the Second Intermediate Period. The country again separated into its two natural geographical parts, Upper and Lower Egypt. The two sections fought from time to time; each was beset by internal squabbling, and one weak leader followed another.

Egypt Divided

The country disintegrated into petty kingdoms, of which Thebes was the largest in the south where a regime maintained itself for about two centuries, holding a short strip of territory of about 125 miles in the area of Thebes.

Without central power to administer its irrigation system, the nation's resources became dissipated and authority weakened. Hence, Egypt was easy prey for foreign invaders when, about 1730 B.C., the Hyksos, an Asian tribe, swept over the northern portion of the land, leaving vast destruction in their wake.

Historians are not entirely sure about the origins of the Hyksos, known as the Shepherd Kings, but they generally agree that they were mostly Semites, probably from Palestine, who came across the desert, settled near the eastern border of Egypt and from there eventually controlled most of the Delta. Apparently they had little difficulty overcoming local opposition, since the Egyptians were not as advanced in warfare as their invaders.

The Hyksos became Egyptianiazed rapidly, and although their rule lasted only about a century, they had a profound impact on Egypt—mainly because they brought with them new tools of war and taught the Egyptians warfare on a large scale. Of the new weapons introduced by the Hyksos, the most important was the horse-drawn chariot. When the Egyptians finally expelled the Hyksos they did so by learning to use their enemy's weapons.

In spite of their military advantage, the Hyksos were unable to extend their rule beyond a point midway between Memphis and Thebes, and their inability to dislodge the Theban regime proved their undoing.

The family that founded the XVIII Dynasty (mid-16th century B.C.) was one of history's most remarkable. Under Ahmose I, their powerful army stormed the Hyksos capital in the eastern

Delta and drove the foreigners out of Egypt about 1580 B.C. It was not, however, until a half century later that the Hyksos were finally defeated, when Thutmose III won the battle of Kadesh in Syria.

Under the XVIII Dynasty, the first of the New Kingdom, Egypt was once again united and its rulers laid the foundation for the greatest period in Egypt's history. Under these pharaohs Egypt became an empire—the world's first—extending its rule in the south beyond the fourth cataract of the Nile in the Sudan and the Euphrates River in the northeast.

In rebuilding the country, Ahmose I faced a task that differed substantially from the reorganization by the pharaohs of the XII Dynasty at the start of the Middle Kingdom. The latter had only to manipulate to their own ends established political power without destroying its base. Ahmose began by building a completely new fabric of government, shaped somewhat by events that had culminated in the expulsion of the Hyksos. He was now head of a strong, well-organized army, which in turn determined the character of the government—Egypt became a military state.

In spite of their traditionally unwarlike nature, the Egyptians in the long war with the Hyksos had become soldiers. The army, after years in Asia, had learned not only the art of war but also the enormous wealth and power to be gained by conquest. The whole country was aroused by the ambitions of empire building.

Ahmose I restored the boundaries that Egypt had held in the Old Kingdom. He destroyed the power of local nobles and confiscated their lands for the crown. In effect, all Egypt became the pharaoh's personal estate, and thus he created a new order that his successors further consolidated.

Hatshepsut and Egypt's Glory

Amenhotep I, the son of Ahmose I, moved the nation's boundary farther south and started the country on a period of prosperity that lasted for 150 years. Thutmose I, the third pharaoh of the Dynasty, pushed the frontiers still farther south beyond the fourth cataract and northeast to Palestine and Syria. After his reign, Egypt's military expansion was suspended for two decades by Thutmose's daughter, Hatshepsut, one of the most remarkable women in history.

Hatshepsut was married to Thutmose II, her half-brother—not an unusual practice in ancient times. When Thutmose II died after a short rule, she took over the government as regent during the minority of Thutmose III, a child her husband had fathered by a lesser wife of the harem. He had become pharaoh by a bizarre incident in which the priests had singled him out during a feast.

Nominally, Thutmose III was pharaoh and at first Hatshepsut ruled in his name, but she soon abandoned the pretense and established herself as pharaoh. Historical evidence is too inconclusive to state for certain what took place, but Hatshepsut and Thutmose III were on and off the throne for over a decade.

The nomination of Hatshepsut to the succession and her descent from an old and illustrious Theban family apparently made her position strong with the nobles of her party. Although unable to eliminate Thutmose III entirely, Hatshepsut ultimately seized power and ruled as supreme co-regent. Thutmose III was relegated to the background while the queen played the leading state role. Both she and Thutmose III numbered the years of their joint reign from the first accession of Thutmose III.

Clearly, Hatshepsut could not have wielded so much power without powerful supporters. Chief among them was Senmut, the architect of the Queen's temples at Deir el Bahri and the Temple of Amon in Karnak. It is said that he held eighty titles.

Hatshepsut was the first queen to assume the godship with the kingship and to wear the Double Crown, indicating sovereignty over the two lands of Upper and Lower Egypt. In addition, statues show her in the masculine attire of the kingship. One of the surest proofs of her amazing ability was her success in dominating Thutmose III so long. For twenty years the man who was to become one of Egypt's greatest pharaohs lived in her shadow.

Finally, when Thutmose III was able to gather the backing he needed to unseat her, he did so with a vengeance. After her death he had her name removed wherever it was written, especially at Deir al Bahri, Hatshepsut's famous mortuary temple at the west bank at Luxor—among the highlights of a visit today.

Thutmose III has been called the Napoleon of antiquity—a brilliant military strategist, leader of men, superhero of the then civilized world. His reign, known as the Imperial Age, marks the crest of Egyptian history. He built the first real empire and became the first universal personality in history.

At the time of his death the Egyptian empire stretched from Syria to the Sudan. His reign marks an epoch not only in Egypt but in the whole East, for never before in history had one person controlled the resources of so great a nation. Thebes grew into a great metropolis from which, amid great wealth and splendor, the pharaohs of the XVIII and XIX Dynasties ruled their vast domain for 230 years.

Thutmose III administered the empire so well that the machinery he set in motion ran successfully for a full century after him. Egypt was at peace and trade flourished. Except for putting down a rebellion in Nubia, his successor had no need of military ventures. Instead, Amenhotep III went on a building spree that included the creation of colossal statues and temples throughout the land.

By 1375 B.C., at the end of his reign and during that of his son, Amenhotep IV, a combination of adverse influences both within and without led ultimately to the empire's destruction. From information contained in a collection of clay tablets discovered in the ruins of Tell el Amarna, events that would later weaken the empire were taking place at the extreme edge of Egypt's territory. In particular, the Hittites from Asia Minor were advancing into Syria, and at the same time Egypt had loosened its hold on Palestine. Unaware or unconcerned about the situation, Amenhotep IV became absorbed in social and religious reform that caused internal convulsions such as the country had never before endured.

The World's First Universal God

Amenhotep IV may have been a religious fanatic; certainly he was an ascetic. He was physically weak, with a long, thin face and a misshapen body. He immersed himself in philosophy and theology and gradually developed ideas that made him the most interesting of all the pharaohs and the first prophet in history. In his immediate circle were his mother, Queen Ti; his wife, Nefertiti (known to us because of her famous sculptured head which now rests in the Berlin Museum), and a favorite priest, Eye, the husband of his childhood nurse.

Whether his original intention was toward a social revolution or a religious one is not clear, but with single-minded determination he collided with the bureaucracy and the clergy, institutions that had become deeply entrenched and powerful since the time of Thutmose III. But to understand Amenhotep IV's role, one must place it in context.

Egypt's imperial position had had a profound influence on all of the country's life and ideas. Even before the conquests in Asia the priests were beginning to interpret the gods in a more philosophical way. James Breasted, in his *History of Egypt,* notes that it was no accident that the concept of a universal god arose in Egypt at the moment when her pharaohs ruled a world empire. A priest of this age had in the person of the pharaoh a tangible form of a world concept—a prerequisite to the notion of a world god.

None of the old divinities of Egypt had been proclaimed the god of the empire, although the sun-god Re of Heliopolis was highly esteemed. Already under Amenhotep III an old name for the material sun, Aton, had come into use and occasionally the sun-god was designated as "the god."

In a move to reassert a pharaoh's authority, Amenhotep IV openly challenged the priesthood, the most powerful and conservative group in the empire, with his new ideas. Under the name Aton, Amenhotep IV introduced the worship of one supreme and universal god, and he did not even try to camouflage the new deity with the old sun god Re. He attributed the new faith to Re as its source, but claimed to have been himself the channel of its revelation. The new religion was not merely sun worship. Amenhotep IV had identified the source of life as the heat that he found to be present in all life. He concluded that Aton was everywhere through his rays. He used as Aton's symbol a disk whose ray resembled many outstretched arms ending in cupped hands.

In a further affront to the priests of Amon, the pharaoh built a temple to Aton between the temples of Karnak and Luxor in the garden of Amon, which had been created by Amenhotep III. (Amenhotep IV is supposed to have built eight temples in Thebes. One was uncovered only recently in the vicinity of Karnak Temple at Luxor.)

Other gods were still tolerated but it was inevitable that the priests of Amon would be jealous of the new strange god, especially since the wealth formerly lavished on Amon's sanctuary was now being spent on the usurper. To make matters worse for the priests of Amon, Amenhotep IV had the support of the Memphis and Heliopolis priests who for so long had had to take a back seat to Thebes.

It was not long before Amenhotep IV found Thebes intolerable and decided to make a complete break. In one move he swept aside centuries of polytheism. The priests were dispossessed and official temple worship of various gods ceased. In particular, he replaced the traditional worship of Amon with that of Aton, the source of all life. With the frenzy of a fanatic he had the names and images of Amon removed from all temples and tombs, including even that of his father.

Then, as the coup de grace, he changed his name from Amenhotep, which meant "Amon is content," to Akhenaton (Ikhnaton), meaning "serviceable to the Aton." (This is the name by which he is known in history). He moved the capital to the site of Tell al Amarna, about 200 miles south of Cairo near the present town of Minya, and called it Akhetaton.

A new spirit prevailed in Egypt. Ikhnaton perceived his god as the creator of nature through which his beneficence for all creatures was revealed. According to Breasted, he called Aton "father and mother of all that he had made," and he saw in some degree the goodness of that All-Father as did he who bade us consider the lilies. He pointed to the all-embracing bounty of the common father of humanity. It is this aspect of Ikhnaton's mind that is especially remarkable; he is the first prophet of history.

"While to the traditional pharaoh the state god was only the triumphant conqueror, who crushed all peoples and drove them tribute-laden before the Pharaoh's chariot, Ikhnaton saw in him the beneficent father of all men. It is the first time in history that a discerning eye has caught this great universal truth."

While Ikhnaton recognized the power and the beneficence of God, he did not have a very spiritual conception of the deity nor did he attribute to him ethical qualities beyond those that Amon had possessed. Nevertheless, he placed a constant emphasis upon "truth." His search for truth and the naturalness of his daily life had a great impact on the art of the time. It was more perceptive than any art had been before and reflected a simple and beautiful realism. It opened a new chapter in art history and was to have a profound influence on future artists of Egypt. (Evidence of these changes are apparent when one compares the tomb and temple carvings during the period of Ikhnaton with earlier ones.)

It is not entirely clear what happened after Ikhnaton's rule, but he was first succeeded by his son-in-law, Smenkhkara, who died soon after and was followed by his half-brother, Tutankhaton, a mere child of nine. For the first three years of his reign, Tutankhaton remained at Tell al Amarna, but finally he succumbed to the power of the Thebean priests and returned to the old capital. He changed his name to Tutankhamun and revived the old religion. We know very little about him except that he died young, probably no more than eighteen. His tomb is the only one of the pharaohs' tombs from the Middle Kingdom or earlier pericds ever found intact.

The army had enabled Ikhnaton to break with tradition, and now it was the army that returned Egypt to tradition. Harmhab, one of the able commanders under the fallen dynasty, survived the crisis and finally seized the throne. Under his vigorous rule the disorganized nation was gradually restored to order.

The army made peace with the civil service and the clergy and all three institutions shared power. In the new age which followed, the throne paid careful attention to the rights and prerogatives of all three. Harmhab was followed by the pharaohs of the XIX (1350-

1205 B.C.) and XX Dynasties (1200–1090 B.C.), eleven of whom bore the famous name of Ramses.

The period spanned by these two dynasties was Egypt's most productive age, and because so many of its colossal monuments have survived until now, it is often taken to be her greatest period. Actually, it was the beginning of the end of Egypt's greatness as a major power.

Harmhab's immediate successors began the recovery of the lost empire in Asia, but the Hittites were too firmly established for them to regain Syria. Neither Seti II nor Ramses II was able to push the northern frontiers much beyond Palestine.

In some part Egypt's decline was brought about by forces over which the pharaohs had no control. Great movements of people were taking place throughout the east. But at the beginning of the 13th century B.C. when Ramses followed his brilliant father, Seti, no evidence of decline was discernible.

Climax of the Age of Pharaohs

Ramses, who has been called the king of kings, ruled Egypt for 67 years and from the evidence he was one of the most spectacular men in history.

He entered into diplomatic negotiations with the Hittites, with whom he signed what is probably the earliest recorded treaty in history. He campaigned in Syria and Palestine and raided the south. Accounts of his valor and courage survive on the walls of almost every major temple of his time.

He covered Egypt from one end to the other with monuments and temples. Among them are the Great Hypostyle Hall at Karnak; the Ramesseum, the funerary temple to himself and the god Amon at Thebes; the great temple at Abydos, dedicated to the god Osiris; several structures at Memphis and the most famous of all—the temple of Abu Simbel with its four colossal statues of Ramses.

The age of Ramses, with its imposing statues, grand temples and great feats, marks the climax of the age of the pharaohs. From this period to the conquest by Alexander the Great, the history of ancient Egypt is one of steady decline. Although the country would enjoy occasional periods of prosperity and unity, never again would it be a world power.

After 1100 B.C., internal dissension again split the country into its traditional north and south halves. At first merchant princes from Tanis ruled Lower Egypt, and the high priests of Amon who succeeded the last Ramses held Upper Egypt.

Around 950 B.C. Sheshank, a Libyan who belonged to a family of high priests from Heracleopolis, seized control of both Upper and Lower Egypt. Under him the XXII Dynasty tried to restore Egypt's prestige and the country prospered. He raided Palestine and in about 930 B.C. plundered the Temple of Solomon in Jerusalem.

But rivalry between the powerful priests at Thebes undermined the dynasty and by 730 B.C. Egypt was once again ripe for foreign invasion, which came this time from the south. The Nubians remained in power seventy years, but were driven back to their homes by the Assyrians, who invaded from the east in 663 B.C.

Within the year, the Assyrians were tricked into leaving Egypt by a prince of Sais, Psamtik I, to whom they gave authority. He established the XXVI Dynasty, sometimes called the Renaissance period, and for 54 years the country enjoyed peace and prosperity once again. His successors were also able leaders and Egypt continued to prosper until 525 B.C., when the country was invaded by the Persians. In 332 B.C., as part of his campaign to destroy the Persian Empire, Alexander the Great conquered Egypt.

With this, the last of the pharaohs—the XXX Dynasty—was swept away.

Greeks and Romans

Ptolemy, the general whom Alexander left to govern Egypt, established a new dynasty that ruled Egypt for over two centuries. Cleopatra, the seventh Ptolemaic queen to have this name and the most famous queen of ancient times, was the last of the line. Alexandria became the capital and most important center of Hellenism. Its university and library were the most celebrated of their time, and among the great scholars who went there to study and work were Euclid, Eratosthenes and Herophilus.

The Greek period closed with the arrival of the Romans in 30 B.C. They turned Egypt into the personal domain of the emperor and the wheat basket of his empire. Within a short time of the Roman takeover, however, Christianity began to spread in Egypt. Alexandria was to become a great center of the new faith, second only to Rome and Constantinople. Particularly important in Egypt was the development of monasticism, the first in Christianity.

Arrival of Islam

In 641, only a few years after the birth of Islam, Egypt was conquered by the Arabs. The majority of Egyptians quickly adopted their faith, and Arabic replaced Greek and Coptic as the language of the country. With the center of the faith in Arabia and the capital of the empire first in Damascus and later in Baghdad, Egypt did not play as significant a role in the early days of Islam as it did in its later history.

In 969, the Fatimids, who were Shiite Moslems from North Africa, invaded Egypt and established their capital at Cairo. Under their reign Al Azhar was begun, later to become the first university and the most important center of Moslem learning in the world.

During the time of the Crusades, a new dynasty, the Ayyubid, was established by Salah ed-Din, known to the west as Saladin. Under his rule Egypt became once again an important power in the east and extended its rule to Palestine and Syria.

With the last of the Ayyubids in 1245, and through the conniving and manipulations of a most unusual slave who became queen, a new group known as Mameluks came to power and, in one form or other, ran Egypt for the next seven centuries. The Mameluks were mercenaries and former slaves of Turkish and Eastern European origin who became influential soldiers and advisers. The ruthless Bahri Mameluks and later the even worse Circassian Mameluks ruled Egypt until it was conquered by the Ottoman Turks, most tyrannical of all, early in the 16th century.

Mameluk rule was characterized by incessant warfare and political chaos resulting from continuing palace intrigues. Seldom did a ruler last more than six years before he was eliminated by a rival. Despite this, the Mameluks lived lavishly and were patrons of the arts. Islamic art and architecture in Egypt reached their zenith under their rule, and many of Cairo's greatest mosques and mausoleums date from this period.

Egypt, long the benefactor of east-west trade, suffered the same fate as other countries of the area when the discovery of America and the circumnavigation of the globe revolutionized world trading patterns.

In the later days of Turkish rule Egypt again fell to the power of influential mercenaries, yet another group of Mameluks. Egypt remained nominally part of the Turkish Empire until World War I.

French and English Invasions

In 1798, as part of his effort to outflank the British and establish a trade route to the east, Napoleon occupied Egypt. His mission was a disaster for the French but it opened a new chapter in Egypt's history and marked the start of modern history in the Middle East.

Napoleon's expedition included an army of scholars as well as soldiers. Their studies were the start of research into the mysteries of Ancient Egypt that later developed into the science of Egyptology. On the other hand, the opening of Egypt to the west also meant exposure to western ideas, which set in motion a chain of events that is felt to this day.

After the French withdrawal, Muhammad Ali, a soldier of Albanian origin at the head of the Turkish Army, was appointed by the Ottomans to rule Egypt. One of his first moves was to eliminate the power of the Mameluks once and for all—by having them massacred. Afterward he set about to modernize Egypt. He introduced cotton from India, redistributed land and improved and expanded irrigation. He and his successors gradually obtained autonomy from the Ottomans.

Although history has tended to glamorize this chapter of Egyptian history, the fact is that Muhammad Ali dealt with the Egyptians as ruthlessly as he had with the Mameluks and in effect made Egypt into his personal estate. The nation became almost entirely dependent on its cotton crop. The combination of the concentration of power in the hands of his successors and the one-crop economy were to plague Egypt with many problems and much distress for the next century and a half.

In 1866 Isma'il, the grandson of Muhammad Ali, was granted the title of Khedive (viceroy) by the Turks, and during his reign the Suez Canal was completed. But by 1875, through his own extravagance and the charlatanry of the British, French and powerful European banking interests, Isma'il had become so heavily in debt that he was forced to sell his Canal shares to Britain. And in 1880 his successor, Tewfiq, had to submit to joint British-French control over Egypt's finances. (A full account of this period is available in James Aldridge's *Cairo*, and it helps one understand the background of events that followed over the next half century and that finally erupted into the revolution of 1952.)

European manipulation of the Khedive, Egypt's economy and the general mismanagement of the country caused unrest throughout the land. What started as an army protest headed by Ahmad 'Arabi, a lieutenant, developed into a revolt, and, unfortunately for the Egyptians, it provided a pretext for British intervention in 1882. For the next four decades, Britain ruled Egypt through her High Commissioners, the most famous—and most infamous—of whom was Lord Cromer, who ruled the country almost singlehandedly for twenty years.

During World War I, Britain declared Egypt a protectorate and brought Turkey's rule to an abrupt end. At the close of the war

Egyptian nationalists led by Said Zaghul agitated for independence, with an appeal by Zaghlul to the League of Nations convened in Paris. A treaty providing for a constitutional monarchy under Fuad I (the father of Farouk) was concluded in 1922; but despite promises of independence, the British protectorate remained until 1936 when another treaty promised eventual withdrawal of British troops.

In World War II, Britain undertook the defense of Egypt and defeated the Germans in a decisive battle at Alamein in 1942. After the war, friction between Egypt and Britain remained. The nationalist movement continued to grow and the Moslem Brotherhood became very strong. The aim of both was full independence and final withdrawal of the British. Outwardly, disputes centered around the Suez Canal and the Sudan, which had been under a joint Anglo-Egyptian condominium since 1899. Also, Egypt bitterly opposed the United Nations' partition of Palestine in 1948.

Independence in 1952

Finally, as a result of long frustration in their attempts to gain full independence and disillusionment with the corrupt Farouk government, a group of young army officers staged a bloodless coup in 1952. The following year Egypt was declared a republic, the dynasty of Muhammad Ali came to an end, and for the first time in 2,000 years Egypt was again in the hands of Egyptians. Muhammad Naguib, a respected elder statesman, was made head of the new government, but the following year Gamal Abel Nasser emerged as the power behind the coup and remained head of state until his sudden death in 1970.

At the beginning of his regime, relations between Egypt and the United States were very good. The United States supported Egypt's effort to enforce Britain's commitment to withdraw its troops and to turn over the administration of the Suez Canal to Egypt. However, as the conflict between Egypt and Israel heated up and the issue of U.S. participation in building the Aswan Dam erupted, American-Egyptian relations deteriorated.

When Egypt nationalized the Suez Canal Company and demanded the removal of British troops, the result in 1956 was a joint British, French and Israeli attack on Egypt, which was halted amid U.S. and Soviet threats and counterthreats that were complicated by the Hungarian uprising at the same time.

For the next decade, the U.S. position steadily declined as Russian influence grew. The Russians helped the Egyptians build the Aswan Dam, and supplied and trained the army, while becoming very active in the educational and cultural fields.

In 1958, and again in 1963 and 1971, attempts were made to form an Arab Union, first with Syria, then with Iraq and later with Libya.

From the time of the Six Day War in June 1967 to a renewal of the fighting in October 1973, diplomatic relations between Egypt and the U.S. were broken. But with the U.S. role in mediating the Sinai agreement and the reopening of the Suez Canal, relations greatly improved and were dramatized by Nixon's visit to Egypt in 1974 and the visit to America of Egyptian President Anwar Sadat the following year and a second visit in April of 1977. Indeed, the normally good relations that have characterized the historic intercourse between the two countries have returned.

British visitors will find a warmer welcome than before, thanks to the desire of most Egyptians to forget the unpleasantness in the past, and to the respect and admiration for Britain that is still strong in cultural and business circles.

Recent Events

Since the October War of 1973, events in the Middle East have taken many unpredictable turns and always Egypt has been at the center of them. The war itself was a turning point for the Egyptians. It helped them regain their confidence so badly shattered by their humiliating defeat in the Six-Day War of 1967. In practical terms, Egypt regained the Suez Canal and the desperately needed revenue from its traffic and began rebuilding the cities in the Canal Zone, enabling those who fled the war zone to return.

In 1974, President Sadat surprised the West by tossing out the Soviets, and in 1977 he dumbfounded the world by making his precedent-breaking visit to Israel. This was followed by the famous 1978 Camp David talks, and President Carter's visit to Egypt in 1979 was the gesture needed to bring the peace treaty with Israel into reality.

Efforts at achieving such a treaty have been the cornerstone of Egypt's policy since Sadat came into power in 1970. While Egypt's relationship with the rest of the Arab world has been greatly strained by the signing of the agreement, Sadat's peace initiatives have had the overwhelming approval of the Egyptian people, and following his tragic death in 1981, his successor Hosni Mubarrak has continued the pursuit of peace.

Isis, Goddess of Heaven and Earth

EGYPTIAN FOOD AND DRINK

Coffee, Fool *and* Zibib

Egyptians usually eat a light breakfast and have their main meal about 2 or 3 P.M. Many take afternoon tea about 5 or 6 P.M., and have a light supper. When Egyptians go out for dinner or invite guests to their home, the invitation will be for about 9:00 but dinner will probably not be served before 10:00 or 11:00 P.M.. Those who have the good fortune to be invited to an Egyptian home for a meal have a treat in store.

Restaurants serve lunch between 1:00 and 3:00 to 4:00 P.M. and dinner from 8:00 P.M. to midnight.

In most hotels, unless you specifically order an American breakfast, you get a Continental repast of toast, rolls, butter, jam and strong French coffee or tea. Juice is extra. Breakfast is usually served in your room with no extra charge for room service.

Sliced bread for toast is available, but is not as soft as American bread. Native Egyptian bread is a flat, round loaf called *aiysh*.

If you cannot start the day without a cup of American coffee, or if you can't handle strong French style morning coffee, pack a jar of instant coffee in your suitcase. Also, Nescafe or powdered coffee is available in most restaurants and hotels.

Drinking coffee is a tradition throughout the Middle East. You will always be offered a cup of Egyptian or Arabic coffee when you visit a friend or a business associate or stop at a shop in the bazaar.

Arabic coffee is thick and ordered according to the amount of sugar: sweet (*ziyada*), medium (*mazboota*), bitter (*saada*). In Egypt the local coffee house has been traditionally a meeting place for men who at the end of the day join their friends to smoke a *nargili* (hubble-bubble), listen to Arabic music, discuss politics and recite poetry.

Egypt has a variety of native dishes, and most good restaurants serve both western and Oriental selections. Menus will be available in English or French along with Arabic. The maitre d'hotel will speak English.

Appetizers

Batarikh: Egyptian caviar, pressed, dried and preserved in salt and oil, is served in small thin slices to be eaten with bread or crackers.

Baba-ghanoug: baked eggplant mashed and mixed with sesame paste, flavored with lemon, garlic and olive oil. The same dish is found in several Middle Eastern countries, but in Egypt its preparation and flavor vary slightly from that found in Lebanon or Syria. It is served as a dip with toasted bread chips or as an hors d'oeuvre or as a first course vegetable dish.

Leban zabadi: Egyptian yogurt—thicker, creamier and better than any yogurt you can get in the States. (Eating *leban zabadi* regularly helps to diminish intestinal upsets.)

Mish: dried cheese with spices added is made into a paste and served as an hors d'oeuvre.

Taameyya (or *falafel*): patties of mashed *fool* (fava bean) with finely chopped parsley, highly seasoned and deep-fried in oil. Excellent with cocktails. This is an Egyptian specialty and prepared better in Egypt than in any other Middle Eastern country, although many others claim it as their own.

Taheena: The oil paste from the sesame seed is often used as an ingredient in Arabic food. In Egypt, taheena alone is combined with lemon, garlic and spices and served with toasted bread chips as a dip for hors d'oeuvres.

Turshi (often called *bickley*): mixed vegetables pickled in a spicy sauce. Especially good with cocktails.

Waraq anab: rolled grape leaves stuffed with rice and meat or lentils. Known to Americans by its Greek name, *dolma*.

Main Courses

Fool mudhammas: This is the national dish of Egypt. *Fool* (fava bean) is cooked with spices, and sometimes tomatoes, into a thick sauce (something like chili con carne without meat). It is often eaten with a fried egg on top for breakfast, or without the egg for other meals. Very few restaurants frequented by tourists serve *fool mudhammas*. The Hilton coffee shop has it, and Tabie, a restaurant in downtown Cairo, is famous for it.

Kebab: Egyptian shish kebab is made of chunks of lamb or minced lamb (*kufta*) with spices added. In Egypt the flavor of kebab is different from that in any other Middle Eastern country. Lean pieces of lamb are cut into small cubes, then seasoned in a marinade of thin shavings of onion, parsley, marjoram, some lemon juice, salt and pepper. The marinaded pieces of lamb are then placed on a skewer and grilled over hot charcoal. When the meat is minced or ground and formed into finger patties around a skewer for broiling, it is called *Kufta*.

Moulukhiya: a steamed green vegetable (something like spinach), which may be eaten separately or used as a sauce on other dishes.

The plant closely resembles mint, and is known scientifically as Corete or *Carchorus alitorius*. The leaves are chopped and added to chicken or rabbit broth. *Moulukhiya* can be served as a soup or with crushed pieces of bread and some rice; the latter is known as *fattett moulukhiya*. The dish is available in several versions in other Arab countries, but to any Middle Easterner, *moulukhiya* is Egyptian.

Pigeons are broiled on an open spit, which gives the meat a smoky flavor. Several outdoor garden restaurants in Cairo specialize in the preparation of these birds. Casino des Pigeons by the Nile is the most popular.

Roz Bel Khalta: fried rice mixed with currants, nuts, meat and liver.

Grilled Shrimp: huge, succulent and delicious shrimp from the Mediterranean and the Red Sea, more like small lobster tails. This is probably the best dish for American tastes to be found in Egypt—a real treat. Small shrimp are available too.

Other Eastern Dishes: Many of the better known Lebanese dishes are available in Egypt and are often served in Egyptian homes. Curry, presumably brought from India by the British, is available in several Cairo restaurants as mild or as hot as you like.

Fruits, Desserts and Cheese

There is a year-round variety of fruit—citrus, melons (especially Ismailia melon), pomegranates, apricots and figs. All are excellent. Eat whatever fruit is in season—peel it for caution. If you are lucky enough to be in Egypt when mangos are in season, you will have an unexpected treat.

Egyptian sherbet, *dondurma,* is a white milk ice that is very sweet. *Umm Ali,* a bread pudding topped with pine nuts and milk, served hot, is also an Egyptian specialty. *Aish el saraya* has a custard on the bottom, cake on top; *ata'if* is a special dessert for the month of Ramadan, and *kanafa,* a sweet resembling shredded wheat stuffed with chopped nuts, is flavored with syrup and rose water. All are very sweet, popular desserts of Syrian origin. *Muhalabiya* is a particularly good dessert made from creme of rice and decorated with pistachios.

The local cheese, *gibna beida,* is similar to what is called Greek or *feta* cheese in the U.S.

Beverages

Several good, inexpensive table wines are made from Alexandrian grapes. Omar Khayyam (dry red), Rubis d'Egypte (rosé) and Gianaclis Village (dry white) are the best, and run about L.E. 2.75 a bottle in retail shops. The markup in hotels and restaurants may be 200 percent or more. Quality is variable, and there are other labels of inferior quality.

As a matter of interest, it is not known whether grapes were indigenous to the Nile Valley or whether they were imported to Egypt in ancient times. Both tree- and vine-growing were known, but from ancient drawings, the latter appears to have been more widespread. As far back as the Third Dynasty (about 2730 B.C.) Egyptians were planting grape trees in their gardens. One of the most interesting tombs in the Valley of the Nobles at Luxor is that of Sennefer. Its ceiling is designed to represent a grape arbor.

Local brandy comes in a variety of prices and grades, but the best, suitable for punches and mixed drinks, costs L.E. 3 for a large bottle. There is also a rum, Zattos, for L.E. 2.

Zibib is the Egyptian version of Lebanese *arak,* Turkish *raki,*

Greek *ouzo,* or French *pernod* and makes an excellent before-dinner drink, either on the rocks or diluted with water, which turns it a milky color. The anisette flavored aperitif comes in two sizes: L.E. 2.50 large bottle; 1.50 pt. for a small one.

All the above wines and liquors can be purchased at the Egyptian Vineyards and Distilleries, 41 Talaat Harb Street. At the resthouse and gasoline station halfway between Alexandria and Cairo on the desert road, the Gianaclis Vineyards maintain a shop for their wines and spirits, as well as their olive and date by products. The wines, especially, are cheaper than in Cairo.

Imported liquors, including whiskey, normally cost L.E. 15 to 20 per bottle in retail shops and will be marked up 200 percent or more in hotels and nightclubs. Visitors should plan to bring the one duty free bottle allowed upon entering. Drinks in bars vary from L.E. 3 to 5.

The local beer is good and inexpensive—70 pts. for a large bottle. Stella is a light lager in green or brown bottles. Stella Export is sweeter, more expensive (L.E. 2 in bars) and comes in smaller brown bottles. You will almost always be served a large bottle. The small ones seem to be in short supply. Bock beer is available briefly in the spring season and is called *marzen.* Aswali is a dark beer made in Aswan. Major hotels and European-style restaurants have a limited selection of imported beers, which are very expensive—L.E. 3 and up per bottle!

There are soft drinks, soda, tonic mineral water and a variety of exotic fruit juices available year round and seasonally. Again, one should be cautioned that imported soft drinks cost L.E. 1 and up; a locally made lemon soda is 30 to 50 pts. depending on where it is purchased. Coco-Cola and 7-Up are now locally made.

One of the most popular Egyptian refreshments is *Karkade,* a pretty rasberry-color drink made from a plant grown in Aswan. Guests are often served this in government or business offices and in Egyptian homes. Local tradition says it is good to calm the nerves. It is served cold in summer or hot, like tea, in winter.

THE FACE OF EGYPT

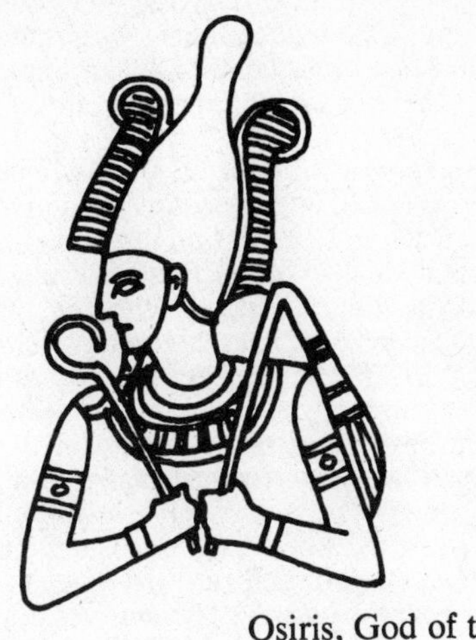

Osiris, God of the Dead

CAIRO

City of a Thousand Years

The graceful minarets of stately mosques vie with slim modern buildings along the skyline. Shady parks overlooking the river and flowering gardens along wide boulevards refresh the eyes against the desert edges of this magnificent city astride the Nile.

Cairo, Egypt's capital and largest city in Africa, sways with the movement of ten million people—the ever-present multitudes. Located at the apex of the Delta, this great metropolis is the meeting place of Africa and Arabia, Europe and Asia.

Throughout most of its history, Cairo has been the bank and warehouse of east-west trade. Because of its location, it was the most convenient junction for the transshipment of goods, which arrived by ship from the East via the Red Sea and from there were carried overland the short distance to Cairo. Here they were stored, bought or sold, then floated down the Nile to the Mediterranean and on to Europe.

Few capitals in the world have quite the same all-encompassing position as Cairo does today. It is Egypt's economic, political, administrative, cultural, educational, entertainment, military, transportation and historical center—all in one. Almost nothing happens in Egypt that does not happen in Cairo. This is at once its blessing and its curse.

Cairo's four universities attract men and women from all over the Middle East, Asia and Africa, as they did in ancient times. Al Azhar, considered the oldest continuous university in history, is the most important center of religious learning in the Moslem world. Cairo has fabulous museums, churches and mosques. Its bazaars are the best in the eastern Mediterranean, set in narrow winding alleys in an atmosphere permeated with spices and incense.

Actually, there have been many Cairos in the history of this great city. The first is so ancient historians do not know when it was begun or by whom. Known as "On" in antiquity, it was called Heliopolis, the city of the sun, by the Greeks. On was the center of worship of Re, the sun-god, and reached its peak about 2500 B.C. For hundreds of years it had the ancient world's most advanced university. After the rise of Thebes, On lost its preeminence but remained an important center of the empire. Today, an obelisk in Heliopolis, a modern suburb of Cairo, marks the site of ancient On. Ironically, Heliopolis in Arabic is called Masr Gadid (New Cairo). Another city is believed to have grown around the royal farm and dwelling place of the workers building the pyramids in the period between 2700–2500 B.C. Today, this settlement is somewhere under the homes and apartments of Cairo suburbs, which stretch unbroken from the Nile to the shadow of the great Pyramids of Giza.

After the Persians under Cambyses razed Heliopolis to the ground in 525 B.C., the long history of the city was broken for a thousand years—significant for Egypt as much as for the city. The Greeks, who followed the Persians, shifted the capital to Alexandria and with one stroke lifted Egypt out of Africa and placed it on the Mediterranean. With it, the era of the pharaohs ended and a European era began. Athens was a village, but Alexandria was the capital of the empire.

All the more reason that a thousand years later, when the Arabs streaked across the desert to pitch their tents at Fustat, the forerunner of today's Cairo, the shift was more than geographic. It signaled the end of Greek culture and the Christian era and the beginning of a new Egypt—Arab and Islamic.

The oldest part of the city is still known by the Egyptians as Old

Cairo. Here, the Persians built a fort on the strategic point of the Nile and the Romans fortified the site known as Babylon. Near the Roman fortress where the Arab army camped, a mosque was built and around it the city grew. Over the next three centuries the city shifted its center slightly—to Askar and to Katai. Then in 969, the Fatimids from North Africa conquered Egypt and established their capital in the area they called al Qahira, the victorious. Finally, in the 12th century under Saladin, all four locales were made into one.

While the name did not change, Cairo changed many times during the next five centuries under the Mameluks and expanded north along the Nile. Finally, in the period after the French invasion and the arrival of the Europeans, the city crossed the river to its west bank. But even after a thousand years the city's greatest expansion of all times has been in this century and more particularly since World War II.

Today, Cairo stretches so far in each direction that the only place from which one can see its great expanse is the Tower of Cairo on the island of Gezira, in the middle of the Nile. In the panorama the history of Egypt and the tale of Cairo unfolds: from the south, the Nile comes up from Africa to just north of the city, where it divides to form the great Delta, and from there it continues to the Mediterranean. Behind the soaring minarets of the Muhammad Ali Mosque and the Mukattam Hills in the east, there is the desert stretching to Arabia. To the west, beyond the Pyramids, another desert stretches across the Sahara wasteland. The green, fertile land created by the Nile is sharply edged on both banks of the river.

From this dramatic scene a visitor can also spot the center of the modern city, Midan al Tahrir (Liberation Square), which is the best place in which to orient oneself to the city. From the square the roads on the north and northeast lead to Cairo's main business district, the fashionable shopping streets of Kasr el Nil and Talaat Harb, and the cinema district. Beyond is Bulac, Opera Square, the Ezbekiya Gardens, the heart of Cairo at the time of the Napoleonic invasion, and the Mouski.

Directly south of Midan al Tahrir lies Garden City, the former palatial residence of colonial Egypt, and farther south are Old Cairo and the island of Roda. The Corniche drive by the Nile leads south to Maadi, a suburb of beautiful villas and gardens.

East of Midan al Tahrir is the Bab el Luk district and beyond that the Citadel commands the city from the foot of the Mukattam hills. This area is the most historic part of the city. Visitors will find many of the great mosques, old houses and museums.

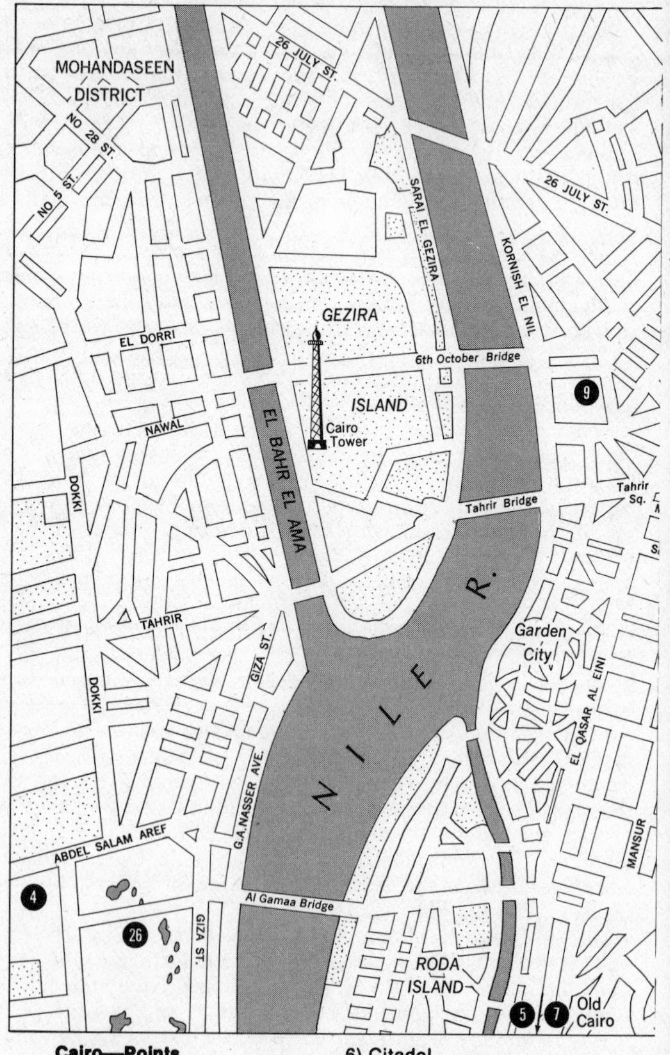

Cairo—Points of Interest

1) Abdin Palace
2) Azbakiya Garden Theater
3) Blue Mosque
4) Cairo University
5) Church of Abu Serga
6) Citadel
7) Coptic Museum
8) Egyptian Library
9) Egyptian Museum
10) El-Azhar Mosque
11) Islamic Museum
12) Khan el-Khalili (Bazar)

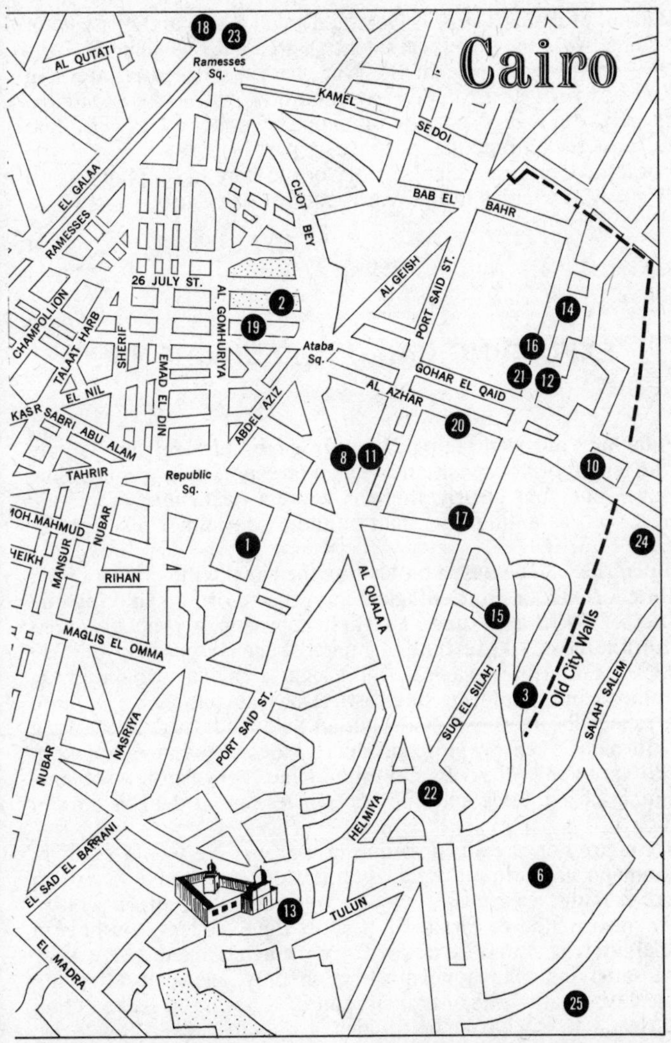

13) Mosque of Ahmed Ibn Tulun
14) Mosque of el Akmar
15) Mosque of el Mardani
16) Mosque of Kalaun
17) Mosque of Sultan el-Muayyad
18) Railroad Station
19) Royal Opera
20) School-Mosque of El-Ghuri
21) School-Mosque of Sultan Barkuk
22) School-Mosque of Sultan Hasan
23) Statue of Ramses II
24) Tombs of the Caliphs
25) Tombs of the Mamelukes
26) Zoo

West of Midan al Tahrir is Gezira, a small island in the middle of the Nile, with the lovely residential area of Zamalek. Beyond Gezira on the west side of the Nile are the residential areas of Dokki and Giza, Cairo University and the road to the Pyramids. This area, although a separate municipality under the governorate of Giza, is for all practical purposes a part of Cairo.

For a traveler in search of history or pleasure, a shophound or a sportsman, few cities in the world compare to Cairo.

EXPLORING CAIRO AND ENVIRONS

Planning Your Sightseeing: What to see in Cairo depends largely on the length of your visit and your interests. There is something for everyone, but clearly there is a great deal more of certain things, such as antiquities, than in almost any other place in the world.

Itineraries can be based on visiting the sites in the order of their historic, artistic or archaeological importance or by exploring one district of Cairo at a time. The first approach is probably more useful for those whose time is limited because one can quickly make a list of priorities and design a sightseeing day around it. On the other hand, exploring one district of Cairo at a time is more fun, especially for those who plan an extended visit. In the long run, it might even be more productive because Cairo is a very large, sprawling city. It has the same congestion problems afflicting all big cities and one can waste a great deal of time in traffic.

If you are not already traveling in a group, we would strongly recommend you join an organized city tour on your first visit to Cairo. It is the least costly way to tour and it will enable you to cover most of the essentials in a short time. Unless you have a special interest in one aspect of Egypt, a generalized tour will be more satisfying than concentrating on only one aspect for the whole day. If, after one or two city tours, you want to strike out on your own, you will have a better idea of what to see and how to see it.

Hiring a car or taxi with or without a guide and planning your own itinerary enables you to see and remain at the places that interest you most, but it can be expensive. If you do decide to go off on your own, be sure to set the fee *in advance* for a hired car, guide, donkey, camel, carriage, horse or whatever.

If at any time you should have trouble with a taxi driver, peddler, vendor, guide or dragoman, you should report it immediately to the Tourist Office or the nearest Tourist Police.

A list of local travel agents in Cairo and Alexandria is available in a local publication entitled *Cairo By Night and Day,* available from hotels and airlines. We have not included the list here as the number of new agencies is growing by the day. Some, but not all, operate their own tours of Cairo and Upper Egypt or can arrange them on short notice. The large companies, such as American Express and Misr Travel, have regularly scheduled tours that you can purchase and join with other travelers. As an example, the half-day Pyramid and Sphinx tour is L.E. 14. An all day Memphis and Sakkara, Pyramids and Sphinx tour is L.E. 24. Either a city tour or a tour of Old Cairo is L.E. 10 each and the evening program for the Sound and Light show at the Pyramids is L.E. 10. Be very careful about the agency with whom you deal. Many of the new ones are inadequately staffed and incompetent and are charging ridiculous prices.

Tourist Police and Guides: At ports, airports, hotels and major tourist areas, tourist officers selected from the police corps are on hand to assist tourists on arrival and during their visit in Egypt. They might not always have the answers to your questions, but they are willing to help. Most speak enough English to help you or to help you find someone who can help you. They wear a regular policeman's uniform (black for winter; white for summer) and can be distinguished by a small light blue bar worn on the chest pocket, which reads "Tourist Police."

There is also a guides' association (although we have yet to discover precisely where it is or who administers it), which gives practical training to candidates chosen and licensed by the Tourist Office, 5 Adly Street, Phone: 79394. On a recent trip to Egypt, we were with a young guide who had taken a tourism degree at a local university. She was sweet and charming, but her knowledge of Cairo was not extensive. If you are genuinely interested in history and antiquities, you should be very exact about this with your travel agent. There are good, knowledgeable guides in Egypt, but the best ones must be booked in advance. A list of guides/phone numbers appears in the *Practical Guide to Cairo*.

On the other hand, even with the best guide in Egypt to show you around, there is no substitute for reading in advance. There is much more to Cairo than the Pyramids. We urge you to investigate it on your own, hopefully with this guidebook in hand and the specialized aids that we recommend where appropriate. If you rely solely on tourist guides, you will have nothing but the most superficial look at this great city.

Dragomen: If you cannot see Egypt's antiquities in the company of a full-fledged Egyptologist, archaeologist, historian, architect or Islamic expert, then your next choice is a *dragoman*. These are the traditional, handsomely robed and turbaned men who have been guiding around antiquity sites and through the bazaars for at least a century—and they are now a dying institution.

The word *dragoman* is a corruption of the Arabic word *terjiman,* meaning interpreter. In olden days that is what they were, but at the turn of the century, with the arrival of the rich Europeans and Americans who came to winter in Egypt, the dragoman expanded his services until he became all things to all people. He filled the role of guide, mentor, father confessor, bodyguard and, with luck, lasting friend. Most of the old gentlemen have never been to school, but they often know more about the sites of antiquity than some of the new guides who have not had proper training, and they are certainly more entertaining. Their information is often inaccurate in detail, but never mind; the good ones tell their stories with great drama and with such excitement that they pique your interest and make a good show of it. Most of the time you are glad to have them with you to call off the hounds of peddlers and the kids after *baksheesh.*

Most dragomen are reliable, but, as with everything else in Egypt, you should agree on the price beforehand—and don't pay until you are finished. The usual fee is about L.E. 10 for half a day and L.E. 20 for a whole day, although the price seems to be going up rather rapidly these days, and many will insist on more. You can be sure that if you go shopping with him he will take you to his favorite shop (one that his cousin owns) and he will get a 25 percent kickback, or more.

For easy reference, the following section on the capital city has been divided into **Pharaonic, Coptic, Islamic** and **modern** Cairo. Visitors would be unlikely to visit the sites in this order, but it helps to read about them and to refer to them with some historical perspective.

Museum hours and entrance fees are as reliable as we have been able to make them. The opening and closing times are notoriously inconsistent. Often we have gone to a museum after closing hours to discover that it is still open. The one that seems to be the most strict about its hours is the Egyptian Antiquities Museum.

The itineraries at the end of this section are designed to enable visitors to see the most in the shortest time. If you are planning an extended stay, you might want to consult a travel agent or the Tourist Office in Cairo for more information and to help you make a detailed itinerary.

A word of caution: Do not overdo your sightseeing. Even if you are a history buff or an archaeology freak, there is so much to see that you could easily become saturated with viewing tombs and temples and lose the thrill and the wonder of ancient Egypt. Try to mix some of the Egypt of today with your tours through the Egypt of yesterday.

PHARAONIC CAIRO

Summary of Pharaonic Cairo: Within easy reach of the city are the Pyramids and Sphinx, Memphis and Sakkara. These should be preceded by a visit to the Egyptian Antiquities Museum.

The Pyramids

Located nine miles west of Cairo. Admission: L.E. 3; Solar Boat Museum: L.E. 6. Hours: 8:00 A.M. to 5:00 P.M.

On arrival in Cairo by plane or train, the excitement of your visit will be heightened as soon as you have the first glimpse of the gigantic peaks of the three Pyramids of Giza rising in the distance on the western horizon. At a closer range, your first look at them—the last of the Seven Wonders of the Ancient World—will be surprising and perhaps even disappointing.

The Pyramids are the ultimate travel cliche and, what's more, they look exactly like their picture. But don't worry, the disappointment is fleeting. Within a short time, your mind will start to grasp the size of the Pyramids, the precision of their structure, and the effort it took to build them, and you will begin to marvel at them. Then, suddenly, the impact of their majesty and symmetry will overwhelm you and leave you speechless.

Famous writers down through the ages have written about this experience. One of our favorites is Julian Huxley in *From an Antique Land* (New York: Harper & Row, 1966):

"Familiarity . . . had led me . . . to discount [the Pyramids]. They had become international commonplaces, degraded to the level of the tourist souvenir. They had passed through so many million minds as one of the 'Wonders of the World' that their sharp edge of real wonder had been blunted. . . . I was sure I was not going to be impressed by them.

"But in actuality, they make an overpowering impression. It is not one of beauty, but on the other hand not one of mere bigness, though size enters into it, and there is an element of aesthetic satisfaction in the elemental simplicity of their triangular silhouette. But this combines with an element of vicarious pride in the magnitude of the human achievement involved . . . to produce an effect different from that of any other work of man."

Jomrad, one of the scholars on Napoleon's expedition, described his experience thus:

"Seen from a distance they produce the same kind of effect as do high mountain peaks. . . . The nearer one approaches, the more this effect decreases. But when at last you are within a short distance of these regular masses, a wholly different impression is produced; you are struck by surprise, and as soon as you have reached the top of the slope, your ideas change in a flash. Finally, when you have reached the foot of the Great Pyramid, you are seized with a vivid and powerful emotion, tempered by a sort of stupefaction, almost overwhelming in its effects."

The Pyramids stand on a hill overlooking the Nile Valley and are a testimony to the ancients' belief in the immortality of the soul. It took 20 years to build one.

Although there are some 80 pyramids in Egypt, the three at Giza are the most important and the most famous. The first in size and chronological order is Cheops (Khufu), erected about 2690 B.C. Its original height was 481 ft. and its base covered 13 acres. Cheophren (Kheophren), Cheops' son, built the second pyramid about 2650 B.C., slightly smaller in size. The third pyramid, smallest of the three, was erected about 2600 B.C. and named after Menkaru (Mycerinus).

The Great Pyramid is estimated to contain 2.5 million tons of stone; each stone weighs an average of 2.5 tons. According to Napoleon, its cubic content is enough to build a wall ten feet high and a foot thick entirely around France. The area of its base is said to be large enough to hold St. Paul's, Westminster Abbey, St. Peter's and the Cathedrals of Florence and Milan all at one time. To put it in American terms, that means that the base of Cheops' pyramid covers the same area as the four city blocks taken up by Lincoln Center in New York.

The Great Pyramid is still the largest and most massive stone structure in the world. The stones, put together without mortar, are fitted so perfectly that not even a razor blade can be passed between them.

The interior of Cheops' pyramid has several long empty corridors without decoration. The most important is the Grand Gallery,

153 ft. long and 28 ft. high, leading to a simple funeral chamber. Two openings pierce the entire structure and let in outer air. Above the King's Chamber, five other compartments formed by huge granite blocks were designed to relieve the chamber of the structure's tremendous weight. The climb up into the chambers of the pyramid is not for the faint-hearted, the claustrophobic or the out-of-shape. One can walk erect for quite a way into the pyramid to inspect the walls and passageways and then turn back.

Details on the history and building of the Pyramids are covered in many scholarly tomes, and the speculations over how and why they were built have been the basis of many popular books. Among those included in the "Suggested Reading List," one of the best and easiest to read is *The Pyramids,* by Ahmed Fakhry, one of Egypt's leading scholars who spent his life studying them.

East of the Pyramids lie the tombs of the princesses; on the west, those of nobles and courtiers. Such tombs are known as *mastabas,* because their shape resembles a bench (mastaba) still found against the doors of village houses. Some scholars think it was, in fact, from these simple structures that the design of the Pyramids grew.

At the foot of the Great Pyramid, a former royal resthouse in pharaonic style is now a museum. It has a pleasant outdoor garden and commands a magnificient view of the Nile Valley and Cairo. The view from here clearly shows the meaning of the Nile to Egypt: the great, green valley created by the waters of the Nile halts abruptly at the barren desert's edge.

New discoveries are constantly being made in the area of the Pyramids, but none have been more exciting than the two well preserved wooden funeral boats that were uncovered in 1954 south of the Great Pyramid. They are the only vestiges from Cheops' reign, other than the Pyramid itself, that have been discovered, and they are considered the most sensational archaeological find of recent years.

The first boat, which has been reassembled and stands in a museum next to the Cheops' pyramid, actually carried the body of the pharaoh from Memphis to Giza. Although the museum building has caused authorities a great deal of trouble in their attempt to stabilize its climatic condition to prevent further deterioration of the wood, ropes, canvas sails and reed mats, authorities finally decided to open the museum to raise money to correct the building's structural problems.

The Sphinx

Five hundred feet southeast of the Great Pyramid is the Sphinx, a recumbent lion with the head of a man. It was carved from natural rock, presumably *in situ.* Over the centuries as parts eroded or broke off, they were replaced, but the additions were fitted so well they are hardly perceptible.

The body of the lion—the symbol of kingship—represented might. The Sphinx's human head symbolized intelligence. Its headgear is called the Klaft, a striped hood with two flaps that are placed behind the ears and brought forward to rest on the shoulders. The Sphinx has a total length of 190 ft. and is 66 ft. tall at its highest point. The face alone measures 16.6 ft. Its paws seem out of proportion with the rest of the body, but the Sphinx was meant to be viewed from the front at the bottom of the valley. From there the paws are in proper perspective. The Sphinx faces east from where it was meant to watch the rising sun—the return of life—each day.

The Greeks called the statue the Sphinx because it resembled a legendary hero by a similar name. It is probable that Abu-al-Hul, as he is known in Arabic, has the head of Cheophren, his builder. Successive pharaohs down to Roman times restored, venerated and admired this remarkable statue. Some considered it the god of death.

Adjoining the Sphinx is the funerary temple of Cheops. At this temple the body of the dead pharaoh was mummified and sanctified by the priests. It is believed this process could have taken as long as a year. From the temple, you may look up the causeway to the site of another temple at the base of the pyramid, where religious ceremonies took place before the body was entombed.

Son et Lumière (Sound and Light): The evening program for the Pyramids and Sphinx was one of the first in the *Son et Lumière* repertoire and is still one of the best. While floodlights play on the Pyramids, recorded voices apparently coming from the Sphinx tell their history. The lights display many unusual aspects of the Pyramids and vividly reveal their beautiful form and majesty. Check locally to verify the exact schedule. Admission: L.E. 4. Phone: 27553.

Buses leave nightly from the Son et Lumière Booth at Tahrir Square in front of the Hilton Hotel and return to the same location after the program. You can also hire a taxi to take you there, wait and return you to town. Be sure to settle the price in advance. L.E. 12 is reasonable. Local tour operators offer the excursion for L.E. 10 by motorcoach. Limo Misr will provide a car and driver for L.E. 16.

A word of warning—modernity has come to the Pyramids.

Those who knew the area a decade or two ago will be startled to see it now. A four lane highway runs from town to the Mena House and a two lane asphalt road continues up the hill to the Great Pyramid, enabling tour buses to disgorge groups at its very base! Progress—it is enough to make one weep.

Memphis and Sakkara

The ancient city of Memphis lies 20 miles southwest of Cairo. Admission: L.E. 3. Hours—8:00 A.M.–5:00 P.M.

Very little remains of the ancient city of Memphis, for centuries Egypt's capital. Near the little village of Meit Rahini, an ancient Egyptian name meaning "the ram-headed sphinx road," a small museum houses a magnificent recumbent figure of Ramses II, carved in alabaster. On the grounds nearby are a large alabaster sphinx from the XVIII Dynasty, which stands on the site where it was excavated, and several ancient statues.

Memphis was the city of the living; Sakkara, the city of the dead. The name Sakkara is derived from the word *sakr* (hawk), the god of necropolis in the nether world. The necropolis contains over 14 pyramids, hundreds of mastabas and tombs, art objects and engravings dating from the first to the XXX Dynasty. Here, the oldest mummy and the oldest papyrus were found.

The Step Pyramid, thought by some to represent a staircase to heaven, was erected by Zoser, a pharaoh of the III Dynasty, and predates the Pyramids of Giza. Indeed, the Step Pyramid at Sakkara is considered the forerunner of the architectural style of the Giza Pyramids. It was the first major building in stone and was considered the greatest structure known to man at that time. Its architect, Imhotep (later known as the god of medicine), was the first to investigate the mystery of the Nile Flood about 3000 B.C.

A funeral chamber probably belonging to Sekhemkhet and an unfinished step pyramid (2750 B.C.) were discovered a few years ago near the Step Pyramid. The tomb is underground and composed of a main passage leading to a funeral chamber. Inside the chamber a large alabaster sarcophagus was found, but with no mummy. In addition, vases and various pieces of furniture were uncovered. Dozens of compartments, probably storerooms, surround the chamber.

Southeast of the Step Pyramid are the remains of an ancient colonnaded temple, probably the first of its kind in the world.

The largest and most beautiful mastaba in the necropolis is the Tomb of Teti, an important figure at the royal court in the late period of the VI Dynasty. The wall decorations have been extremely valuable to scholars in studying the life and customs of the ancient Egyptians in the early Dynastic period.

The Serapeum is the most curious tomb of the whole necropolis. It was dedicated to Apis, the ox, which was mummified in exactly the same ceremonial fashion as a human being.

Many excavations have been undertaken at Sakkara in recent years, but scholars estimate that only a third of the area has been studied.

Egyptian Antiquities Museum

Located on Tahrir Square (next to the Nile Hilton Hotel). Admission: L.E. 3. Hours: 9:00 A.M.–4:00 P.M. daily, Friday until 11:30 A.M. and from 1:00–4:00 P.M.

This museum contains the world's most important collection of Egyptian antiquities, dating from earliest times to about the 6th century A.D. The collection includes some of the artistic masterpieces of the world, including the famous mask of Tutankhamun.

The Department of Antiquities was created, and conservation and excavation services started, in the mid-19th century. The French savant August Mariette was appointed its first director, and the antiquities were housed and exhibited in a building in Bulaq. In 1891, the collection was transferred to Giza, and finally in 1902 they were placed in the present building. The collection has long since outgrown the space. A building ten times larger would be only adequate—that's how much the collection has grown. What's more, the museum suffered for several decades from Egypt's hard times. In planning your sightseeing, you may find the museum less crowded with visitors early, although the tour group crunch starts about 9:30 A.M. or after 1:00 P.M.

At the entrance of the museum a guidebook is available, and it is essential for viewing the exhibits on your own. Each exhibit in the museum is labeled with a number. The descriptions in the guidebook correspond to the numbers of the exhibit. More elaborate, expensive books and color slides and photographs are also on sale. Special permission is required to photograph in the museum. At least two hours are needed to see the main exhibits.

Guides can be hired for L.E. 5 for a tour that will take approximately two hours. Be sure to settle this price in advance.

The museum is in the shape of a rectangle. At the main entrance, turn left and follow its four sides. This will give you a chronological survey of ancient Egypt, beginning with the earliest period of recorded history, the Old Empire, about 3200 B.C., followed by the Middle Empire and the New Empire comprising the XVIII, XIX and XX Dynasties.

In the north gallery is the Akhenaten Room, and in the east gallery are numerous rooms containing monuments of the Ramasessid, Saite, Persian, Greco-Roman and Nubian periods. On the second floor, the collection from the Tomb of Tutankhamun is displayed.

The museum is so full of marvels you will want to return many times. From the paintings, statues, furniture and models in the museum, visitors can draw a vivid impression of the ancient Egyptians. It would be impractical to describe all the exhibits in this museum, there are so many. We will point out only some of the most important.

The Rotunda at the entrance contains exhibits from recent excavations and those of the most colossal size. You may wish to save this section for the last stop as you will have several opportunities to view it from the balconies of the second floor.

Turning left at the entrance, you come to the monuments of the first pharaonic period, the Old Kingdom (III to VI Dynasties, 2700–2200 B.C.), during which period Memphis was the capital. Its greatest surviving achievements are the Pyramids of Giza. In the galleries and corridors that make up the South and West Galleries on the ground floor there are dozens of statues and exhibits. In particular, note the group of statues in painted limestone representing workers at various tasks. The ancient Egyptians believed that the dead could still be served after death and that their eternal life depended in some measure upon their being properly supplied from earth.

In the first exhibit room on the right, Room 42 of the West Gallery, is a diorite statue of Cheophren (No. 138), who built the second Pyramid. The statue was discovered in the temple of Cheophren by Mariette in 1858. It represents one of the finest pieces of sculpture ever found in the country. Two other excellently preserved painted limestone statues, discovered in 1871, are located in Room 32 on the right. These lifelike statues represent Ra-Hotpe (No. 223), high priest of Heliopolis (IV Dynasty), and his wife, Nofret. Different skin colors are used to denote man (dark or reddish brown) and woman (mustard yellow). This is one of the most photographed of all the exhibits. In the same room, you should note the larger-than-life statue No. 225, the priest Ra-hufer (V Dynasty). It is considered one of the best examples of Memphis art ever found.

The corridors have as many interesting and important exhibits as the rooms on each side. Note No. 286, Queen Nofret; Nos. 180, 158, and 149 of Mycerinus with Hathor. There are also statues in wood, as well as stone. Note especially the statue No. 116, with eyes of translucent stones.

After a period of internal discord in the Old Kingdom, during which time the country was divided into small kingdoms, there was a renaissance with the beginning of the first Theban or Middle Kingdom (2200 B.C.). It ended about 1700 B.C. when the Hyksos invaded Lower Egypt.

The character of the Middle Kingdom (Room 22) is quite different from that of the Old Kingdom, and is reflected in the statues, such as those of Amenemhat III (XII Dynasty) and Senusret I (Sesostris). Notice No. 280, a wooden statue of King Hor (XIII Dynasty), which has the emblem of the *Ka* (two arms raised) placed on his head, signifying that the statue is a double of the king and qualified to receive his soul, if the need should arise.

Further on in the hall is the small sphinx (No. 6152) in painted limestone portraying Queen Hatshepsut (XVIII Dynasty). The headdress is identical to those of the Hyksos sphinx.

Near the entrance of the hall (Room 12) of the XVIII Dynasty, which marked the beginning of the New Kingdom, is the white marble statue of Thutmose III (No. 428), the hero of the battle of Megiddo and the head of the Egyptian Empire at its zenith. During his reign and that of his predecessor, Queen Hatshepsut, architecture developed to a degree equalled only by Ramses II (XIX Dynasty), the greatest monument builder of all time.

In Room 12 are two of the most interesting of all the museum's exhibits: No. 445, a sandstone chapel with excellent reliefs depicting Thutmose III making offerings to Amen-Ra, and No. 446, a statue of a cow representing the goddess Hathor and Amenophis II drinking from the cow's udder, found in the chapel (XVIII Dynasty). Also note No. 6257, a fine ebony statue of Thy with intricate details. It was found at Sakkara, XVIII Dynasty.

In the Akhenaten exhibit, housed in Room 3 of the North Gallery, note exhibits No. 13247, 13248 and 3873. The jewelry in this room is exquisite. Also note the alabaster canopic vases (jars to hold the viscera of the deceased, embalmed separately from the body). There are also Nos. 6015 and 6016, statues of Akhenaten. A stele (No. 487) shows Akhenaten kneeling in adoration before the solar disc. It marks the founding of Tell El Amarna, his new capital. Another, No. 6056, is part of an altar with Akhenaten and his beautiful wife, Nefertiti. Among other important monuments is a sanctuary erected by Ramses II. It consists of two small obelisks bearing inscriptions glorifying the ruler.

Room 14 in the East Gallery is a continuation of the New Empire, XIX and XX Dynasties. You should note especially the statues of Ramses III, Horus and Set found at Medinet Hebu, dating from the XX Dynasty.

Also, No. 930, an alabaster statue standing in the hall at No. 30 position, is of Amenartais, XXV Dynasty.

Among the Greco-Roman antiquities, there is an extensive coin collection (Room 4, North Gallery).

There are fine mural paintings from Tuna El Gebel (ancient Hermopolis) near Minya, depicting the Oedipus legend, along with other art works belonging to the Greek and Roman periods (Room 34, East Gallery).

Also in the East Gallery (Room 44) is the Meroitic exhibit dating from about 300 B.C., when the capital of Ethiopia was transferred to Meroe, an island between the White and the Blue Niles, well situated for control of the routes from Sudan into Egypt.

In the period of the Ethiopian Kings (XXV Dynasty, 750–656 B.C.) Piankhi and Taharqa, the latter was driven back to Sudan by the invading Assyrians. At Begerawien, there are 40 small pyramids, which were the tombs of the kings of Meroe.

This hall also contains Nubian antiquities of the Byzantine period, which came from the royal tombs of Ballana and Qustul in Nubia. They have a strong resemblance to the objects found in the excavations near Wadi Halfa. The collection includes jewels, crowns, bracelets and necklaces of semiprecious stones.

Leaving the Nubian Hall, you are once again in the South Gallery, and pass a number of sarcophagi from the Ptolemaic period.

The center hall contains a lovely painted wall from Tell al Amarna. There are also huge statues of Amenophis III. The stele of Ramses II, which some scholars say was the pharoah of Moses' time, is the first mention of the Israelites found in Egypt.

The Tutankhamun Galleries are located on the second floor. Visitors should note that these rooms are closed 30 minutes earlier than other parts of the museum.

The story of the discovery of the young pharaoh's tomb, whose marvelous treasure today fills a quarter of the museum, is well known. For years, Howard Carter, a British archaeologist, searched for the tomb the length of the Valley of the Kings. Then, in 1922, just as he was about to abandon the search, he came upon the first steps leading to the hiding place.

When Amenhotep III (1402–1365 B.C.) died, his eldest son ascended to the throne as Amenhotep IV; but later he discarded that name, and history knows him best as Akhenaten. A rebel against the powerful priests of Thebes, Akhenaten has always been one of the most fascinating pharaohs of ancient Egypt. Although a great deal has been written about him, in fact very little is known about this unusual man. Only recently one of the temples he is known to have built was found near Luxor.

Akhenaten formulated a new faith which historians describe as the first monotheistic religion in the world. He conceived of Aton, the symbol of which is the sun's disc, as the one god, and he set about to destroy all the other gods, an act which directly threatened the powerful priests of Thebes. The conflict became so bitter that the revolutionary young Pharaoh moved his capital from Thebes to Tell el Amarna, south of Minya, where he built a new capital, which he called Akhetaton (the Horizon of Aton).

Here he lived with his beautiful Queen Nefertiti, who gave birth to daughters only. The eldest married Semenkh-Ka-Re, for whom Akhenaten felt a deep affection and whom he named his successor. Semenkh-Ka-Re died, probably at about the same time as Akhenaten. He was replaced by Tutankhamun, who had spent his childhood at his brother's court and who had married Akhenaten's second daughter. Egyptologists are not sure of the precise relationship between Tutankhamun and Akhenaten. They are alternately described as brothers and half-brothers.

Tutankhaton was thought to be about nine years old when he acceded to the throne in 1334 B.C. For the next three years, he remained at Akhetaton and continued the Aton cult. But the priests of Amon were too powerful for the young king, and he was forced to reestablish the court at Thebes.

This move was the first of a series of concessions that ultimately brought about a total rejection of the Aton faith and the reinstatement of Amon as the state-deity. The boy-king changed his name to Tut-Ankh-Amun and the name of his wife from Ankh-Es-Aton to Ankh-Es-Amon.

Because the ancient Egyptians believed that life on earth was transient and life after death eternal, the first thing a man did when he started to earn a living was to prepare his tomb and its funerary furniture, which included the objects he cherished and those he used in daily life. Tutankhamun is believed to have started work on his tomb when he came to the throne; but it was still rough when he died suddenly of an unknown cause in 1324 B.C.

All the royal tombs in the Valley of the Kings were robbed except Tutankhamun's; this was spared unaccountably, and it is the only one to have been discovered almost intact. Because he died at an early age, about 19, his tomb might have been passed over as not containing enough treasures for the tomb robbers to bother with. At least this is one theory. Imagine—after you view the masterpieces in the collection—what the tombs of the great pharaohs must have contained!

After completing a tour of the ground floor, it is easiest to climb the east stairway from the south gallery to the second floor. This will put you in the corridor number 49 and 50, where you can begin the tour of the Tutankhamun exhibit. Your walk will take you in descending order of the exhibit hall numbers, but by following the east corridor to the north side, you will have enjoyed the most dramatic way of viewing the collection and saved the best part for last.

At Station 50 at the entrance to the east corridor stand the lifesize statues of Tutankhamun (Nos. 96 and 181), which were found in the antechamber of the tomb. They were posted like sentries to the left and right of the entrance. They are wood painted with black and gold leaf. No. 447 is a carrying chest in the form of the god Anubis. You will notice that the Tutankhamun collection has a separate numbering system from those of the museum's other collections. It starts with No. 1 and runs consecutively in the order the pieces were received at the museum between the years 1922–1932.

Continuing along the hall, you pass five cases containing about 30 small statues in gold that represent the pharaoh and various gods. Each is an exquisite piece of art and you will want to spend time examining them closely, but note especially No. 408—the King is carried on the head of Menkaret; No. 409—the King wears the White Crown of Upper Egypt; No. 425—the goddess Isis; and No. 427—the serpent Neter-Ankh.

Next is No. 1, the pharaoh's throne—one of the most photographed of all items. It is carved wood coated with gold and inlaid with faience glass, colored stones and silver. The legs are in the shape of those of a lion, and the front ones are surmounted by lion's heads; the armrests are in the form of two serpents with wings outstretched for protection. On the back panel the king is portrayed sitting, while the Queen, holding a perfume jar in her left hand, takes some with her right hand to anoint the king's shoulder. Above them, the sun sheds its rays on the royal couple. The seat is covered with papyrus. Across from it is No. 3, a chair in dark wood that is in remarkable condition, and another chair, No. 983, which has exceptionally fine mosaic inlay. Be sure to examine these exhibits closely as they are excellent examples of the master craftsmanship of the ancient Egyptians.

Nos. 6–9, 185 and 543 are lovely alabaster vases decorated with gold and ivory. They depict the symbolic plant of Upper Egypt, the lotus, and of Lower Egypt, the papyrus. No. 435 is the symbol of Anubis, two long stalks ending in a papyrus bud and fixed in an alabaster vase.

In the center of the north corridor at Station 10, there are several beds and couches, each supported by an animal representing a god or goddess, such as Hathor the cow. Note especially No. 521 and No. 221, No. 984, Nos. 437–440 and 455–458, alabaster canopic boxes, are a group of four vases that hold Tutankhamun's viscera.

Among the bowls found in the tomb was a translucent alabaster cup in the form of an open lotus flower. The handles also were shaped like lotus buds and flowers and surmounted by a figure symbolizing eternity. Around the edge of the cup in hieroglyphics are phrases to wish the king long life and prosperity.

A number of toilet articles were found. One is an alabaster ointment jar in the shape of a lion standing on its hind legs, its right forepaw raised aloft, its left resting on the hieroglyphic sign for protection. The base of the jar is decorated with floral designs.

At the entrance to the coffin room is the collection of four funerary chambers made of wood, covered with gold leaf and guarded by the four figures. One of the figures was part of the collection that toured the U.S. and Europe.

The Mask: In the center of Room 4 is the mask of Tutankhamun (No. 220), probably the most dramatic piece of ancient craftsmanship ever discovered. It is breathtakingly beautiful. The more often one sees it, the more beautiful it seems. Perfect in design and execution, it is in an equally perfect state of preservation. (The mask was the centerpiece of the Tutankhamun exhibit.)

The mask, which covered the face of the mummy, is made of solid gold and decorated with inlaid stripes of blue glass. On the forehead are the vulture and uraeus representing the gods of Upper and Lower Egypt; the eyebrows and eyelids are inlaid with lapis lazuli and the necklace with precious stones and glass.

In the case surrounding the mask is the collection of jewelry and other objects that were found on the body of the king. At the side of the mummy, a gold dagger with a richly decorated hilt was found; and the mummy itself was covered with jewels. One of these was a crown formed of a plain gold band in the shape of the vulture and the uraeus, inlaid with carnelian red, bright blue and dark blue glass; the feathers of the gods are outstretched in such a way as to form an almost complete circle.

A rectangular gold frame, filled with three large lapis lazuli scarabs and lotus flowers, made of polychrome glass and set in gold, hung down from one side. From the other, a chain of five rows of gold beads were attached to a plaque of gold that showed a seated man with the pharaoh's name in a cartouche over his head.

Tutankhamun's granite sarcophagus is *in situ* in his tomb in the Valley of the Kings at Luxor. It contained the three coffins: the outer coffin in wood, which in turn contained two more coffins, fitted one inside the other. On the left side of the room is the outer coffin (No. 222), and on the right side of the room is the third, or innermost, coffin (No. 219). Both are exquisite. The middle one is *in situ* and contains the mummy.

The innermost coffin is made of solid gold and weighs 495 lbs. It represents Tutankhamun as Osiris, god of the dead. His arms are crossed over his chest; one hand holds the scepter and the other the flail—the signs of royal power. On his forehead are the vulture and the uraeus (the sacred asp), symbols of sovereignty; around his neck is a wide collar of two rows of multicolored stones; and on either side of the body are the deities of Upper and Lower Egypt represented in the form of a vulture and bird with outstretched wings to protect the body.

Fifty-five out of the more than 3,000 pieces of the Tutankhamun collection were exhibited in the United States, Canada and Europe from 1977–1981. It was the largest such collection ever to leave Egypt. Several of the pieces left the country for the first time. All the exhibit is back on display at the museum.

The Jewel Room has collections from different excavations; jewels of the Greco-Roman period, silver vases, a boat with figures in gold and silver, a falcon head from Hieracopolis (near Abydos, the place where Egypt's first pharaohs originated). It was carved in wood and covered with copper plate. You will want to spend time examining the exhibits in this room, but note especially No. 4170—the links of gold. It would make a Cartier designer green with envy.

Room 2 holds the collection from Tanis in the Eastern Delta. The gold and silver vases and jewelry especially are to be noted.

In the Ostraca Room (from *ostracos,* a Greek word meaning oyster shell) are fragments of stone or pieces of pottery. The collection of figured ostraca is from Deir el Medina.

The Papyrus Room shows the methods used by the ancient Egyptians for writing, drawing and painting on the materials of their day.

Another room shows the utensils of daily life: a collection of musical instruments, toilet articles, spoons for face cream or perfumes, equipment of the jeweler, weights and measures, working tools of the peasants, knife blades, razors and other household objects.

Before leaving, be sure to see the model of the funerary temple and pyramid of Sahu-Ra at Abusir, located on the second floor under the Rotunda dome. This exhibit will help you to understand better the Pyramids of Giza and Sakkara, since it shows how they were built. At the base, close to the Nile bank, was the reception temple, containing the embalming and purification rooms and the funerary chamber, which contained the sarcophagus. The funerary temple was built outside the pyramid, sometimes leaving room behind the pyramid for storerooms, as in the case of Cheops' pyramid. The small pyramid of the queen in the funerary monument of Pepi II at Sakkara is also located outside.

The Mummy Room, on the second floor, is closed and will remain so until a "dignified way to exhibit the mummies can be found," according to one of the museum's directors.

Restaurant and Gift Shop: On the east side of the museum's main entrance is a restaurant and gift shop, which is a branch of *Onnig's,* a well known and long-established jewelry and gift shop in the Mouski. Prices here are fixed and reasonable, and the merchandise is reliable. (See *Shopping* section.)

King Tut in America: A selection of 55 treasures from the vast Tutankhamun collection went on tour in the U.S. in 1976–77 to rave reviews and an unprecedented number of viewers. It touched off a wave of Tutomania, which resulted in the reproduction—good and bad—of ancient Egyptian designs on everything from towels and T-shirts to solid gold bracelets and pendants.

On the first stop on the tour at the National Museum in Washington, people stood in line for six to eight hours to see the exhibit. After that, museums in Chicago, New Orleans, Los Angeles, Seattle, New York, San Francisco and Toronto tried to devise a system that would be fair and efficient without putting museum directors into their graves along with King Tut.

In the midst of the excitement, New York's Metropolitan Museum opened a new Egyptian wing, which enabled the museum for the first time to display its collection adequately. Soon after, the museum completed the installation of the Western Hemisphere's first complete Egyptian temple, the first century B.C. Temple of Dendur. It was one of the monuments that would have been flooded by the lake created by the Aswan High Dam had it not been moved. The temple is a gift from the Egyptian government to the U.S. in recognition of the American contribution toward saving two dozen temples and monuments, including the most famous one, Abu Simbel.

The Temple of Dendur is small, measuring 41′ × 21′ × 21′, with a gateway 11′ × 12′ × 26½′, and is made of Aeolian sandstone. It has been reassembled as it appeared on the banks of the Nile, and is located in the museum's new Sackler Wing.

Phase Two of the Metropolitan's permanent Egyptian collection was completed and went on view in late November 1978. Twenty galleries were opened in all, and they have had a steady stream of visitors ever since. They cover all the important periods of ancient Egypt, and include study-storage areas housing material from the late 18th (Amarna period) through the 29th Dynasties: 1379–380 B.C. The galleries contain exhibits from the time of Akhenaton and Tutankhamun, plus extensive material from the Museum's 21st Dynasty excavations.

COPTIC CAIRO

Summary of Coptic Cairo: There are churches of all denominations in the city, but the most interesting are the ancient Coptic Churches in Old Cairo adjacent to Babylon Fort. Housed in the old buildings around the churches is the Coptic Museum. It is the starting point of the tour. Coptic Art is considered an evolution of pharaonic art—evidence of this as seen in the museum is surprising.

Egypt was one of the first countries to embrace Christianity, which it did with fervor; and it marked the beginning of another period in the country's history: the Coptic Age.

The word Copt (*Gibt,* in Arabic) comes from the Greek *Aegyptius,* meaning Egyptian. The Greek word is said to be a corruption of Ha Ka Ptah (in the spirit of Ptah), the reigning deity and one of the names of Memphis, the ancient capital of Egypt.

The language of the Copts was ancient Egyptian as it was spoken in the early Christian era. After their conversion to Christianity, the Egyptians abandoned their ancient form of pictorial writing and adopted the Greek alphabet. They added seven demotic letters to represent sounds unknown in Greek.

Eventually, Greek became the language of the government and scholars, but Coptic continued to be the common language. In education, it was restricted to religious instruction. At the time of the Arab conquest in the 7th century A.D. there was a brief revival of the ancient language, but by the 11th century Coptic literature had all but disappeared. Today, Coptic is used only in the liturgy.

The history of Christian Egypt began officially with St. Mark, who founded the Church of Egypt about the middle of the first century. To this day, the Coptic Patriarchs of Alexandria trace their succession directly from him. In 1968, St Mark's relics were returned from Italy and reburied in a new Coptic cathedral, said to be the largest in Africa.

Traditionally, of course, Christianity goes back to the time when the Holy Family sought refuge from Herod in Egypt. The family is thought to have traveled along the route usually taken by merchants coming from the east. They arrived first at a place near Ismailia, from where they continued to the small town of Tal Basta, an ancient site near the present-day town of Zagazig. Here they met Aqloum, one of the townsfolk, who took pity on them and invited them to his home. Aqloum's wife, who had been an invalid and bedridden for a long time, was healed by Jesus. Today the Church of the Virgin stands on the traditional site of the miracle.

When news of the miracle reached Jerusalem, Herod sent more soldiers to pursue the family and bring them back to Palestine. The family continued their flight until they reached the outskirts of Belbeis, where they saw a woman crying over her son who was dying. Jesus approached the crowd and, addressing the dying child, said "Rise, Jacob, for thou art well." Upon which, according to tradition, Jacob rose to his feet.

The family continued to Meniet Genah, near the present town of Samanoud, and then to Al-Sabbah. Finding no water to drink, Joseph asked Jesus to strike the earth with a piece of stone. He did, and water flowed immediately. Tradition has it that a church was built in the 4th century A.D., where the stone was kept.

Near Senga, the family crossed the Rosetta branch of the Nile to the west bank and then traveled southward on the desert road (now the Cairo-Alexandria highway) till they reached the village of Hoaker (located near the Desert Road Rest House).

In Matarieh (Heliopolis), the Virgin's Tree is located where, according to tradition, Jesus made water spring from the ground. The well is still there and the faithful drink from its waters or douse themselves for blessing.

Traveling southward, the refugees arrived at Babylon (Old Cairo), where they found shelter in a cave. The Church of Abu Sergah is built above the sacred crypt. The family resumed their journey until they arrived at Maadi (a suburb of Cairo), where they spent the night at one of the temples and in the morning continued to Upper Egypt by boat. Tradition says that on the site, Jesus told His mother a church would stand that would commemorate her name to the end of time. At present, the convent of the Sacred Virgin overlooks the Nile at the spot where the temple once stood. In the convent, a staircase leads to the water where the Holy Family took the boat. Patrons of the church celebrate the event annually, and the father of the church takes a boat on a short Nile cruise in commemoration.

According to tradition, the family arrived by boat at the small town of Al Fashn, 108 miles from Cairo, where they traveled by land to a village called Babar el Betouh (near present Bahnasa). Authorities claim that historical evidence in the region shows there were more than 360 churches here at the beginning of the 5th century.

From there the family journeyed southward to the village of Attsa, then to Hemopolites (now Ashmonin), Al-Qiussieh and the nearby village of Qousqam, where they lived in a little room for six months. Word spread of the Child's miracles and people rushed to Him from all over the countryside to be cured. A church named after the Virgin has its altar in the room in which the family is said to have lived. The church has a slab of stone said to have been used by Jesus as a bed and a pillow.

Al Muharraq was the family's last stop. Here the angel appeared to Joseph to tell him about Herod's death. Before leaving Egypt, tradition says, they spent a night in a cave overlooking Assuit. Today it is known as the Virgin's Cave. The family returned to Palestine by the same route they had come.

In the 4th century Deir Al-Muharraq, once considered the greatest monastery in the East, was built. Near the monastery there is a church where, tradition holds, the Virgin appeared to Pope Theophilus, 22nd Patriarch of the Coptic Church (376 to 403). When he awoke he is said to have written the history of the Holy Family in Egypt as the Virgin told it to him in his dream. The church is said to date back to the 1st century and is older than the monastery.

Coptic Churches

Babylon Fort in Old Cairo (about one mile south of the Meridien Hotel) is surrounded by many old and interesting Coptic churches. El Mouallaqa, Abou Serga and St. Barbara are the ones most often visited by tourists, although there are seven old churches in the area that may be seen. Between the churches is the Coptic Museum. *A Guide to the Ancient Coptic Churches of Cairo* by O.H.E. Khs-Burmester (Cairo, Societe d'Archeologie Copte, 1955) is one of the few books available with detailed information on these churches. The book is difficult to find, but you might be able to locate a copy through a Cairo bookstore.

El Mouallaqa Church (The Church of the Holy Virgin): The name *Mouallaqa* (hanging) was given to this church because it is built over the Roman fortress as though suspended from it. The church, located next to the Coptic Museum, is the largest and loveliest in Old Cairo. It probably dates from the late 4th or early 5th centuries. Up to the 11th century it was the patriarchal seat of the Bishop of Alexandria.

To visit the Hanging Church, a visitor must climb a flight of 24 stairs to the entrance. On the wall on the right after entering is a group of three icons. The large one in the center depicts St. George. On the south wall is a series of icons, beginning with a 10th century one of the Virgin carrying Jesus on her lap, before whom St. John the Baptist kneels to kiss the Child's feet. The series ends with an ancient icon of St. Mark.

The door next to St. Mark's icon is made of carved wood inlaid with an intricate pattern of translucent ivory crosses. South of the sanctuary and in a direct line is the baptismal font.

In the main part of the church, and facing the altar at the eastern end, there is a wide iconostatis made of wood inlaid with ivory and ebony. Unlike their counterparts in other churches, the crosses in the design here do not consist simply of bands of ivory framed with ebony contours. Instead, they are elaborately carved and interwoven. From the ceiling and in line with the iconostasis hangs a row of ostrich eggs. An alabaster pulpit in the center of the church rests on 13 marble pillars, one of which is black marble, meant to symbolize Judas. The pulpit is used only once a year, on Palm Sunday.

Abou Serga Church: According to tradition, this church occupies the spot where the Holy Family stayed after its flight to Egypt. The church was founded in the late 4th or early 5th centuries and was dedicated to Sergius and Bacchus, martyred soldiers who died in Syria early in the 4th century. The most interesting features are the altars over the manger on the east side, the main nave separated from the two lateral naves by three rows of marble pillars, which bear the likenesses of saints, and a grotto, 30 feet below the surface of the ground, containing a tiny chapel. The Crypt, where tradition says the Holy Family stayed, is under the altar, but water from the Nile has seeped in and the chapel is not open to visitors at the present time.

From the Abou Serga Church you can go through a doorway in the garden to a Jewish synagogue that was a Coptic church until the 9th century. The caretaker happily whisks visitors through, rattling off facts and fiction at a rapid pace. The synagogue owns a beautiful collection of ancient Hebrew manuscripts that he will gladly show you.

St. Barbara Church: In the vicinity of Abou Serga Church and the Coptic Museum is a church originally built in the late 4th century and rebuilt in the 10th century with some of the materials being used at the time to restore Abou Serga. According to legend, when the Caliph learned that a second church had been built, he ordered the builder, Yuhanna, to demolish one of the two. Unable to decide which to destroy, Yuhanna paced from one church to the other until he collapsed and died from exhaustion. Upon hearing the sad news, the Caliph reversed his order and declared that both churches could remain.

The Saint Georges' Church (Greek Orthodox Church): Built on a bastion of Babylon Fort in the 6th century, the church was rebuilt several times and renovated again recently. It is approached by a great marble staircase from which there is a splendid view of Old Cairo. Inside is a Byzantine Icon Museum. It is one of the few examples of a circular church in the east.

The Coptic Museum

Coptic Museum, Old Cairo, adjoining the ancient wall of Babylon Fort. Admission: L.E. 1 daily; L.E. 1.50 for a visit to the ancient churches. Hours: 9 A.M.–4 P.M. Fridays to 11 A.M.

The museum was founded in 1908 to house the large collection of Coptic art and antiquities dating from 300–1000 and previously kept in the Antiquities Museum. Excavations at Baouit and

Sakkara resulted in the discovery of two ancient monasteries, St. Appollon and St. Jeremia, from which many of the museum's objects were taken.

The exhibits are divided into seven groups: architectural fragments and funeral stelae; woodwork; glass and earthenware; textiles, considered the ancient Copts' greatest artistic achievement; metals; an interesting and valuable display of icons and frescoes; and manuscripts. A brief guide is available at the door.

The architecture of the museum building is in keeping with the collections it houses. The woodwork, taken from old houses belonging to the Coptic community, was adapted to the different rooms in the building. Particularly outstanding is the collection of *mushrabiya* windows.

The exhibits are well displayed on two floors of the Museum. The ground floor is devoted mostly to architectural fragments, while the second floor rooms contain the famous textile fragments (the best, however, are in Paris), old manuscripts and icons (none older than the 15th century).

Visitors are not allowed to take pictures inside the Museum, and, unfortunately the selection of photographs and slides on sale is of poor quality. You will need at least one hour for a hurried look at the museum, several churches and the synagogue.

Within the compound of the Coptic Museum is Babylon Fort, the only Roman vestige in Cairo, dating back to the 1st century A.D. The Romans chose the site because of its strategic location. In those days, the area overlooked the edge of the desert on the east and was guarded by the Nile on the west, north and south. According to historical records, Babylon Fort covered an area of one acre. In the 7th century the Arab armies battled for seven months to conquer it.

A stairway in the garden of the Museum leads down to the south gate of the fortress. This gate, which is flanked by two great bastions, used to open on to the Nile. In addition to this gate, there are traces of other gates and towers.

Coptic Art

The evolution of Christian and Islamic art from pharaonic motifs is in evidence in many exhibits. For example, the Christian cross is said to have developed from the *ankh,* the pharaonic key of life, and the elevated pharaonic chair became a pulpit for the church and a mimbar for the mosque.

Properly speaking, Coptic art flourished from the 5th to the 7th centuries and formed a transition between the Roman period and Byzantine art. It was influenced by the classical art of Alexandria as well as Persian and Syrian art.

Alexandrian art itself had been an evolution of the Hellenistic tradition, but with a difference—as a creation of the Ptolemaic court, it was half Greek, half Egyptian and the Oriental element is pronounced.

The influence of Persian art resulted from a renaissance of ancient styles in the 3rd century A.D. under the Sassanid Dynasty in Persia. From it, Coptic art is said to have derived a number of characteristics: floral designs, animals, horsemen, hunting scenes and the contrast of colors.

The influence of Syria on Coptic art might be called spiritual. In the beginning Christian art in Egypt was Alexandrian, but it was to Syria, geographically associated with the birth and life of Christ, that Egyptian monks looked for inspiration. Egypt, transformed by monasticism, which it had conceived, considered itself the spiritual heir of Christianity. In the monk's mind Alexandria was the refuge of Hellenism, and Hellenism was synonymous with paganism. From the 5th century, Egypt's affinity was with Syria and it was hostile toward all things Alexandrian.

By the 7th century, when it was beginning to develop in a new direction with an independent identity, Coptic art was redirected by the Arab conquest.

Monasteries

As many as 50,000 monks are said to have lived in approximately 500 monasteries in the Western Desert. The best known are located in Wadi el Natroun, where only four monasteries have survived. These are Deir Amba Bishoi, Deir es-Suryani, Deir el Baramus and Deir Macarius.

There are also some in the vicinity of Aswan that are accessible.

St. Anthony and St. Paul monasteries are about 132 miles from Cairo near the Red Sea and may be reached by car.

Visitors to any of the places where there are monasteries or their ruins will be impressed by the devout and austere life the monks led in the solitude and serenity of the wilderness.

Tourists should request permission from the Coptic Patriarchate in Cairo to visit the monasteries. His office is located at 1 Atfet el Ezba, Clot Bey Street. Phone: 822256.

ISLAMIC CAIRO

Summary of Islamic Cairo: The oldest and most interesting of Cairo's mosques and other Moslem monuments are covered here, but this only scratches the surface. There are over 650 designated by the Islamic Monuments Preservation Society. Your visit to Islamic monuments and mosques should be preceded or followed by a visit to the Islamic Museum.

From the time of the Arab conquest in 641 Cairo became a stronghold of Islam, but it was not until the decline of Damascus and later of Baghdad as Arab capitals that Cairo grew into one of the most important cities in the Moslem world. Ruler after ruler embellished it with mosques and monuments to the glory of Islam.

Islamic art is a tradition completely foreign to western art after the Renaissance in Europe. No place is a better school for studying the development of this art then Cairo, whose ancient mosques are themselves an evolution of Islamic architecture and design and whose museums trace the history of this development.

Among the arts in which Islamic craftsmen excelled were calligraphy, textiles (a continuation of the Coptic tradition), carpets, lustreware, crystal and ornamental decoration on metal and wood.

There are many excellent books on Islamic art and architecture that can be read in advance of your visit, but once you are in Cairo, the most useful book for sightseeing is *A Practical Guide to Islamic Monuments in Cairo,* by Richard B. Parker and Robin Sabin, American University in Cairo Press, Cairo, 1974. It is available in city bookshops.

No matter how fascinating you find the pharaonic antiquities, you cannot have seen Cairo or known Egypt without a look at its Islamic heritage.

Cairo Mosques

Cairo's mosques, said to number more than 500, represent some of the finest examples of Islamic architecture in the world. Each has a slight variation and point of interest, but only those of the most historic or architectural importance are described here. They are also those most likely to be visited by tourists. Even this number requires several days, but certainly no trip to Egypt is complete without seeing some of them.

Visits to mosques are not recommended at prayer time. Tickets to those mosques, which are designated as monuments, are sold by the caretaker and cost 50 piasters, unless indicated otherwise.

As a compromise with the Moslem tradition of removing one's shoes before entering the sanctuary, visitors are asked to cover their shoes with large cloth slippers provided by the mosque's caretaker. You are expected to tip 20 piasters for each pair. In mosques where slippers are not provided, as well as in mausoleums which are considered sacred to Moslems, you must remove your shoes before stepping over the threshold. Women must cover bare arms with a scarf.

Amr ibn el-As: In Old Cairo. Built by the Arabs in the 7th century following their conquest, this mosque was the first sacred place to Moslems in Egypt. It is situated in the heart of Old Cairo on the site of Fustat, the "first" Cairo. At that time the mosque overlooked the Nile. From the structure of this mosque came the model of an early style of minaret used in Egypt. Subsequently, it evolved into the final style of minaret now used throughout the Middle East. Reconstruction and expansion of the mosque were undertaken by later rulers. Today it is in a ruined state.

Ibn Toulun: In the area of the Citadel. Completed in 879, it is considered to be the oldest mosque in Cairo because it has not been altered from the original building (as has Amr's Mosque). The mosque was built of brick coated with stucco. The minarets are joined to the main structure by carved stones elaborately fitted to one another. The simplicity and perfect symmetry of the mosque make it one of the most beautiful buildings in the world. Its special features are the kufic writing in bold, massive strips along the wall and the detailed stucco carving of its windows and arches, each in a different pattern from the other. Experts believe that the minaret was inspired by the minaret of the Samarra Mosque north of Baghdad and is therefore an evolution of the *ziggurat*. In 1296 the mosque underwent considerable restoration, and a school for teaching the Koran, medicine and the four schools of Moslem law were added. Visitors whose time is limited might select this mosque to visit, as it is one of the best examples of pure Islamic architecture in the world.

Al-Azhar: Entrance: L.E. 1. In the district and street of the same name. Al-Azhar ("the splendid") celebrated its millenium last year. The structure was started in 969, soon after the Fatimids took control of Egypt, and was completed in 971. It is considered one of the best examples of Islamic architecture in the world and is intimately associated with the history of Cairo itself.

Throughout its long history, Al-Azhar has been a seat of learning, as well as a place of worship. Its university, considered the oldest in the world, has educated and trained the leading scholars of the Moslem world since the early days of Islam. The ulema (learned men) of Al-Azhar are considered Islam's most influential group of theologians. Today, over 90,000 students from every Moslem country come here to study. The teaching staff numbers 3,600. Al-Azhar is also a place of shelter where the poor and Moslem pilgrims are given a free night's lodging.

Originally the mosque was intended simply as the main mosque of the capital, but in a short time judges began lecturing there on Shi'ite jurisprudence, the official sect of the Fatimids. In 988, under the second Fatimid Caliph, Al-Aziz, the first professors were formally appointed and Al-Azhar became a seminary as well.

At first, instruction was restricted to Shi'ite doctrine. Secular subjects such as philosophy, medicine, chemistry and astronomy were taught at another university, Dar El Hekma, founded in 1005 by the Caliph Al-Hakim. For a century the two vied for academic leadership.

At the end of the 12th century the Fatimids were succeeded by Ayyubites, who were Sunni (orthodox) Moslems. They abolished all Shi'ite teachings and traditions. Salah ed-Din, known in the west as Saladin, even went so far as to cancel Friday prayers at Al-Azhar, thus divesting it of its status as the city's major mosque. Freed from sectarian restrictions, it was able to broaden its courses in medicine, astronomy, philosophy and logic.

Then in the 13th century, with the fall of the Abbassid Caliphate in Baghdad in the east, Cairo assumed unchallenged leadership in Islamic scholarship and Al-Azhar became the foremost university in the Moslem world.

For centuries under the Mamelukes, Al-Azhar continued to be a great center of Islamic and Arabic studies. Along with its academic prestige it enjoyed immense political and social influence until the Ottoman conquest in 1517. Its ulema (professors) occupied top legislative and juridicial posts, and sometimes key political posts.

Even under the Turks, Al-Azhar was able to maintain its academic prestige and remain the stronghold of Moslem thought. This stability, as a focal point, is considered its greatest contribution to Islam and to the Arabic language.

The Turks, who feared its influence and regarded its professors and students with suspicion, could do no more than keep a vigilant eye on it. Al-Azhar became the refuge for the progressive and liberal students from Arab countries dominated by the Turks. It could even be said that the university nurtured the seeds of the Pan-Arab movement.

When the French invaded Egypt in 1798, they formed a council for governing Cairo made up of the ulema of Al-Azhar, regarding them as the political leaders of the people and hoping to gain popular approval through them. But the plan backfired. Al-Azhar sheikhs and students were responsible for many uprisings which provoked the French into retaliation. They bombarded the school, stormed the mosque with the cavalry and occupied it for three days. The Egyptians were outraged and finally got their revenge the following year when an Azhari assassinated Kleber, Napoleon's commander-in-chief in Egypt.

As the influence of European education and culture began to grow in Egypt and other Moslem countries, Al-Azhar's influence slipped. It needed reform.

The first move for reform started in 1872, and other steps to reorganize and revise its system followed. Finally in 1936 Al-Azhar was transformed into a modern university made up of three faculties: theology, Islamic jurisprudence and the Arabic language. Prior to admission to any one of these faculties, students have to complete general studies in such subjects as physics, chemistry, mathematics and physiology, as well as foreign languages.

Al-Azhar stands on the same site on which it was founded a thousand years ago. Over the centuries, the mosque has been altered, expanded and restored many times. The present entrance dates from the 14th and 15th centuries. On the left of the entrance is the library, containing some of the oldest and most valuable manuscripts in the world. It contains more than 250,000 ancient and rare handwritten manuscripts, some penned in gold. The section behind the large courtyard, is the oldest part of the building. The *mihrab* (prayer niche) dating from the Fatimids has been preserved.

The cultural influence of Al-Azhar is still immense, and it remains the most prestigious center for the study of Moslem theology and jurisprudence and Arabic. There are students from other Arab and Moslem countries as far away as Mauritania and Indonesia. Scholars from abroad are lodged without charge and many receive allowances in addition.

A detailed history is available in *Al-Azhar,* by Bayard Dodge, Middle East Institute Press, Washington, 1961.

El Hakim bi Amr Illah: Entrance: L.E. 1. In the Bab Nasr area. Completed by the Fatimid ruler al-Hakim in 1010, this mosque has many features in common with the Ibn Toulun Mosque. At one time it was a grand and graceful structure, but today most of it is in ruins. The most interesting architectural features of the mosque are the two minarets (no longer thought to be original) and the entrance. This was the first mosque in Egypt with a monumental entrance that jutted out from the facade. The mosque is located next to the old walls of Cairo between the two old gates Bab al-Futuh and Bab al-Nasr. The mosque was recently restored after six centuries of disrepair.

The Citadel and Muhammad Ali Mosque: Entrance: L.E. 1. The Citadel is situated on the slope of the Mukattam Hills and commands a complete view of Cairo, the Nile, and, in the far distance, the Pyramids of Giza. The Muhammad Ali Mosque (also called the Alabaster Mosque) within its compound is frequently used as an outstanding example of Islamic architecture. Its domed cupola and graceful minarets are second only to the Pyramids and Sphinx as favored subjects for picture postcards for Egypt.

The Citadel was started by Salah ed-Din (Saladin) in the 12th century as a fortress and was constructed of stone taken from small pyramids at Giza. In later years, the Citadel was used as headquarters and official residence of the sultans until 1850, when Khedive Ismail transferred them to Abdin Palace.

The military career of Saladin conditioned his concept of city planning. In addition to the Citadel, he ordered all four of Egypt's earlier capitals—Cairo and its predecessors, Al-Fustat, Al Askar and Al-Qatae'e—to be enclosed within one fortified wall. Many sections of that wall still stand today, particularly the southeastern portions.

The Ayyubites, the family founded by Saladin, ruled Egypt for 80 years, during which time they embellished Cairo with new buildings of outstanding architecture that had a great impact on succeeding ages. Among the developments were the addition of halls and galleries in mosques, in place of the earlier cloisters, and a mastery of military construction.

In the early 19th century, Muhammad Ali rebuilt much of the inner part of the Citadel and doubled its area. He added the mosque bearing his name, the Jewel (Gawhara) Palace, the Law Court, the Mint and Archives situated opposite El Bab el Gadid and the New Gate.

The Muhammad Ali Mosque was designed by a Greek architect from Turkey and is a reproduction of the Nur-ed-Din Mosque in Istanbul. Its walls, both inside and out, are covered with alabaster. The facade is ornamented with quotations from the Koran and with the names of the caliphs of the Rashid dynasty. The minarets measure over 255 feet in height. The chandeliers of the Mosque consist of dozens of crystal balls hung from huge rings suspended from the ceiling (the caretaker never seems to tire of illuminating them for visitors).

The mausoleum at the southwest corner of the mosque contains the tomb of Muhammad Ali, who died in 1848. In the tower to the west is a clock presented to him by Louis Philippe of France.

Most of the Gawhara Palace, within the compound of the Citadel, was destroyed by fire over a decade ago. Guides used to show visitors the room in which Muhammad Ali is said to have feted the Mameluk sultans before having them beheaded—all except one, who escaped by the daring feat of riding his horse over the wall of the Citadel. A more accurate account of the grim incident is related in *Cairo,* by James Aldridge. The only Mameluk who survived never got to the party. He was en route to the palace when news of the massacre reached him and he fled.

Bir Youssef (Joseph's Well) was built by Saladin to ensure an adequate water supply in case of siege. The well is about 300 feet deep and is made of two superimposed sections, each fitted with a waterwheel driven by oxen. You may walk down the steps of the well to see the waterwheels with their fittings. Fee: 25 piasters.

On the new drive to the Citadel from the south and east side, the road passes the remains of a long aqueduct originally built by Saladin to supply the Citadel. It was rebuilt by Sultan el-Ghouri in the early 16th century.

At press time, the Citadel was closed to visitors because it was being used to hold the persons being tried in connection with the plot against Anwar Sadat. There is no indication when it will be open to the public again.

Ibn Qalawun: In the Mouski area. This 13th century mosque was formerly one of the leading places of worship in Cairo. It was begun in 1269 by Sultan el Mansur Qalawun and completed by his son, el-Nassir. Connected with it were a famous law school and a *maristan* (hospital). The mosque was once covered with beautiful marble and mosaic works. Except for the vestibule containing el-Nassir's tomb, the buildings are now in ruins. The vestibule has lovely stained glass windows and elaborately decorated walls and ceiling, parts of which have been restored. The interesting feature of this complex of buildings is its architectural appearance of being a Crusader church rather than a mosque. The archway entrance was taken from the Crusader Church of St. John in Akka.

El-Barquq: In the Mouski are. Adjacent to the Ibn Qalawun Mosque is a 14th century mosque. Although most of it has deteriorated badly, the ceiling and decorative glass windows of the diwan (now restored) and the vestibule containing the tomb of Barquq's daughter are worth viewing.

Mosque of El Zaher Baybars: El Zaher Square. One of the most outstanding monuments of the Mameluk age, this mosque was built in 1269. The wood and marble are said to have come from the Fortress of Jaffa, which Baybars captured from the Crusaders.

El Aqsunqur (also known as the Blue Mosque): In Bab Zuweila area. Sometimes called the Ibrahim Agha Mosque, the mosque was built in the mid-14th century by Emir Aqsunqur but restored three centuries later by Ibrahim Agha. It takes its name, the Blue Mosque, from the panels of blue and green Persian tiles that decorate the east wall.

Sultan Hassan: Entrance: L.E. 1. In the Citadel area. This mosque, standing at the foot of the Citadel, is the most colossal one in Cairo and a masterpiece of Islamic architecture. It was built in 1356 in the form of a cross, each section representing one of the four schools of Moslem jurisprudence. The structure is massive. The gateway alone measures 85 feet in height and the minarets are the tallest in Cairo. In the mosque the *kursi,* a stand on which the Koran is laid open for reading, is the oldest of its kind in Egypt. In the courtyard there is a lovely fountain surrounded by marble columns.

Behind the diwan of the Shafii wing is the room containing the tomb of Sultan Hassan. Note especially the window and ceiling decorations in this room.

Although the mosque is in poor condition, it is regarded by many as the masterpiece of the Mameluk Age and of Islamic architecture generally. It combines grandeur with grace and perfectly blends proportion with dimension. The mosque offers excellent examples of the art of carving in stone, wood and marble. Note the brass inlaid with gold and the stained glass.

Al Hussein Mosque: In Al Azhar area. The mosque is named for Sayyedna al Hussein, the son of Ali and grandson of the Prophet, and is the principal congregational mosque of Cairo. Thousands of Moslems come to Cairo during the week of the Prophet's birthday to celebrate the occasion here. It houses some of Islam's most sacred relics, including articles that are said to have been used by Muhammad. It also houses a Koran that is said to have been written by Ali, the son-in-law of the Prophet.

El Muayyad: At Bab Zuweila. The mosque was built in the early 15th century and extensively restored in the late 19th century. The huge bronze gates were taken from the Sultan Hassan mosque. The roof is supported by marble columns taken from nearby churches. One of the columns bears a cross in its capital. The restored walls, ceilings and windows offer elaborate examples of Islamic art during the Mameluk period. The minarets rise high above the mosque on the two bastions of an 11th century gate known as Bab Zuweila.

Imam el-Shafii: Imam el-Shafii, a descendant of the Prophet, was the founder of one of the four schools of Islamic law. In 1278 Saladin erected a mausoleum to the famous scholar. In the mid-18th century the mosque was built and was later reconstructed by Khedive Tewfiq. The canopy that surmounts el-Shafii's tomb is made of small geometric panels with carved Kufic inscriptions from the Koran and incidents from the Imam's life.

The Tombs of the Caliphs

In a huge burial ground known as the City of the Dead there are numerous mosques, mausoleums and tombs, many of which are elaborately decorated. For those who have the time, this is one of the most interesting parts of Islamic Cairo. However, because the area has now become very crowded, you will need a guide or someone with a knowledge of Arabic to help you find your way around. Parker's book will also be very useful.

Mausoleum of Qait Bey: Located in the northern cemetery behind the Citadel, it is considered one of the most outstanding examples of Moslem architecture anywhere in the world and is especially famous for its minarets and elaborate dome. It was built by Sultan Qait Bey in 1474 and combines many features that are characteristic of Islamic architecture and art—marble, inlay, gilded ceilings, lattice wood and colored glass.

The Gates of Cairo

The two most famous city gates are Bab-al-Futuh (Gate of Conquest) and Bab al-Nasr (Gate of Victory), both of which were built by Gowhar, the Fatimid general who founded Cairo. Between the two gates run the old city walls (now restored), and adjacent to the walls is the mosque of Hakim bi Amr Illah.

All that remains of the southern wall of the medieval city is the Bab Zuwayla, a most remarkable gate through which centuries of commerce have passed. You may climb to the top of the wall through the Muayyad Mosque that adjoins the gate on the western side.

Museum of Islamic Art

This museum is located on Ahmad Maher Square and Port Said Street. Hours: daily 9:00 A.M. – 4:00 P.M.; Fri. to 11:30 A.M. and 1:30 P.M. – 4:00 P.M. in winter, to 11:30 A.M. in summer. Entrance fee: L.E. 2. Phone: 903930.

In the late 19th century a museum was created by Khedive Ismail to house the valuable objects of Islamic art scattered around in various Cairo mosques. The collection was kept in El-Hakim Mosque until 1902 when it was moved to its present location.

The museum's collection is said to be the most valuable and comprehensive display of Islamic art in the world. At the time of its opening, the museum had only 7,029 pieces, but over the years the collection has grown through donations and purchases and archaeological discoveries, especially the finds at Fustat. The museum now has over 78,000 pieces representing every type and school of Moslem art, although only about 8,000 pieces are on view. After years of neglect, the museum has recently been cleaned and painted and some of its treasures restored. A new group of textiles and other discoveries from Fustat have been put on display.

The museum is something of an institution for studying the history of Egypt in the Middle Ages. The names of the cities that played an important role in shaping events, the famous artisans and artists who formed schools of art, and the wide range of styles of Oriental art in different Moslem countries are available for those who want to learn about the development of Islamic art.

Exhibits from the 7th century, at the time of the Arab conquest, through the 19th century are displayed in 23 galleries and are grouped according to style and subject. Those according to subject are arranged chronologically.

A careful study of these exhibits is useful for later visits to the mosques and other Islamic monuments throughout Cairo. The woodwork, rugs and enameled glass are among the most interesting and extensive displays. A booklet describing the exhibits is available at the entrance to the museum.

Exhibits Representing Various Styles: Each of the Moslem ruling dynasties established in Egypt fostered its own artistic school, which developed a particular style and characteristics. The Umayyad style, Room 3, originated in its capital of Damascus. Nature is faithfully represented, and there are marked traits borrowed from other styles that prevailed in pre-Islamic Egypt, Syria and Iran. One of the museum's oldest and most important pieces is a water jug of bronze dating from the 8th century at the time of Caliph Marwan II, the last of the Umayyad rulers.

The Abbasid and Tulunid styles are also represented in Room 3. Abstraction in art, as it is understood now, finds a forerunner in arabesque. The decorative styles that evolved from writing were based on abstractions from nature. Among the most notable on display are the stucco decorations from Egypt and Iraq. About that time lustreware was first used for making vessels, instead of gold and silver, which were distasteful to strict Moslems. Ostentation was considered contrary to the true teaching of Islam.

Room 4 presents the Fatimid style, which was rich in decoration and detail. Most of the art works in this style are scenes of daily life, such as hunting, dancing, drinking and singing. The Fatimid calligraphers excelled in the Kufic style of writing. There is also an impressive collection of ceramics.

Room 5 shows the Mameluk style of Egypt and Syria, especially copper and brass inlaid with silver and gold. This tradition continues to this day. One of the most extensive displays is that of mosque lamps (*mishkat*) enameled in a variety of colors and bearing minute decorations.

Colored mosaics in marble laid in geometric patterns and decorative forms are one of the best known of the Islamic arts. Among the most famous examples of this art is Al Hambra in Granada and the Cathedral of Cordova in Spain.

The Turkish style in Room 20 shows the European influence, especially in faithful representation of nature, and is thus a departure from the true Arab style. Also in this room is a collection of silver and glass pieces and a collection of prayer carpets.

The Iranian style, in Room 22, is characterized by an exactness in detail and a profusion of decoration and shows the influence of Chinese art on the Islamic art of Moslem Asia.

To view the ways Moslem artists have used materials over the ages, Rooms 6, 7, 8, 9 and 10 are devoted to displays of furniture from houses, palaces and mosques. There is also a display of combs and jewelry boxes in different styles. Some are inlaid with ivory or mother-of-pearl or woods of different colors, others are painted.

Rooms 9 and 11 contain metals that were used in making vessels and water jugs shaped like birds and animals. There are also statuettes, mosaics or tools for ornament, candlesticks and censers with filigree decoration inlaid with silver and gold. A collection of weapons is displayed in Room 12.

The Museum's porcelain collection is one of the most important and can be seen in Rooms 13, 14, 15 and 16.

The textiles in Room 17 were made in Yemen, Egypt, Iran and Turkey. These include a wide variety of embroideries, some with Kufic inscriptions of prayers and the name of the city of origin. Tiraz, as the textile industry was then called, was of two types, one working for the Caliph and his family and the other for the public. Both were directed by the government.

Room 17 also contains capitals with their bases and tombstones with Kufic and Naskhi inscriptions representing the development of Arabic writing in various stages.

Examples of marble mosaics that covered the floors in houses, palaces and mosques are also on display.

Among the most outstanding artistic achievements of Islam were book illustration and calligraphy. Books penned in beautiful handwriting and abundantly illustrated are on display in Room 19. Some of the most elaborate are book covers and copies of the Koran.

Glassware, displayed in Room 21, includes vessels and fragments. It was an art in which Egypt and Syria excelled from ancient times. This hall has over 60 lanterns (*mishkats*) that belong to the Mameluk period and form the largest collection in any museum. Room 23 has a large collection of carpets belonging to different periods and places.

Woodworking: Historically, woodwork was one of the most important branches of Islamic art, and it flourished in Egypt. Even though Egypt has never been a producer of rich wood, and has always had to import good qualities from neighboring countries—cedar from Lebanon, teak from India, and ebony from the Sudan—Egyptian craftsmen have shown great skill in woodwork since ancient times.

The museum has a good collection of wood objects belonging to different Muslim periods. Many pieces were uncovered at Fustat and Ain es-Sira and had been used in buildings and as furniture.

Umayyad woodwork (661–750) continued to follow the Sassanid and Hellenistic traditions both in its deep cutting and its realistic style, such as the bunches of grapes, vine leaves and scrolls with decorative motifs derived from Hellenistic art.

Those of the early Abbassid age (8th–9th centuries A.D.) can be distinguished by their decorations with concentric circles, interlacing arches and small pierced oblongs with open work. But in 868, when Ibn Tulun became ruler of Egypt, an artistic evolution began and a new style was developed in both design and method. It was the slanting or beveled method and used scrolls and lines that formed a stylized design of an animal or a bird. The technique was similar to the Abbassid stucco decoration found at Samarra.

The Fatimid woodwork (969-1171) is in good condition. It came from palaces, mosques and Coptic churches, and the conditions under which it was produced make it obvious that it represents the highest artistic standards of Fatimid art.

During the reign of the Khalifs Al-Zahir and Al-Mustansir (1020–1094), the art of woodcarving reached its peak. Carving became more accurate and scrolls and leaves were more elaborately carved. Nature was honestly represented in rendering birds and animals.

The best examples of this style are the richly carved boards discovered in the Maristan of Qalaun. They are decorated with human figures, hunters, dancers and musicians and other scenes that give one an insight into the life and customs of the Fatimid period.

The woodcarving style that begins with the reign of Al-Musta'li (1094) was a new method of decorating larger surfaces. The decoration did not form a continuous pattern but was split into small units such as hexagons and stars, each containing a separate design. An elaborate example is the beautifully carved mihrab of Sayyida Rukayaa. The *naskhi* style of calligraphy replaced Kufic script. Decorative animals and birds continued to be used, but the workmanship became less careful, and the figures were often treated as silhouettes with little surface detail.

During the Ayyubid period (1171), woodcarving maintained the late Fatimid traditions, but the arabesque became more elaborate and some of the early Ayyubid wood carvings from Syria show Seljuk influence.

Under the Mameluks, carving became even more elaborate. Geometrical patterns of small panels became popular and usually consisted of hexagons arranged around central stars, all covered with intricate patterns of arabesque. The artists created outstanding works on pulpits, chests, doors and chairs.

Another type of woodwork popular during this period was turned latticework, or *mushrabiya,* which has come to be known in the West as harem screens. The screens were used on the fronts of private houses and also to separate the sanctuary in mosques and churches. By varying the arrangement of the pieces, the artist was able to produce a great variety of designs.

With the weakened economic and political conditions of Egypt after the 15th century, the art of woodcarving, along with the other Islamic arts, gradually declined.

MODERN CAIRO AND OTHER SITES OF INTEREST

Summary of Modern Cairo: Several old houses and former palaces have been made wholly or partly into museums and now serve as centers for art and handicrafts. They give a visitor the chance to meet Egyptians and to glimpse a side of the cultural activity. There are also innovations such as the Papyrus Insitute and the village of Harraniya, and attractions such as the zoo and botanical gardens and excursions to Helwan and Fayoum.

Museums

(Entrance fee in most cases is 25 or 50 piasters.)

Agricultural Museum, Ministry of Agriculture, Dokki, hours: daily, summer 9:00 A.M.–2:00 P.M.; Fri. till 11:30 A.M.; winter 9:00 A.M.–4:00 P.M.; Fri. till 11:00 A.M. Phone: 702687.

Displays of village life, collection of stuffed animals and a variety of agricultural processes. Cotton Museum is adjacent.

Art and Life Center, Manisterli Palace (Roda Island next to Nilometer), hours: daily 9:00 A.M.–2:00 P.M. except Fri.

A home that once belonged to a member of the royal family has been made into a center for the study of man through art from pharaonic times to the present, and is sponsored by the Ministry of Culture. Students' works are available for sale and include, among other things, kaftans with pharaonic designs for L.E. 30 and up. Watercolors by director Ihsan Khalil are lovely. There are also paintings, batiks, sculpture and other art objects on display.

Egyptian Civilization and Gezira Museum, Gezira Exhibition Ground, hours: daily 9:00 A.M.–1:30 P.M. Paintings and sculpture on the history of Egypt from prehistoric times to the present.

Ethnological Museum, Sharia Kasr el Aini, hours: daily 9:00 A.M.–1:00 P.M. except Fri. Displays of village crafts, utensils and implements.

Khalil Museum, Sharia el Sheikh el Marsady, Zamalek, hours: daily 9:00 A.M.–1:30 P.M.; Fri. to noon. A private collection of paintings and sculpture is open to the public. Exhibitions of contemporary artists are held regularly.

Modern Art Museum, 18 Sharia Ismail Abul Fetouh, Dokki, hours: daily 9:00 A.M.–2:00 P.M.; Fri. to noon. Permanent exhibits of many leading contemporary Egyptian artists and new shows at intervals.

Mukhtar Museum, Gezira, hours: 9:00 A.M.–1:30 P.M. Housed in a building designed by the famous architect, Ramses Wissa Wassef, it houses the works of Mahmoud Mukhtar, Egypt's best-known modern sculptor. The most famous piece is known as *The Winds of Khamsin,* often pictured in books on modern Egyptian art. The museum is worth a visit, though unfortunately, it is in wretched condition. The building is easily reached by walking from the Cairo Sheraton Hotel.

Papyrus Institute, Sharia el Nil, Giza (near Sheraton Hotel), hours: daily 9:00 A.M.–7:00 P.M.

At the research center, founded by Dr. Hassan Ragab, visitors learn how the ancient Egyptians made paper from the papyrus plant. Dr. Ragab spent seven years researching and perfecting the method. When he began in 1962, he had to bring the papyrus plant from Chad as Egypt no longer had the plant growing naturally, its importance having died in the 10th century with the introduction of rice paper.

The institute is situated in houseboats and adjoining buildings and includes an exhibition hall, museum library, and laboratory for research. Copies of drawings from tombs and temples painted on papyrus and other souvenirs are available for purchase at reasonable prices. This institute is one of the few places open late in the afternoon. Visitors often combine it with a sail on the Nile. Due to visitor interest stimulated by Dr. Ragab's pioneering efforts, "Papyrus Institutes" have opened all over the city; despite their pretensions, they have no purpose other than commercial, several having been started by Dr. Ragab's apprentices. Dr. Ragab also has a shop at the Nile Hilton and another on a houseboat in Luxor where guests may learn about the making of papyrus.

Old Houses

Anderson House, near entrance of Ibn Toulun Mosque, hours: winter: 8:30 A.M.–4:00 P.M.; Fri. to noon. Entrance fee: L.E. 1.

Two houses built by Hajj Muhammad al-Jazzar in the 17th century are in excellent condition today because of the restoration by Major Gayer-Anderson, a British resident of Cairo during the 1920s. Anderson joined the two houses into one and lived here for many years. He furnished his home with interesting pieces of furniture and objets d'art he collected. After Anderson's death, the house was turned into a museum by the government. It gives a visitor a good idea of how a prosperous Cairo family in the 17th century lived. Attached to the house in the garden is a *sabil,* a public fountain from which members of the community could draw water, and a small tomb of a sheik who was venerated as a holy and wise man by people of the neighborhood.

Beit el-Suheimi and Beit el-Tablawi: Two adjoining houses dating from the 17th and 18th centuries are located in the Mouski area on a street halfway between the mosques of Barquq and al Hakim. Entrance fee: 50 piasters.

Beit Sennari, off Midan Sayyeda Zeinab on Haret Monge, a lane south of Saneyya Girls' School, 9:00 A.M.–2:00 P.M. except Fri.

An old Islamic house is now used as a center for research in applied arts from the pharaonic period to the present. You may watch students at work and visit an exhibit of textiles, ceramics, batiks, kaftans, glass, silk screen prints and other handicrafts.

Musaferkhana, in a small lane several blocks from El Hussein Mosque, hours: 9:00 A.M.–4:00 P.M. Entrance fee: 50 piasters.

A grand old house built in 1779 was the birthplace of Khedive Ismail. It was restored by the Ministry of Culture a few years ago and now serves as an art center where several artists have studios. The building is difficult to find without a guide.

Wekalet el Ghouri, 3 Sharia el Sheikh Abdu, near El Ghouri Mosque, one block before entrance to Khan Khalili, hours: daily 8:00 A.M.–2:00 P.M. except Fri.

A 16th century caravanserai has been restored by the Ministry of Culture and is used to house a permanent exhibit of local crafts and folk arts from the different areas of Egypt. It also serves as a center where a number of artists display their works and as a workshop where pupils learn the traditional crafts of the country.

Former Royal Palaces and Rest Houses

Abdin Palace: Begun during the reign of Khedive Ismail and completed in 1874, Abdin Palace is a community within itself. In addition to the private living quarters of the former royal family and the reception rooms, there is a motion picture room, theater, electrical workshop, carpentry sections and radio shop.

The Salamlek was the ladies' reception rooms. Other rooms were the dining hall and living quarters of the former king and queen, the Belgium wing used for state receptions, the Byzantine hall and the gardens. The gilded bathrooms, with their sunken tubs, always draw comment. At present, the building is being used by the government and is not open to tourists.

A Military Museum contains exhibits pertaining to ancient as well as Islamic Egypt; the French expedition under Napoleon; and the reigns of Muhammad Ali and Khedive Ismail, among others.

Qubbah Palace: Built in 1863 under Khedive Ismail, Qubbah Palace was used as the official residence of his successor, Tewfiq. The palace has some 400 rooms, including a museum, extensive gardens, swimming pool and tennis courts. A railway station and engine shed accommodated the ex-king's train, in which he took trips incognito. The palace now houses apartments used for state occasions.

Pyramid Rest House: Built in 1941 by ex-King Farouk, the rest house is pharaonic in style and contains some interesting pieces. A visit should be planned with enough time to relax in the museum's tea garden with the Pyramids as a backdrop and Cairo stretching out to the horizon.

Helwan Corner: Of all the former royal houses in Cairo, this small, unpretentious home built in 1942 by Farouk is the most pleasant. After the gilded and ostentatious palaces in Cairo and Alexandria, Helwan Corner is a delightful change. Its beauty is in its simplicity and its serene setting. It has a wide veranda overlooking the Nile and is surrounded by flowering gardens. Located about 12 miles from Cairo on the Helwan Road, it may be reached by car or boat. The pier in front of the palace is a popular docking place for small boats on a cruise from Cairo.

Manial Palace and Museum, Roda Island, hours: daily 9:00 A.M.–1:00 P.M. Entrance fee: L.E. 1.

Those people whose stay is too short to see many palaces and museums in Cairo might opt for a visit to the Manial Palace. It gives one an idea of the grand style in which Egyptian royalty lived. The palace was built in 1901 by a prince of the royal family, Muhammad Ali. It is located on Roda Island and surrounded by lovely gardens. The palace is a mixture of Persian, Ottoman, Moorish and Arab styles. It is divided into reception, residential, throne and regency wings and the museum. Every inch of the palace is covered with mosaics, mushrabiya or some intricate work of art—any one of which can be admired for its beauty. Taken together, it is overwhelming.

The reception quarters are located in a two-story building above the main gate. The west wing of its upper floor is in the Moorish style, the east wing in Syrian design. Its walls and ceiling are covered with wood taken from El Azm Palace in Syria and fitted by Syrian artisans brought to Egypt for the purpose.

The Mosque is regarded as the loveliest of the palace's buildings. Its walls are plated with glazed tiles framing panels inscribed with the attributes of Allah. Around the walls are hollowed marble casements and stained-glass windows, and the floors are covered with Oriental carpets. The minaret is in the Moorish style and has a clock that chimes.

In the residence the massive oak doors are framed in brass and inlaid with gold and silver. The ceiling designs, different in each room, are outstanding.

The Throne Room, 100 feet long and 21 feet wide, has white marble floors covered by red carpets. In the center of the ceiling an arabesque knob of hollowed wood inlaid with gold lets in the light in a symmetrical pattern. The decor is in the Ottoman tradition.

The palace museum consists of 14 galleries and contains masterpieces from the various periods of Islamic civilization: gold-decorated Korans, manuscripts penned by some of the most renowned calligraphers, Turkish carpets of the 17th and 18th centuries, ancient weapons and candelabra. Also found here are costumes, a rare collection of nargilehs (waterpipes), furniture that once belonged to the Turkish Sultan Abdel Hamid and a thousand-piece set of table silver engraved with the initials of Mohammed Ali, the Caliph to whom it was presented as a gift from Louis Philippe of France.

The palace grounds now house a Club Mediterranee, which has an entrance on the west side.

Moses and Gardens

The Nilometer, a graduated column said to date back to 715, was used to measure the water level of the Nile and to anticipate the strength of the annual flood. Located at the southern tip of Roda Island, it is situated on the spot where, according to legend, the infant Moses was found in the bulrushes. Entrance fee: 50 piasters.

Zoological Gardens: Open daily, 9:00 A.M. to 5:00 P.M. Cairo's 21-acre zoo is located on the Pyramid road and contains a rare collection of African and Sudanese animals and a museum of stuffed species. There is also a tea garden with restaurant.

Other Places of Interest

American University in Cairo: Founded in 1920 by a group of private citizens, the school has about 1,600 students, of which 80 percent are Egyptian. It offers bachelor of arts and science degrees as well as masters' in both disciplines. It has a large library and is especially proud of its Islamic Art and Architecture library and the Debanne Collection on Egypt, which is available for use by scholars. The University's Division of Public Service offers an adult education program and sponsors cultural events throughout the year and has 9,000 students.

AUC is centrally located in the modern part of Cairo, only two blocks from the American Embassy and a short distance from the Nile Hilton and Shepheards' hotels.

Cairo University: With a student body numbering 100,000, Cairo University is the largest institute of higher learning in the Middle East and receives students from throughout the Arab world for study. Courses are primarily in Arabic. Among its leading faculties are medicine and engineering. The main gate to the campus is directly in front of the bridge leading from Roda to Giza.

Cairo Tower: Located on Gezira Island in the center of Cairo, the slim, modern structure dominates the skyline. The observation deck at the top offers a spectacular 360° view of the city. There's also a restaurant at the top. Entrance: L.E. 1.

Suburbs of Cairo

Cairo has now grown in every direction so that places that were once separate towns or villages are now part of the city. On the west side, Dokki and Giza, both of which are mainly middle class residential areas, now stretch to the foot of the Pyramids, and the green fields which once surrounded them have given way to high-rise apartment buildings. Another rapidly growing district on the northwest is Mohandaseen.

South of the city is the elegant residential district of Maadi, connected by a superhighway. Further on, the road leads to Helwan, which is both a spa and a developing industrial complex. The east side of the city is hemmed in by the Mukattam Hills, but the city is creeping in this direction too. The greatest growth in the past decade has been in the area north of the city, especially with the addition of Nasr City, a low-cost housing project, and the expansion of Heliopolis, one of the oldest continuously inhabited sites and one of the main cities of Egypt throughout its ancient history.

Today, Heliopolis—in Arabic, *Masr al Gadida* (New Cairo)—is 15 miles from downtown Cairo and is considered one of its suburbs. Its wide boulevards, spacious villas and abundant gardens make it one of the loveliest sections in the city.

The old city of Heliopolis is referred to in the Bible as the city of On. Its only remnant is an obelisk. The section known as Matariya, once a village, stands on the original site of the ancient city. Located here is the Tree of the Virgin, which tradition holds to be the resting place of the Holy Family on its flight to Egypt. Visitors are also shown an old well from which, tradition says, the Holy Family obtained water. The Church of the Nativity is within walking distance of the sacred well.

SUGGESTED ITINERARY FOR CAIRO

The hours suggested on these programs will vary according to season. Those listed below are for winter; in summer, visitors should avoid sightseeing in the hottest part of the day—between noon and 4:00 P.M.—and should adjust the schedule appropriately.

First Day, Morning: Visit Egyptian Antiquities Museum—a brief survey of both floors will take two hours. (Prior to a visit, be sure to read the exciting account of the discovery and opening of the tomb of Tutankhamun in C. W. Ceram's *Gods, Graves and Scholars*. The museum is located at Midan Tahrir, which is an excellent place to orient oneself to the city.

After the museum visit, drive to the Citadel, at the foot of the Mukattam Hills. View the Mosque of Muhammad Ali and enjoy an 180° view, or go to top of Cairo Tower for the 360° view of Cairo and the Nile Valley.

Afternoon: Drive to the Mouski to visit the bazaars of Khan Khalili, where you can wander through the labyrinth of lanes and alleyways, watching craftsmen and chatting with shopkeepers. Afterward drive to the Pyramids and Sphinx. Some may want to ride around the Great Pyramid on a camel or have tea at the cafe nearby and stop for awhile to enjoy the view.

You can remain at the Pyramids for the Son et Lumière program. To pass the time before the show, enjoy drinks at the Mena House, where you have a spectacular view of the Pyramids.

Alternatively, you might stop at the artist village of Harraniya or Kerdassa, a short side trip off the Pyramids road before going to visit the Pyramids.

Evening: Dinner cruise on the *Nile Pharoah,* a large cruise boat in pharaonic decor offering dinner and dancing during cruises from Cairo to Maadi.

Second Day, Morning: Drive to Memphis and Sakkara. Visit the Step Pyramid, the mastabas of the nobles and the tomb of the sacred bulls. (There is plenty here to fill a morning.)

Afternoon: Visit the Islamic Museum and the mosques of Sultan Hassan, Ibn Toulun (and the adjacent Anderson House) and Al Azhar. Some visitors may wish to make a second trip to the bazaars that are located in the vicinity.

Evening: A felucca sail on the Nile at sunset.

Third Day, Morning: A visit to the Coptic antiquities in Old Cairo. Babylon Fort, old churches and the Coptic Museum are located next to each other and the tour does not consume a morning. The extra time can be used for a shopping tour of downtown Cairo or a return visit to the Egyptian Antiquities Museum.

Afternoon: Visit to Manial Palace and the Papyrus Institute. Those who have not yet been on a felluca might include a sail on the Nile.

Evening: Dinner and dancing at one of the nightclubs featuring an oriental dancer.

If you are planning five days to a week in Cairo, we would recommend the same itinerary but at a slower pace, to allow one to spend more time at the museums and antiquity sites, shop, relax over meals, enjoy a sport and to sense the serenity that is Egypt.

EXCURSIONS FROM CAIRO

Helwan

This spa, about 15 miles south of Cairo, may be reached by car on the Corniche or by train from Bab al-Luk station. Helwan's six sulphur springs, gushing water at 90° F., are considered to have excellent curative powers. Visitors may swim for health or pleasure in open-air pools fed from the springs. Helwan has several reasonably priced hotels.

The town of Helwan is on a plateau 275 feet above sea level and enjoys a delightful winter climate.

The quarries of Tura and Ma'sara near Helwan are today, as in pharaonic times, a source of supply for limestone. At the quarries you can see interesting old drawings depicting the ancient methods of stone working. Between Helwan and Ma'sara at Ezbet al Waldu, tombs of the first three dynasties contained exquisite vases and other artifacts that are now in the Egyptian Museum.

Wax Museum in Helwan: Established in 1934 and originally housed on Gumhuriya Street, the museum was moved to Helwan in 1955. It depicts the highlights of Egypt's history, especially under the pharaohs and Islam. The rooms include exhibits of Akhenaton in company of his wife Queen Nefertiti, their children and retinue on their way to Aton Temple at Tell-al-Amarna; Saladin's visit to his ailing enemy, Richard the Lion-Hearted; Caliph Umar Ibn el-Khattab making a charity call on a poor family; a wedding scene of the 19th century; Pharaoh's daughter sheltering the infant Moses rescued from the rushes.

The Japanese Garden: This is the only garden of its kind in the Middle East. There are statues of Buddha and Japanese-style arcades, as well as artificial pools. Unfortunately, it is in a run-down condition.

Helwan Rest House Museum: Situated on the Nile bank about four miles from Helwan, it lies between the Pyramids of Dahshur on the west and the Helwan sulphur springs in the east. The Rest House belonged to ex-king Farouk and is open to visitors as a museum.

Helwan Observatory: The ancient Egyptians were the first to establish observatories, and records show that the scribes of the pharaonic university of Ain Shams, thought to be the first university of antiquity, were able to plot the stars. The present observatory in Helwan was built in 1903.

Fayoum

The largest oasis in Egypt, Fayoum lies 75 miles southwest of Cairo and can be reached by train or car. Fayoum is a popular hunting and fishing region. Its wooded countryside, flowering trees, old waterwheels and cultivated fields offer a picturesque landscape in contrast to the barren desert surrounding it.

Fayoum was the center of one of Egypt's most ancient cultures and the earliest known site of pottery making and cultivation. Records of Fayoum's history indicate that the period of the XII

Dynasty was the most prosperous. At that time Lake Qarun, known to ancient Egypt as Moeris Lake, occupied almost half of the Fayoum depression. Over the years the lake gradually shrank, although to judge from the ruins of Greek cities in the area it was still large during the period of the Ptolemies.

The Greek capital was called Crocodilopolis, after the local god Sobek, who was conceived as a crocodile. The province as a whole was called Arsinoite Nome, after the sister and wife of Ptolemy II. By the first century A.D. the oasis had come to be known as Bion in Coptic, which later evolved into Fayoum, the present name of both the town and the province.

A few miles before the lake, near the turnoff south to Fayoum, there is the **Kom Oshim Museum,** which houses a small collection of antiquities found in the Fayoum region. Entrance fee: 50 piasters. Immediately behind the museum is a huge site dating from Roman times, which was excavated by the University of Michigan.

Fayoum is noted for the famous wax-painted portraits, dating from the Roman period, found on mummies in place of the mask. The lifelike portraits, meant as pictures of the deceased, have astonishing force and character. Nothing similar has ever been found elsewhere. Some of the best are in the **Cairo Antiquities Museum** and the **Greco-Roman Museum** in Alexandria.

Among the monuments at Fayoum one of the most important is the Pyramid of Amenemhat III, XII Dynasty, 19th century B.C., located 9 miles southeast of Fayoum. It is made of dried bricks rather than stone. In 1956 the Tomb of Nefru-Ptah, daughter of Amenemhat III, was discovered a mile from the father's pyramid.

At Lahun, 30 miles southeast of Fayoum, are other pyramids and mastabas belonging to princesses and nobles. In the tomb of Princess Sat-Hathor were found exquisite pieces of jewelry, now in the Egyptian Museum.

Cairo travel agents can arrange a Fayoum tour, or one can negotiate a half- or full-day trip with a Cairo taxi.

A new road continues south from Fayoum to the main highway along the Nile leading to Beni Suef, Minya and Upper Egypt.

HOTELS: *Auberge,* initially built as a rest house and hunting lodge for the king, was turned into a hotel after the revolution but allowed to deteriorate completely. It is now being completely renovated and will be managed by the Oberoi group, which runs the Mena House in Cairo. Situated on Lake Qarun, the hotel will become the nucleus of a resort which will have health club and extensive sports facilities for tennis, riding, boating and windsurfing and a hotel/clubhouse with 55 guest rooms and two suites. Completion is scheduled for later in the year. *Panorama,* 26 beds, price L.E. 18, dwb, is tourist class. A new restaurant, *Gabal Zeina,* is being completed near the Auberge.

Towns and Antiquity Sites South of Cairo

Minya: Located on the main road on the west side of the Nile, Minya is a 4-hour drive from the capital. The road passes through Beni Suef, where a new paved road to the west leads to the pyramid at Meidum. The pyramid may be seen from the main road as well. Entrance fee: L.E. 1.

Minya, the capital of the governorate, has one of Egypt's 12 state-run universities. At the municipal building, which adjoins part of the University of Minya campus on the Corniche, the office of the inspector of the Antiquities Service is located on the first floor of the north wing. He is helpful and informed, and in lieu of any sophisticated tourist services, will be able to point you in the right direction to explore the antiquity sites on your own.

On the west bank, 24 miles south of Minya and west of the village of Mallawi, is **Hermopolis,** the site of a fabulous temple whose ceiling was supported by statues of huge baboons; these have been placed together at the site. The patron of the city was the god Thoth, who was depicted as a baboon or an ibis. Hermopolis is also the site of a Greek agora, which has been restored by the Antiquities Service.

The necropolis for Hermopolis was **Tuna El-Gebel,** which is west of the city. Entrance fee: L.E. 1. Here, tombs of ibises and baboons, animals sacred to Thoth, were excavated in the rock foundation of the desert and extend in catacombs for many miles underground. Thousands of mummified ibises, baboons, ibis eggs and the workshop of an embalmer have been found. A small museum in Mallawi displays many forms of the ibis. Entrance fee: 50 piasters.

The outstanding building at the necropolis is the Tomb of Petosiris, whose sarcophagus is now in the Egyptian Museum in Cairo.

North of the tomb is one of the stelae of Tel Al Amarna, which designated the city's boundaries. Tel Al Amarna was the city of Akhenaten and Nefertiti, who abandoned Thebes and the worship of Amon and embraced a new worship centered on one god, Aton.

To reach **Tel Al Amarna,** drive eight miles south of Mallawi to the point where you cross the Nile. On the east side of the Nile the distance is less than a mile and can be covered on foot or on donkey. Behind the present village, at the ancient site of Tel Al Amarna, the ruins known as the Palace of Nefertiti are among the very few remnants from the Akhenaten period. Tablets in cuneiform writing, which contained military correspondence between Egypt and Syria, were found here and are now in the Cairo Museum. It is a very long hike up the limestone hills behind the site to the tombs dating from the Akhenaten era. Five of the 25 tombs that have been found are open to visitors. The drawings are badly damaged but do provide evidence of the profound changes in art and philosophy this unusual pharaoh had begun.

To see any sights on the eastern bank of the river you must cross by ferry, which carries cars along with the usual donkey carts and local traffic. The ferry docking station is located at the southern end of town. You should arrive there at least a half hour before the first 6 A.M. crossing. The ferry does a brisk business, and you will need every available second for sightseeing.

On the east bank, 9 miles north of Minya, is the site of the Monastery of the Pulley. A new Coptic church stands on the foundation of the ancient monastery, where centuries ago the monks were lowered in baskets from the high rock by pulley to the banks of the river, to bless the journeys of the feluccas.

Across from Minya, on the east bank at **Beni Hassan,** is one of the largest Christian and Moslem cemeteries in Egypt, used since the time of the Persian invasion. The cemetery with its beehive domes stretching far into the distance fills the land between the limestone cliffs and the water.

Just south of the cemetery in the limestone cliffs are several tombs of the Middle Kingdom—unusual because they are in the east rather than the west, as are all other Pharaonic tombs. Some of these tombs are still unregistered. The Antiquities Service representative can arrange for you to visit them. Entrance fee: L.E. 1. They are particularly interesting because of the sporting scenes, which clearly show that the ancient Egyptians knew judo, karate and wrestling, among other sports we practice today.

One of the main problems of visiting the area of Upper Egypt from south of Cairo to Luxor is the lack of hotel facilities. There are no first class hotels and most of the tourist or economy ones are old and inadequate. There is a plan under development by the Ministry of Tourism which would expand the road network, add hotel and other facilities to enable visitors to travel to Upper Egypt by car or camper with ease and convenience. Until the project is further along, the only hotels available are the *Beach, Ibn Khattab, Lotus* and *Nefertiti,* all of which are Tourist B class, at best. Ask to see your room before booking and look at several before you decide.

PRACTICAL INFORMATION FOR CAIRO

HOW TO GET AROUND. Taxis may be your best bet, in which case see information on that subject in the *Facts at Your Fingertips* section.

Trams (street cars): Trams connect Bab El Louk station (near the American University) and Helwan with a stop in Maadi. A ticket to Maadi is 5 piasters. The train also stops at Mari Girgis (Old Cairo) only a few yards from the ancient Coptic churches. Station names are written in Arabic only. Before you board, ask someone to verify the train's destination. There is also tram service to Heliopolis, though the cars are in such dilapidated condition we do not recommend use.

City Buses: City buses are simply too crowded to be recommended for tourists' use. However, Bus No. 13 is a line of 21 passenger minibuses which make regular runs from Zamalek to Bab-al-Louk, via Midan El Tahrir. These buses are strict about limiting the number of passengers. Deluxe and large first-class hotels in the suburbs have courtesy buses to Midan Tahrir in the city center.

Walking: With a good map in hand, you can find your way around the major parts of downtown Cairo without difficulty. At major intersections, street names are posted in Arabic and English. Maps are available from the Tourist Office, travel agents and bookshops. Egyptians are very willing, even eager, to help. You can stop in any shop and ask for directions. The shopkeeper will often leave his business to show you the way or send his helper along to guide you. People on the street who spot a foreigner looking lost will often offer to be of help. The *Practical Guide to Cairo* has 10 maps detailing the different parts of the city.

HIRING A CAR. You may rent a car with or without a driver, to be picked up at the airport on arrival. *Hertz* and other international car rental firms have offices at Cairo airport and major hotels. This is a new and very welcomed development and can go a long way to help foreigners cope with the taxi shortage and/or overcharge.

On the first visit to Egypt, we do not recommend renting a car without driver. Language becomes a problem when you strike out alone, and driving in Cairo is not easy. Besides, the cost of an English-speaking driver is so little (L.E. 7 per day from Hertz) that it is worth it. We strongly recommend it for those who are not on an organized tour, and for business travelers who need to move around the city a great deal. In the latter case, it is smart to hire a car and driver by the week or longer, especially if you are likely to have several appointments each day. A car and driver can save you hours of frustration as well as time. It is important to hire a driver who knows at least a little English. You can ask your hotel doorman or travel agency to arrange for one, or if you find a taxi driver you like and with whom you can communicate, strike a deal with him on your own. But be sure to set the price in advance. On the other hand, you will probably do as well by going to a rental company, or at least checking their prices before putting your bargaining skills to the test.

Taxis can be hired by the hour, half day or full day. By the hour the cost is about L.E. 5; for a half day, L.E. 15–20, depending on your ability to bargain. For an eight-hour day, the cost will range from L.E. 30–40, including driver and gas, and more if the day stretches late into evening. Because of the great demand for hired cars, students and others with cars are free-lancing. They charge whatever price the traffic will bear, so do not hesitate to bargain with them.

In addition to car rental firms, *Limo Misr* (described earlier in Part One) has cars for hire. Rates are higher than the usual tariff but they are fixed prices.

HOTELS. After a decade of hotel shortage, Cairo is now well equipped with hotels in all categories. Seven well-known American and several European chains are represented and other hotels are nearing completion this year. Even so, during the high season, it is wise for visitors to have confirmed reservations, especially between December and April, and to have their confirmation notice in hand upon arrival in Egypt.

Hotel prices are set by the government and should be valid through 1984. With the boom and inflation which Cairo is experiencing, prices might be increased, and therefore those listed here should be taken as an indication only. *Under no circumstances do we guarantee these prices*. The following are representative in each category:

Deluxe: single with bath L.E. 45–52; double L.E. 49–60.

First Class: single with bath L.E. 23–30; double L.E. 30–35.

Tourist: single with breakfast L.E. 17–23.

Pension: single with bath and half board L.E. 13–15.

A 12 percent tax is added throughout Egypt on the hotel and meal charge, and a municipal tax of 2 to 5 percent, depending on the city.

English is widely spoken in hotels throughout Egypt.

The government designates hotels by stars, ranging from five (deluxe) to one (pension). In our experience all but a few hotels are overrated by at least one and sometimes two stars. Maintenance is a problem even in the hotels belonging to reputable international chains. The Ministry of Tourism has begun a review to re-evaluate the rating of each hotel; however, it will be several years before the review is completed and new ratings assigned.

A current list of all hotels, their facilities and official rates may be obtained from the Egyptian Government Tourist Office in New York. Those hotels listed here are the best in each category.

Key to Abbreviations: swb—single with bath; dwb—double with bath; a/c—air-conditioned; TV—television; sw/ob—single without bath.

Note: All prices are approximate and subject to change.

Deluxe (five star)

Cairo Concorde, next to Cairo International Airport, 412 rooms. Price: L.E. 54.35 swb; 60.25 dwb. Phone: 664242; 690077.

The French chain's first hotel in Egypt, which is partially owned by EgyptAir, is Cairo's newest deluxe property in the rapidly expanding airport area. The impressive lobby is complemented by attractively furnished, sound-proofed rooms, all equipped with mini bar, TV, direct-dial phone, and air conditioning. Facilities include three restaurants, one of which is open 24 hours, large swimming pool, two tennis courts, nightclub featuring The Reda Group, Egypt's best dance group, hair salon, boutiques, convention hall, meeting rooms and parking space. There is a free airport shuttle bus.

Cairo Marriott, P.O. Box 33, Sharia al Gezira, Zamalek, 1,250 rooms. Price: L.E. 56 swb; 65 dwb. Phone: 650840.

Two high-rise towers have been added around a famous old palace, originally built by Khedive Ismail as a guest house for the Empress Eugenie at the time of the Suez Canal opening in 1869. It was later bought by a wealthy Egyptian pasha of Lebanese origin. The palace must have been considered grand at the time; it warranted a description in the 1895 edition of Baedeker's *Guide to Egypt*. The interior was elaborately decorated and gilded. The palace was made into a hotel in the 1960s. It quickly became a favorite for wedding receptions—brides could make their grand entrance on the carved marble staircase of the main entrance hall, its most outstanding feature.

In the design of the new hotel, the palace has become a central pavilion that includes a ballroom and reception rooms. Marriott has gone to great effort to restore all the old furniture, wood, marble, rugs, tapestries and objets d'art, most of which date from the late 19th century. These are used in the decor throughout the hotel where they are appropriate.

The facade with its original latticework porticos is the most impressive. Inside, Damascene painted high ceilings, elaborate arches and mammoth old oriental chandeliers help to retain the mansion's former grandeur.

The palace houses the specialty restaurant, coffee shop, cocktail lounge and bar, an indoor nightclub, a summer terrace club, and casino.

Situated on 12 acres, overlooking the Nile, the gardens include a swimming pool, fountains and extensive facilities. There are two lighted tennis courts, health clubs with gym. Most guest rooms have twin beds, but there are some fitted as businessman's suites with desk and work area; and there are elaborate suites on every floor. The towers are connected to the palace by arcades of boutiques and services.

Cairo Sheraton, 2 Galaa Square, Giza, 400 rooms. Price: L.E. 50 swb; 55 dwb. Phone: 983000.

Opened in 1969, the hotel is located in one of the most attractive parts of the city, on the west bank of the Nile at Giza, a few blocks from the house of the late president, Anwar Sadat.

Rooms overlook the Nile or the public gardens and Gezira Island. They are equipped with air conditioning, TV, and direct-dial phones. Rooms are large and nicely furnished. Facilities include bank, travel agency, swimming pool. The hotel's fine restaurants are among the best in Cairo, and its casino the liveliest. The shopping arcade has a very good bookstore and camera shop among other boutiques, a patisserie and a quick snack, stand up bar.

Nearby, the 522-room Gezira Sheraton is being added and is expected to open sometime in 1984.

Holiday Inn Pyramids, Alexandria Desert Road, 536 rooms. Price: L.E. 48 swb; L.E. 51 dwb. Phone: 856477.

The attractive hotel has the standard Holiday Inn amenities, plus a great view of the Pyramids. It is laid out in pyramid shape around a garden and outdoor pool. Guest rooms are large and nicely decorated and have direct dial telephone, air conditioning, radio and color TV. All 536 guest rooms are large, nicely decorated and have direct-dial phone, air conditioning, radio and color TV. A businessman's center offers secretarial and translating facilities among other services, and the hotel has banquet and conference facilities for 500 people. There are bars, 24-hour coffee shop, restaurants, shopping arcade, car rental—and camel rental—service, and one of the city's most popular nightclubs where the country's leading oriental dancer usually performs.

Holiday Inn Pyramids and Holiday Inn Sphinx face each other on a boulevard near the Pyramids, which are in view from many vantage points of each hotel. Regular shuttle bus service to/from the city center is available.

Holiday Inn Sphinx, Alexandria Desert Road, 246 rooms. Price: L.E. 34.70 swb; L.E. 38.50 dwb. Phone: 854700.

All rooms are in garden settings with oriental architectural accents and have air conditioning, color TV, radio, direct-dial telephone and two double beds. Sports facilities include two flood-lit tennis courts, swimming pool; horseback riding and golf are available nearby. It has a grill restaurant, 24-hour coffee shop, ice cream parlor, and disco. The two hotels complement each other in facilities, which are shared by guests.

Hyatt El Salam, 69 Abdel Hamid Badawy, Heliopolis, 328 rooms. Price: L.E. 45–55 swb; 56–68 dwb. Phone: 692155; 695155.

Located in suburb of Heliopolis near airport, the Georgian-style hotel is situated on 7 wooded acres and adjacent to El Shams Sporting Club, with which it has arrangements to use squash and tennis courts and riding facilities. Rooms have air conditioning, sound-proofing, TV with in-house movies and direct-dial phone. There is a 24-hour restaurant pool and dining terrace, bar/lounge, supper club, conference facilities with simultaneous translation facilities; business center, ballroom, theater. The Hyatt Fitness Center for men and women has two gyms, sauna, hair salons. Free bus service to city and airport. The hotel is being expanded and redecorated, and additional restaurants and other facilities are being added.

Mena House Oberoi, Sharia el Haram (Pyramid Road), Giza, 310 rooms. Price: L.E. 50 swb; 55 dwb; L.E. 125–275 suites. Phone: 855444; 856222.

Originally built as a royal hunting lodge for Khedive Ismail, Mena House is located at the base of the short, steep rise to the plateau on which the Pyramids and Sphinx stand. The building was enlarged by the free-spending monarch and converted into a guest house in 1869 in preparation for the festivities marking the opening of the Suez Canal.

A decade later the property was made into a hotel, expanded and further embellished. The most outstanding feature of its arabesque decor was its windows of intricate woodwork, known as *mushrabiya* in Arabic and called harem screens by Westerners. These were said to date back to the 14th century.

Over the century, Mena House came to be one of the most popular places in Egypt, with a guest list that included kings, queens, statesmen, writers, actors and other celebrities from around the world. The Empress Eugenie of France, King Zog of Albania, King Gustav of Sweden, King Umberto of Italy, King Alphonso of Spain, Emperor Haile Selassie, Mohamed V of Morocco all stayed here. Winston Churchill met President Roosevelt here.

From the hotel's front terrace, once the favorite place for British colonists and elite Cairenes to sip afternoon tea, visitors once had a superb view of the Pyramids. In bygone days before the road to the Pyramids was paved, visitors would mount camels at stables in front of Mena House to carry them up the hill. It was a romantic scene, especially for the spectators who enjoyed their tea on the hotel's veranda while they watched the sun set behind the Pyramids. Today, the terrace is the coffee shop, enclosed with large glass windows. The view is the same, but cars and motorcoaches breeze by and—no, it really is not quite the same.

The Oberoi Hotel chain of India took over the 44-acre property on a 20-year management contract in 1972, and completely renovated the old hotel and the 200 room extension that had been added in the 1960s. Oberoi has upgraded all the hotel operations and added many new features and facilities. Another expansion program, nearing completion, has added restaurant, meeting and banquet facilities. The rooms on the front, or south, side of the main building have spectacular views of the pyramids.

The guest rooms in the original buildings are deluxe doubles with private bath, television and air-conditioning, and a group of them have recently been redesigned into the most lavish, spectacular suites in Egypt, if not in the Middle East. They are furnished with authentic antiquities that were discovered in one of the hotel's storerooms, and completely restored to mint condition.

The main restaurant, bar, coffee shop and halls have retained the original decor, although all the old wood had to be replaced and much of it has been painted gold. The walls of the public rooms, once painted white, have now been covered with white marble. The effect is more that of a maharajah's lavish palace than a small royal retreat.

Complete new kitchens with the latest American equipment were installed to supply *Al Rubaiyat,* the main dining room serving continental food; the *Moghul Room* offering Indian specialties; *Khan el Khalili,* the coffee shop open 24 hours daily; the *Saddle Room,* a stereo nightclub; *Abu Nawas,* the inside winter nightclub; and the *Mameluk Bar,* the main bar of the old part.

Another building, encompassing the reception area, shops and administrative offices, forms a connection between the old buildings and the garden sections and is being enlarged to include a full-service executive business center.

Rooms in the garden buildings were refurbished and upgraded. These rooms face the Pyramids and overlook the swimming pool. Another 200 rooms have been added as an extension to the back side of the garden buildings. These rooms overlook the desert and the road to Alexandria.

The hotel's facilities include two tennis courts, a nine-hole golf course, a health club and a large swimming pool with a terrace restaurant which becomes the *Oasis,* an outdoor nightclub, in summer. There are several lovely meeting rooms, including one where presidents Carter and Sadat met to discuss peace.

While the location of the Mena House is fantastic, it could be a drawback for those who want to spend time in the city. The drive to Tahrir Square in the city center takes 30 to 45 minutes depending on traffic. The hotel offers shuttle bus service for guests. It should be noted also that much of Cairo has grown in this direction, especially the restaurant and nightclub area. Because of the hotel's extensive grounds and facilities, Mena House should be thought of as a resort on the edge of town rather than a city hotel.

Meridien, Corniche el Nil, Roda Island, 295 rooms. Price: L.E. 52 swb; 57 dwb. Phone: 845444.

The hotel was taken over by Air France's Meridien Hotel chain in 1971, and it completely renovated the property. It has the most fabulous location of any hotel in the city, sited on a two-square kilometer island in the Nile.

Rooms are spacious and comfortable; all are currently being refurbished and new bathrooms are being installed. The semicircular shape of the building gives each of the rooms a magnificent view of the Nile and Cairo. Rooms are equipped with air conditioning, direct-dial phone and TV with 2 in-house video channels. Each room also has a nice-sized terrace on which guests may enjoy breakfast, sunbathe, watch the *feluccas,* the graceful sailboats of the Nile, or see the sun set over Cairo.

The hotel has several restaurants and a rooftop dining room, featuring a nightly combo for dancing and a top-rated Egyptian belly dancer.

Facilities include photo, souvenir and book shops, florist, jeweler, several attractive dress and accessory shops, travel agent, car rental, bank and airline office. There is a beauty salon, winter and summer swimming pool, sauna and massage. The hotel has a Business Service Center, with telex, copying machine, secretarial service and private office space for rent. The hotel has a constantly changing exhibit of Egyptian art.

The hotel is near the British Embassy and within walking distance of the American Embassy. It is a short taxi ride from the Egyptian Antiquities Museum and the downtown shopping district.

Nile Hilton, Corniche el Nil, 466 rooms. Price: L.E. 61–84 swb; 72–91 dwb. Phone: 740777; 750666. The Hilton has become something of an institution in Cairo. Terrific location overlooking the Nile on one side and Tahrir Square on the other. The Egyptian Antiquities Museum is next door and the hotel is within walking distance of the downtown shopping district and the American Embassy.

The Hilton has long been a favorite meeting place for foreigners, press and top level government and business people, and its bars, poolside restaurant and cocktail lounge are usually crowded with Egyptians and visitors alike. The rooftop nightclub is tops. In summer it moves to an outside garden by the swimming pool. Its disco, *Jackie's,* is the leading one in the city. There is also a casino. Dining facilities include several restaurants, coffee shop, pizzeria, and rotisserie.

The hotel uses a modern adaptation of ancient Egyptian motifs and colors throughout its decor. Most of the fabrics, furnishings and objets d'art were made in Egypt. The hotel has many shops and services; prices tend to be higher than elsewhere but the selections are good and the atmosphere pleasant. Several airlines and travel agents have offices in the hotel lobby. There is a beauty salon, barbershop, health club, sauna, swimming pool and two tennis courts.

Rooms are large and comfortable with terraces offering panoramic views of Cairo. For a view of the Nile, ask for a room on the west side. Rooms are equipped with air conditioning, TV, in-house movies, mini-bars, and direct-dial telephones—an important advantage for business travelers. Reservations must be made and confirmed in advance.

A three-story extension, the Nile Hilton Centre, has added 66 rooms to the main building and a wide range of shops and services. There are nine suites with kitchenette; space for 47 offices, and 23 shops including a bank, car rental, airline offices—including *Air Sinai*—and a parking garage.

Nova-Park Cairo, 10 Aisha Taymuria St., Garden City. Phone: 29977. A large luxury hotel overlooking the Nile by the same group, which recently opened the Green Pyramids Hotel, is scheduled to open in 1985.

Ramses Hilton, Corniche el Nil, 900 rooms. Price: L.E. 58.50–73.40 swb; L.E. 69.50–81 dwb. Phone: 744400. A completely separate hotel from the Nile Hilton, located on the Nile about 3 blocks from the latter and within walking distance of the Antiquities Museum, it is the tallest hotel and one of the tallest buildings in town. The rooftop lounge is a popular spot for cocktails and a panoramic view from where, on a clear day, the Pyramids of Giza are visible on the western horizon, nine miles away.

Throughout the hotel touches of Egyptian motifs from all the important periods of its history are reflected in the decor. The walls of the lobby and main corridors are faced with a pharaoh's ransom of rose granite and Portoccino marble from Aswan. In the *Garden Court* of the central lobby, one can enjoy drinks under columns which soar to the second and third floors and resemble the great columns of Karnak Temple in Luxor.

A stairway curves up to the *Terrace Cafe,* a 24-hour coffee shop on the second level, which overlooks the Nile as well as the Garden Court. Nearby, the *Citadel Grill,* the main dining room, combines Egypt's Islamic heritage in design details taken from traditional tiles and in the use of mushrabbiyah latticework, with the village tradition of weaving, as seen in the beautiful tapestries from Harraniya. Enormous copper chimneys over the open grill are reproductions of bread ovens still in use in Upper Egypt.

To the right of the grill is a cozy bar.

The lobby level and first floor have meeting rooms and a ballroom. A nightclub and an oriental restaurant/nightclub are on the swimming pool level as are the hair salons, health club and gym for men and women.

Guests can also ride from the lobby to the first and second floors in what might be the world's plushest elevator. The two-ton glass and brass lift was made by the famous British manufacturer, Basingstoke. Its interior is finished in genuine suede leather and, according to one British newspaper report, so "lifted" the pride of the firm's employees, they invited their wives to the factory to see it.

Guest rooms are located on another 30 floors, and because of the building's unusual triangular shape, 80 percent of the rooms have views of the Nile. The rooms are beautifully decorated, even to the point of having original paintings by modern Egyptian artists and handmade ceramic wall plaques in Pharaonic design in the bathrooms. Rooms have air conditioning, TV, in-house movies, direct-dial telephones and refrigerators/bars. Two rooms are especially designed for the handicapped. There are a variety of shops.

Semiramis Inter-Continental, Corniche el Nil, 800 rooms. Situated on the site of a famous old hotel it is replacing, the hotel is scheduled to be completed in 1984 and operated by the Grand Metropolitan group.

Shepheards, Corniche el Nil, Sharia al Hamy, 290 rooms. Price: L.E. 30 swb; 40 dwb. Phone: 33800. Under the government rating system, Shepheards is listed as a five-star hotel, but in its present condition it doesn't deserve more than three. An $8 million refurbishing and upgrading project to return it to its former deluxe status is underway.

The hotel's modern design is mellowed by arabesque decor. Rooms are large and comfortable and equipped with air conditioning and TV. There are a few shops and services, dining room, bar, roof garden with summer dining and dancing, lounge with a view of the city and a casino.

Samuel Shepheard, an Englishman who came to Cairo in 1841, opened the New British Hotel, later named Shepheard's British Hotel. It catered to travelers en route to and from the Far East, and it thrived. Eventually the hotel was moved to the palace of Alfi Bey in Ezbekieh Gardens, which at one time had been used by Napoleon's commander-in-chief.

In 1861 ownership passed to a Dr. Zach, who restored and enlarged the building to accommodate the increasing number of tourists who came to Egypt following the opening of the Suez Canal. Its guest register began to read like an international *Who's Who,* and included Queen Mary of Rumania, King Leopold of Belgium, King Alphonso of Spain and Winston Churchill. Its reputation was made.

Indeed, few hotels in the world have become so much a part of the history of their times that their destruction could symbolize the end of an era. When Shepheards was burned to the ground during the riots in 1952, it signaled the beginning of the Egyptian revolution and the end of colonialism.

The new Shepheards was built in 1956 in a new location on the Corniche overlooking the Nile. For a brief moment it tried to recapture some of the grandeur of the old one, but it failed. Now, it is just another hotel.

Sheraton Heliopolis, Airport Road, 645 rooms. Price: L.E. 50 swb; L.E. 55 dwb. Phone: 665500; 66700. Built by Gulf Hotels, a Kuwaiti-financed firm, the Cairo property is spread over a large area, allowing for extensive gardens and recreational and other facilities that include a convention center, health club, and one of the best bakeries in the city.

The hotel looks so plain on the outside that it belies its lovely interior. The reception area, shops, restaurants and bars operate around a huge central, sunken garden lobby. Rooms are situated in three wings around the swimming pool and tennis courts; those on the ground level have sundecks. Rooms are beautifully decorated in soft, restful colors, using fabrics with modern adaptions of Egyptian motifs, and have air conditioning, TV with in-house video, direct-dial phones.

The hotel's different restaurants—Italian, German, continental and others—have gained a reputation for being among the best in the city. The hotel is located about 10 minutes from the airport; there is free bus service to Cairo Sheraton in town. Car rental is also available.

Sonesta, El Tayaran St., Nasr City (en route airport/city), 217 rooms. Price: L.E. 45 swb; L.E. 49 dwb. Phone: 604811. An attractive, small hotel on a quiet street, convenient to the airport. Rooms are nicely decorated, air-conditioned, TV. Facilities include 24-hour coffee shop, restaurant, bar, disco, pool, sauna, tennis court, car rental, shops, business services center and meeting rooms.

First Class Superior (four star)

Concorde, 146 Tahrir St., Dokki, 72 rooms. Price: L.E. 24 swb; L.E. 28 dwb. Phone: 813173. (Not to be confused with the new Concorde near the airport. This hotel is located within walking distance of Cairo Sheraton.) A small, modern and very attractive hotel that occupies the first and top 5 floors of a 12-story office/apartment building. It belongs to the same owners as the President Hotel and caters to business travelers and a European clientele. Rooms nicely furnished and have air conditioning, TV; there is a restaurant and bar.

Green Pyramids, Helmiat Alahram St., 78 rooms. Price: L.E. 40 swb; L.E. 48 dwb. Phone: 852600.

A hotel situated in the house and gardens of a former Egyptian actor, Yousif Wahbi, on a quiet street off the Pyramids Road in Giza.

Several buildings housing guest rooms, restaurant/bar and the pool have been added around the house. The hotel is managed by the Swiss group, Nova-Park, which is building a large deluxe hotel on the Nile in Cairo. All rooms have minibars, TV, direct-dial phone and overlook the gardens.

The hotel quickly acquired a good reputation for its restaurant, *Nova Palm*. There's a coffee shop in the former guest house; meeting room for 20 people; and disco, *Rasputin,* named for the role which Wahbi made famous in Egypt.

Jolie Ville, located on the road to Alexandria near the Pyramids of Giza, 250 rooms in 18 bungalows. Price: L.E. 38 swb with breakfast; L.E. 45 dwb with breakfast and including service charge. Phone: 855510. The hotel, operated by the Swiss group Movenpick opened in 1977 and quickly received good reviews. It is a pre-fabricated structure of aluminum panels, built on one level, like a motel. Each room faces onto a small patio and overlooks the property's extensive gardens. All rooms are twin-bedded, have large bathrooms and are equipped with radio, telephone and air conditioning. The hotel's facilities include a dining room, Italian garden restaurant with live entertainment, lobby bar, pastry shop, gift shops and swimming pool with terrace bar and snack service. Food service is available 24 hours daily.

Jolie Ville has an informal and friendly atmosphere; all public rooms, bar, restaurant, etc. are in an open area separated by panels, in one building next to the swimming pool. From the pool and most of the guest rooms, guests have a clear view of the peaks of the Pyramids. Another asset of the hotel is that guests can step from their room almost directly to the pool, only a few feet away.

A sister hotel, *Movenpick Hotel Jolie Ville Luxor,* was scheduled to open in Luxor for the winter season.

Manial Palace/Club Mediterranee, El Manial Street, Roda Island, 183 rooms. Price: on request from Club Mediterranee, New York. Phone: 524535. The palace was the former residence of Muhammed Ali, an uncle of King Farouk and an enthusiastic collector of oriental art. After the revolution of 1952 the palace was turned into a museum, and in 1955 bungalows were added in the gardens to make it into a hotel. The palace is worth a visit even if one is not a hotel guest. It is set in beautiful gardens and has an outstanding collection of oriental art.

Currently, the hotel portion, which has a separate entrance, is being used exclusively by Club Mediterranee and must be booked through them. When the Club is not fully booked, it will accept individual guests upon request. Also, outside visitors are welcome to lunch or dine here, and it serves one of the best spreads in town. Reservations a must.

Novotel, Cairo Airport Rd., 215 rooms. Price: L.E. 33 swb; L.E. 38 dwb. Phone: 661330.

Another French entry for the first time in Cairo, the new hotel is located next to the airport and the Cairo Concorde. It has a restaurant and coffee shop, pool, tennis, shops, 24-hour room service, and guest rooms have air conditioning, and video. Free shuttle bus to the airport.

President, 22 Taha Hussein St., Zamalek, 107 rooms. Price: L.E. 38 swb; L.E. 40 dwb. Phone: 816751. Located on the first and top three floors of a new apartment building in Zamalek, a fashionable Cairo residential district on the west bank of the Nile. Rooms are large and nicely appointed; most have an unusually large balcony overlooking the city. The hotel has a good roof-top restaurant with nice view, bar and 24-hour room service. For newcomers the hotel might be hard to find, although large signs are posted along the way. It has become very popular with businessmen, as it is clean, well run and convenient, with telex and direct-dial for international calls. The hotel has added a pub, The Cairo Cellar, where food and drinks are served in a lively atmosphere.

Radisson Oasis, Alexandria Desert Rd., 260 rooms. Price: L.E. 34 swb; L.E. 37 dwb. Phone: 851506. Situated on nine acres in sight of the Pyramids. All rooms are situated in quiet garden settings and fitted with TV, minibar. There is a restaurant, coffee shop, bar, nightclub, 24-hour room service, an unusually large pool, and tennis courts are being added. The hotel is quiet far from the center of town and offers weekend escape packages for citysiders. Courtesy bus operates 8 A.M. to 8 P.M. to Tahrir Square.

Ramada Inn, Alexandria Desert Rd. The large resort-style hotel is nearing completion and promises to be one of the loveliest in the area. The design of the main building—a modern interpretation of classic Middle Eastern architecture—is particularly attractive.

Siag Pyramids Penta, 59 Marioutia Road, P.O. Box 1037, Giza, 349 rooms. Price: L.E. 33 swb; L.E. 36 dwb. Phone: 850874. The new hotel, situated on the road to Harraniya, is built in a half-moon shape enabling a majority of rooms to have a full view of the Pyramids from their balconies. All rooms have air conditioning, bath, direct-dial phone, television and mini bar. There is a coffee shop, grill room, lobby bar and meeting and banquet facilities. Sports facilities include pool, health center and tennis. The hotel expects to have a shopping arcade and businessmen's center.

Medium (four star)

NOTE: Many of the four- and three-star hotels included in the following sections are really tourist-class hotels. The old ones are often very old, and are included here because of convenient in-town location and price. Most of the new ones are in the new residential areas of Dokki and Mohandaseen, which makes them inconvenient without a car, but they are modern and, hopefully, clean.

Atlas Zamalek, 20 Gameet el Dowal el Arabia, Mohandeseen, 64 rooms. Price: L.E. 29 swb; L.E. 33 dwb. Phone: 805782. Situated in a residential section, the hotel has two restaurants, two swimming pools, roof garden snack bar, coffee shop, disco, meeting rooms, sauna and shops. Rooms are large and have air conditioning, direct dial phone, color TV; 24-hour room service. Same owners as Atlas in downtown, which is not recommended; and Osiris Travel, which has its own fleet of motorcoaches and minibuses.

Cleopatra Palace, 2 Sharia Bustan, Tahrir Square, 84 rooms. Price: L.E. 32 swb or 36 dwb with breakfast. Phone: 759945. A modern hotel with simply-furnished rooms. Dining room and roof garden on the top floor, a/c and bar. The hotel is centrally located on a main square of the city, which makes it very convenient but noisy. Moderately priced coffee shop added recently.

El Borg, Sharia el Gazira, 75 rooms. Price: L.E. 32 swb; 36 dwb. Phone: 816060. Well located on the Nile across the river from the Hilton, this hotel was good when it opened in the mid-1960s. Time has taken its toll. Rooms are equipped with air conditioning and have panoramic views of the Nile; bar and restaurant.

El Nil, Sharia Ahmed Ragheb, Garden City, 232 rooms. Price: L.E. 24 swb; 26 dwb. Phone: 22800. Conveniently located in Garden City on the Nile, near the Meridien and the British Embassy and within walking distance of the American Embassy; a/c bar and pleasant rooftop restaurant with view; disco.

Salma, 12 Mohamed Kamel Morsi St., Dokki, 45 rooms. Price: L.E. 23 swb; L.E. 26 dwb. Phone: 700901. New, very nice small hotel, managed by Swiss group Comana, which has opened two more hotels in Cairo. Located on a quiet street in pleasant neighborhood, rooms are small but nicely furnished and have air conditioning, TV, phone, radio. Small meeting room; restaurant, bar, business service center. The new hotels **Marwa** and **Aman,** both in Giza between the Cairo Sheraton and the Zoo, are also four-star and have rooms equipped with air conditioning, minibar, color TV.

Tourist Class (three star)

Amoun, 26 July Sq., 43 rooms. Price: L.E. 20 swb; L.E. 22 dwb. Phone: 650335. Simple hotel, rooms with air conditioning, TV. Coffee shop, tea garden, *Paxy* restaurant.

Continental Savoy, 10 Opera Square, 176 rooms. Price: L.E. 14 dwb. Phone: 911049. In the past, this hotel overlooking the Ezbekieh Gardens was one of Cairo's best, but now it is worn. It has a convenient downtown location, its lobby is a large shopping arcade, and it's hard to beat the price. The noise during the day is at a high pitch, but it quiets down considerably at night. Rooms vary greatly in size and condition, even at the same price. Most have been renovated and have new bathrooms; others are old and run down. Ask to see room before accepting it.

Cosmopolitan, 2 Saalab St. (off Sharia Kasr el Nil), 90 rooms, all with bath. Price: L.E. 14 dwb. Phone: 743956. The hotel is located amid downtown office buildings, one block off the major shopping street. Rooms are modest. It has a reputation for good food and services; bar, restaurant. This is an old hotel, which was recently renovated. It is a good value for the rate.

Garden Palace, 11 Moudiriet El Tahrir St., Garden City, 65 rooms/suites. Price: L.E. 20 swb; L.E. 25; L.E. 42 suite, up to 4 persons; L.E. 55 suite, up to 6 persons. Phone: 29157; 28435. The first of a chain with another opening soon in Heliopolis and a third being built in Luxor. The Cairo hotel is near the American and British embassies and walking distance of Tahrir Square. All rooms have phone, private bath and air conditioning. Twenty-four hour room service, laundry and bank. Suites of two and four bedrooms are suitable for families and can be provided with kitchenettes for long stay. Hotel has restaurant with European and Middle Eastern dishes; Chinese restaurant and disco.

General, 28 Shagaret el Dor St., Zamalek. Prices: L.E. 15 swb and L.E. 19 dwb. A new hotel in the residential area of Zamalek. Rooms have air conditioning. There's a good pub in the same building.

Golden Tulip/Tonsi, 143 Tahrir St., Dokki. 67 rooms. Price: L.E. 22 swb and L.E. 24 dwb. Phone: 989704. Hotel located on first, second and 16th/17th floors of office building. Rooms have air conditioning, mini-bar, TV on request. Restaurant, bar, roof deck. One block from Cairo Sheraton.

Indiana, 16 El Sarayah St., 120 rooms. Prices: L.E. 23 swb and L.E. 26 dwb. Phone: 800321; 801138. New hotel in Dokki on quiet street two blocks north of Sheraton. Airconditioning units, phone, TV in rooms; restaurant, bar, 24-hour coffee shop, car rental.

International, 3 Abdel Azim Rached St. and Nawal St. (at 6th. of October Bridge), Dokki. Prices: L.E. 16 swb and L.E. 19 dwb, including breakfast. Phone: 806159; 818475. A new hotel with 60 rooms, some without bath; all with phone. Air conditioning and TV are 2.250 extra. Room service, bar, 24-hour coffee shop.

Kanzy, 9 Abu Bakr el Saddeek St., Dokki. Prices: L.E. 18 swb; L.E. 24 dwb. Phone: 709443. New and modern; rooftop swimming pool. Suites and larger singles and doubles available for a few pounds more.

Khan al-Khalili, 7 Sharia el Bosta, Midan el Ataba. Price: 16 dwb. Phone: 900271. Despite its rundown appearance on the outside, the hotel receives good marks from Americans who have stayed there for being a good value. And, despite its name, it is not or even near the Khan el Khalili bazaar of the Mouski. It is, however, in the downtown area and within walking distance of the shopping district and businesses located in the city center. The hotel has air conditioning, restaurant, bar. Not all rooms have private bath.

Raja Hotel, Mohi el Din Abul Ezz St., 83 rooms. Price: L.E. 37 dwb w/ breakfast. Phone: 702250. All rooms are double with two beds; air conditioning, refrigerator, TV. Restaurant; bar, coffee shop and disco; 24 hr. room service.

Rehab, 4 Sharia Fawakeh, Mohandessin/Dokki. Prices: L.E. 23 swb and L.E. 26 dwb. Phone: 703112. The hotel gets good reviews for its *Marhaba* restaurant. Hotel is airconditioned and has a 24-hour coffee shop, bar, 24-hour room service. It is located in the residential district and will be a little bit hard to find. Rooms have large bathrooms, but showers only; very clean linens; caters to European groups.

Scheherazade, 182 el Nil St., Agouza, 240 rooms. Price: L.E. 16 dwb. Phone: 819896. This hotel is upgrading its entire facilities. Overlooking the Nile in Agouza, near the British Council; bar, restaurant, nightclub. Swimming pool being added.

Sweet's, Street 13 (one block from Sharia Mustapha Kamel), Maadi. Price: L.E. 700 per month. Furnished apartments on short-term lease.

Attached to the hotel is a restaurant and pub. Building is located in the suburb of Maadi, 10 miles from downtown Cairo.

Economy and Pension (two star)

Garden City, 23 Kamel ed-Din Salah Street, 38 rooms. Prices: L.E. 17 swb and half board; L.E. 24 dwb and half board. Room without private bath is L.E. 3–5 cheaper. Phone: 28400. An old but pleasant pension, centrally located only two blocks from the American and British embassies, it is a long time favorite of the embassy staffs.

New Horus House, 21 Sharia Ismail Mohamed, Zamalek, 34 rooms. Price: L.E. 21 swb; L.E. 27 dwb. Phone: 803977. Small pension in the heart of Zamalek. Pleasant, friendly and comes highly recommended. (Not to be confused with a hotel in town named Horris). Restaurant, bar, a/c, phones in each room. Same owners as President and Concorde Hotels.

El Hussein, Midan el Hussein (Al Azhar area), 55 rooms. Prices: L.E. 12 swb; w/breakfast L.E. 16 dwb with breakfast. Phone: 918089. A fairly new hotel in the heart of the Azhar and Mouski area at the entrance to the Khan el Khalili bazaar; restaurant, bar. If you really want the atmosphere of medieval Cairo, this is the place to stay. From your room, the minarets of Al Azhar and El Hussein Mosques and the cupola of El Ghouri are in full view.

Longchamps, 21 Sharia Ismail Mohamed, Zamalek, 24 rooms. Price: L.E. 15 swb; L.E. 24 dwb with breakfast. Phone: 802311. Centrally located in the Zamalek residential area; a/c, restaurant, bar, discotheque. Private bath, phone in all rooms; TV and minibar on request.

Lotus, 12 Talaat Harb, 49 rooms. Price: L.E. 14 dwb. Phone: 970360. The pension occupies the top three floors of an office building, one block from American Express, near Sharia Kasr el Nil. It is simple and convenient.

Tulip, 3 Midan Talaat Harb, 20 rooms. Price: L.E. 8 dwb. Phone: 762704.

Good downtown location, but recommended only in a pinch. Some rooms with bath. All with telephone.

New Hotel Developments

Student Facilities: The *Youth Hostel Association,* 7 Sharia Doctor Abdel Hamid Said, Marrouf, Cairo, can assist students in arranging accommodations in youth hostels and a program for visiting Egypt.

Hostels charge approximately L.E. 1 per night per bed, second sheet, hot bath and kitchen facilities. All bookings must be made directly with the hostels by letter stating name, address, dates of arrival and departure. Or ask the association for assistance.

There is a new youth hostel at Sharia Abdel Aziz al Saud, El Manial, at the foot of the Nile bridge leading to the University of Cairo. You should write or call in advance as the hostel is usually full.

The *Youth Travel Bureau* organizes excursions around Egypt to enable students to travel at low costs to most of the historic places and to modern projects as well. The Bureau sometimes organizes excursions to remote places that would be difficult for an individual to visit on his own.

The *Sahara Tourist Camp* is located in the desert behind the Pyramids. It has simple camp facilities in bungalows and tents.

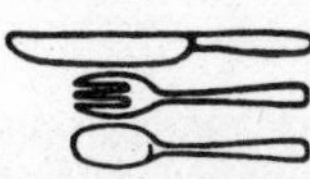

WHERE TO EAT. Some of the best restaurants are in nightclubs and hotels. Those listed here are generally recognized as Cairo's best. With few exceptions, restaurants depend entirely upon local ingredients and offer whatever vegetables and fruits are in season. The variety of cuisine has expanded recently as a result of Cairo's new boom, and new restaurants are popping up daily.

In most good restaurants the maitre d'hotel takes your order. He will speak French and English, often Italian, German and Greek. Waiters usually speak only Arabic and a few words of English pertaining to food.

Breakfast can range from $2 to $3, lunch or dinner a la carte from $4 to $10; double this amount at luxury hotels and nightclubs. Twelve percent is added to the bill. There is almost no difference between lunch and dinner prices. Many restaurants catering to foreign tourists, especially large groups, offer a daily menu which will average from $4 to $6 for lunch and $6 to $8 for dinner and is served at specific hours, i.e. prior to the normal dinner hour of 8:00 or 9:00 P.M.

Egyptian Cuisine

Egyptian cooking is a mixture of native tradition and Turkish, Lebanese and Syrian, Greek, Italian and French cuisine. The choices offered in restaurants tend to be limited. You will only get the wide range in people's homes or at special banquets.

Do not judge an Egyptian-style restaurant by its exterior. Most are simple and specialize in the basic skewered meat and dishes made from *fool* (fava beans). They could be likened to a souvlaki place in Athens or New York. They are not for tourists who need to have special food or those who are not a little bit adventurous about trying new food. All are moderate in price.

Abou Shakra, 69 Sharia Kasr el Aini. Phone: 848811. Specializing in *kofta* and *kebab*, this place is refurbished every year during Ramadan. Home deliveries.

Ali Hassan al Hati, 8 Halim Square (behind Cicure Department Store). Phone: 916055. One of Cairo's oldest and best known restaurants for Egyptian food and up a grade from the others in its decor of crystal chandeliers and white tablecloths. The kitchen with large open ovens and grills is next to the entrance. Moderate prices.

Casino des Pigeons, on the Nile in Giza. Phone: 896299. One of the oldest and best outdoor cafés on the river bank. Specializes in roast pigeon, an Egyptian delicacy. No alcoholic beverages. Moderate prices.

El Chimi (Shimy), 45 Midan Orabi. Phone: 55345. *Kebab* and other Egyptian specialties; long-time favorite.

El Dahan, 4 Kahan el Khalili. Phone: 905086. *Kebab* and *kofta.*

El Dar, Sakkara Road. In a charming house with arabesque decor and garden. Egyptian specialties, pleasant for lunch and dinner. Stereo music for dancing in the evening. Open until 2:00 A.M.

El Domiati, Badrawi Building at Midan El Falaki. Phone: 56753. *Fool* (fava beans) and *taamiya.*

El Rakeeb, 19 Midan el Sayedda Zeinab. Phone: 906659. Specializes in *kofta* and *kebab.* Popular with movie and show business personalities.

El Tabie, 31 Sharia Orabi, near Sharia Ramsis. Phone: 979842. A well established reputation as the best place in Cairo for *fool* and *taamiya.*

Fatarane el Tahrir, 166 Sharia el Tahrir off Midan el Tahrir. Phone: 33596. Specializes in *fateer,* a pastry stuffed with cheese, eggs, meat or sweetmeats. Open all night.

Felfela, 15 Sharia Hoda Shaarawy at Midan Talaat Harb. Phone: 977751. One of the best for *fool,* which is prepared in many ways; other local dishes. Pleasant garden in city center.

Felfela now has a country cousin—it's located on a country road north of the Pyramids Road (opposite the road south to Sakkara). It is a garden restaurant with many features meant to bring traditional Egyptian life to city slickers—a donkey for the kids to ride, a puppet show (one of the country's most popular forms of entertainment), dancing horses and dance troupes performing traditional folk dancing of Upper Egypt. There are also the traditional coffee house, open-spit cooking and a shop for Egyptian crafts. It's all by the same family that owns Paprika. (Incidentally, *felfela* means pepper in Arabic, as does paprika in several languages.)

Hag Mahmoud el Sammak, Sharia Abdel Aziz, opposite Omar Effendi. Phone: 901377. Considered by many to be the best seafood restaurant in the city. Clean, simple; no liquor. Also sells fresh fish and will deliver in Cairo.

Khomais, located in the heart of town, offers Oriental food in an Arabian Nights atmosphere. Be sure to have your meal in the upstairs room. Specialty is *kebab.* Moderate prices.

La Lanterne, Alexandria Road (road north from the Pyramids, opposite the road south to Sakkara). Outdoor garden restaurant, nightclub in the evening.

Mushrabiya, Ahmed Nessim St. (across the street from the Swiss Chalet). Very pleasant, new, clean restaurant serving good Egyptian and other Middle Eastern cuisine. Moderate prices. No alcoholic beverages. An adjacent patisserie for Middle Eastern sweets.

Omar Khayyam, Saray el Gezireh. On a yacht docked near the Omar Khayyam Hotel (but no connection with the hotel). Decor and food are Oriental. The menu is brief. The restaurant is especially pleasant for lunch; in the evening it becomes an intimate nightclub.

European Cuisine

Although the following group of restaurants offer European, American or international cuisine, many also include Egyptian and other Middle Eastern dishes on their menu.

After Eight, 6 Kasr el Nil (next to Aeroflot office). The top choice of Cairo's elite; expensive by Egyptian standards. This is really an insider's place in more ways than one. You have to walk through an alleyway to reach it but don't be dissuaded by the entrance. It is quite attractive inside with panelled walls and furnishings like a pub or private club. Tourists almost never know about it.

Aladin, 26 Sharia Sherif, Immobilia Bldg. One of the best restaurants in Cairo for European cuisine outside of the hotels. It is patronized by Egyptians and resident foreigners rather than tourists. Lunch is served from 1:00–4:00 P.M.; dinner from 8:00–12:00 midnight. Moderate prices.

Aladin, Sheraton Hotel (second floor). Phone: 98300. Not to be confused with the restaurant by the same name (above) located in the center of downtown. Continental menu, attractive decor. Considered one of the best in the city. Small piano bar adjoining dining room. Reservations recommended. Expensive.

Alfredo's, Heliopolis Sheraton, classic Italian cuisine, probably the best in Cairo.

Al Rubayyat, Mena House Oberoi. The dining room generally gets good reviews from patrons. It offers Continental cuisine and Indian specialities and is open for lunch and dinner.

Al Zahraa, Heliopolis Sheraton. Popular 24-hour coffee shop. Because it is so near the airport, it's a good place to wait during times of delay.

Andrea, about one mile north of the Pyramid Rd. at Tereit el Maryutia (opposite the road south leading to Sakkara). Phone: 851133. Specializes in barbecued chicken and *mezzah* (Middle Eastern hors d'oeuvres). Rustic outdoor setting. Crowded on weekends. Considered one of the best in Cairo. Same owner as Seahorse. Moderately expensive.

Arabesque, 4 Kasr el Nil St. (next to Middle East Airlines). Consistently good for food, decor and service. The menu is Continental with a selection of Egyptian specialties. The decor, as the name implies, is Oriental and attractive. Prices are expensive by Cairo, but not U.S., standards. The entranceway is a gallery for local artists.

Arous el Nil Coffee Shop, Sheraton Hotel. American snacks and full meals. Open 24 hours daily. Moderate prices.

Bier Stude, Heliopolis Sheraton. Features German specialties.

Bonito, 25 Mariolia St. off Pyramid Rd. Phone: 851870. Specializes in fish. Moderate.

Borsalino, 1 Latin America (opp. British Embassy), Garden City. Open daily 12:30–4 lunch; 8:30 P.M.–2:30 A.M. for dinner.

Brasserie, Meridien Hotel (ground floor). Coffee shop resembling a Paris brasserie. Nice view.

Cairo Cellar Pub, 22 Sharia Taha Hussein, Zamalek. Phone: 816751. Located in the President Hotel, neighborhood sort of place. Popular.

Caroll, 12 Sharia Kasr el Nil. Phone: 753224. One of the best in the downtown area; pleasant, mellow decor; good service and good food. Small, reservations recommended. Lunch 12:30–3:30 P.M., dinner 8:00–11:30 P.M. Moderately expensive.

Carvery, Sharia Maryuita off Pyramids Road. A new restaurant in a lovely setting about a quarter mile off the road to the Pyramids has quickly become a Cairo favorite. It serves a buffet at set price.

Chateau de Versailles, 12 Sharia Mohamed Sakeb, Zamalek. Phone: 813199. Good French and Lebanese food; pretentious and expensive.

Citadelle, Ramses Hilton. The new hotel's principal dining room overlooks the fabulous central, colonnaded lobby. Main room offers steaks and grilled specialties.

Don Quichotte, 9A, Ahmad Hismet St., Zamalek. Phone: 806415. French cuisine. Small, reservations recommended.

El Nil Rotisserie, Nile Hilton. Phone: 740777. Specializes in imported American meat; offers well-prepared European and Oriental dishes in attractive surroundings. Reservations recommended. Expensive.

Estoril, 12 Sharia Talaat Harb (in passageway), near American Express on Kasr el Nil. Phone: 743102. Good European food; once was one of Cairo's best establishments, but not quite up to its old reputation. Lunch 12:30–3:30 P.M.; dinner 7:30–11:00 P.M. Moderate.

The Farm, Mariolia Street, off Pyramid Road. Phone: 851870. Specializes in grilled lamb and other meat dishes. Moderate.

Flying Fish, 166 El Nil Street, Agouza. Phone: 814867. A new, moderately priced riverside establishment gets good reviews. Conveniently located to Cairo Sheraton.

Le Grillon, in passageway off Sharia Kasr el Nil (near Middle East Airlines). Phone: 41114. French and Egyptian food; generally good, clean and pleasant. Moderate.

Ibis Cafe, Nile Hilton. Open 24 hours daily and almost always full. Serves American snacks and Egyptian dishes, one of the few nonoriental restaurants in Cairo that serves *fool mudhammas* at breakfast. Moderately expensive.

Kasr El Rachid, Meridien Hotel (ground floor). Phone: 845444. International and oriental specialities; open buffet. Moderately expensive.

Khan el Khalili Coffee Shop, Mena House Oberoi Hotel. On the terrace of the old building with a full view of the Pyramids; open 24 hours a day.

King's, 3 Ibrahim el Kabany (opposite Lappas) in heart of town. Variety of European and Egyptian specialities in a blend of eastern and western decor. Reasonable prices.

King Tut Grill Room, Heliopolis Sheraton. Hotel's gourmet restaurant consistently gets good reviews.

Kursaal, 17 Sharia el Alfi. Phone: 918930. Modern restaurant with a wide selection of western and Oriental food from an à la carte menu. This was for many years rated the best restaurant in Cairo. It has an outdoor terrace for summer evenings. Food and service are good, atmosphere pleasant. Moderate.

Liban, 20 Sharia Adly. Phone: 53406. Lebanese dishes, not as good as those at some other restaurants. Moderate.

La Mama, Sheraton Hotel. Italian restaurant with very good food. Lovely view of Nile from window-side tables. Open daily from noon until 2 A.M. Moderate.

La Mediterranee, 13A Mar'ashly St., Zamalek, near intersection of Sharia Willcocks. Specializes in fish. Moderately expensive.

Manial Palace (the Club Mediterranee), Roda Island. Phone: 978495. Buffet style, good quality and quantity in the pleasant surroundings of the Manial Palace gardens. Lunch for L.E. 8, including wine. Non-resident guests may go for lunch from 1:30–2:30 P.M. and dinner from 8:30 P.M.; reservations required.

Moghul Room, Mena House Oberoi. Phone: 855444. Authentic Indian cuisine in beautiful surroundings and excellent service. Recommend ordering complete dinner. Lunch served noon–3:00 P.M.; dinner 7:30–11:00 P.M.

Munchen Lowenbrau, 31 Sharia 26 July. Phone: 57329. German restaurant where food and service are good in Bavarian setting. Moderate.

Naniwa, 3 Sharia Lebnan, Mohandiseen. Japanese restaurant, complete with tatami room. Good classic specialties; moderate prices.

Nile Garden, Corniche el Maadi. Phone: 988121. Continental and Oriental selections. For lunch the restaurant has a very pleasant setting on the Nile with a superb view. The food and service are good. It becomes a nightclub in the evening. Moderate.

Nile Pharoah, floating restaurant by Corniche Giza, near Sheraton. Phone: 726713; 726122. The new fanciful boat in the shape of a pharaoh's barge is operated by Mena House Oberoi. It serves continental and Egyptian dishes. Guests can enjoy a 2½-hour Nile cruise with luncheon or dinner, dancing and entertainment. Check with restaurant for departure times. Reservations required.

Nova Palm, restaurant of Green Pyramids Hotel, has gained an excellent reputation since it opened last year. Swiss and continental specialties. Entrees L.E. 6 to 10. Fridays, buffet by the pool.

Oasis, Mena House. Poolside restaurant with full view of Pyramids offers a very pleasant setting for lunch. It becomes the hotel's nightclub in summer. Indian specialties. Moderately expensive. Nonresident guests can spend the day at the pool with lunch for L.E. 5.

Okamoto, 7 Sharia Ahmed Orabi, Agouza. Phone: 809321. It was a sign of the times when Cairo got its first Japanese restaurant, which came on the heels of the Japanese businessmen invading the city.

La Palme d'Or, Meridien Hotel (second floor). Phone: 84544. Good French cuisine but expensive.

Paprika, 1129 Corniche el Nil (next to the Radio and Television Building). Phone: 972347. Attractive establishment featuring pizza. Lunch from

1:00–4:00 P.M.; dinner from 7:00–12:00 midnight. Moderate.

Paxy, Amoun Hotel, July 26th Sq., open evenings, 6–1. Korean cuisine. Owner began in Iran in home of wealthy family during Shah's days.

Peacock, Holiday Inn Pyramids, good stop en route to the Pyramids.

Pizza Boffo, Mohandiseen. Wide selection of Italian dishes in addition to pizza. Food is tasty and restaurant is very clean; moderate prices.

La Pergola, Meridien Hotel. Summer swimming pool area; simple dishes, snacks and grills. Open from May to Oct. from 9:00 A.M. till sunset.

Pizzeria, Nile Hilton Hotel. Italian specialties, attractive decor. Lunch 12:30–3:30 P.M.; dinner 7:30–12:00 midnight. Moderate.

Pizzeria-Capri, Sharia 26 July, near Munchen Lowenbrau. Wide variety of pizza, including some the Italians might never have heard of; delivers in Cairo. Open till 1:00 A.M. Moderate.

Pub 28, 28 Sharia Shagaret el Dor, near Sharia 26 July, Zamalek. Small, intimate pub atmosphere. Lunch, noon to 3:30 P.M.; dinner 7:00 P.M. to midnight. Good meat; moderate prices.

Rex, 33 Sharia Abdel Kalek Sarwat (at Talaat Harb). Phone: 41763. Their onion soup is the best in town. Reasonable prices.

Scarabee, floating restaurant operated by Meridien Hotel. The bar is open from 11 A.M. to 2 A.M.; departs daily at 1:30 P.M. for lunch and 9:30 P.M. for dinner for two-hour Nile cruise. A la carte entries average L.E. 15.

Seahorse, by the Nile on the road to Maadi. Rustic thatched roof riverside restaurant under same management as Andrea's. Excellent grilled fish. Lunch for two with *mezzah,* grilled fish and beer will run about L.E. 8 plus tip. It's a wonderful spot to enjoy a relaxing afternoon watching feluccas sail by on the Nile against the outline of the Pyramids of Giza.

Sofar, 21 Sharia Adly. Phone: 54360. Old established restaurant, specializing in Syrian and Lebanese cuisine. Moderate.

Steak Corner, 8 Midan Amman, Dokki (near Shooting Club). Moderately priced meat specialties. Open noon to 1:00 A.M.

Swiss Air Restaurant, Sharia el Nil, Giza. Phone: 981488. First floor of Cairo's most luxurious building, one block from former President Sadat's house and about two from the Sheraton Hotel. This is one of Cairo's smartest restaurants, with a wide range of European selections. Expensive. Its less expensive counterpart is on the ground floor for cost-conscious travelers.

Swiss Chalet Bar-B-Q, Ahmed Nessim St. (between Giza and Nile Sts. and not to be confused with Swiss Air Restaurant above). Charcoal-broiled chicken, filet, shrimp and liver. Take-out service for anything on menu. Air-conditioned. This is the first of a chain being developed in Egypt and the Middle East by Canarab, a Canadian/Arabian company. The restaurant is attractively decorated in modern Alpine decor and is very clean. It has become popular as a stop for tour groups, which it can accommodate in a large room at the rear. Prices moderate.

Tokyo Japanese Restaurant, El Sayed el Bakri and El Maa'had el Swissry Sts., Zamalek. Excellent food and very popular with Japanese residents of Cairo. Moderate.

Taverna, 3 Elfi Bey Street. Bar and restaurant. Greek food and seafood.

Taverne Du Champ de Mars, Nile Hilton Hotel (ground floor). The restaurant's authentic Belle Epoque interior was brought piece by piece from Brussels and reassembled in Cairo. It is decorated with beautiful stained glass windows and Tiffany lamps. The waitresses and waiters are also dressed in the style of the period. An interesting feature is a series of paintings done in Egypt during the last century. These apparently hung in the original Brussels tavern, although nothing is known about the artist. Drinks and snacks are served from 12:00 noon to 2:00 A.M.

Terrace Cafe, Ramses Hilton coffee shop. Lovely setting on hotel's second floor with views of the Nile and the hotel's dramatic, central lobby.

Tropicana, Nile Hilton Hotel. Swimming pool area; snacks and grills are served. Open from 9:00 A.M. to sunset.

Union, 28 Sharia 26 July. Phone: 56464. An old pub-like restaurant in the heart of downtown. The food is good, mostly European and moderate. The restaurant is usually crowded, so service may be slow. Moderate.

Vue des Pyramides, Pyramids Rd. near junction of desert road to Alexandria. Phone: 896582. Specializes in grilled fish; casual outdoor atmosphere. Good food, good service. Moderately expensive.

Wimpy and **Kentucky Fried Chicken,** Dokki, Zamalek, Maadi, Heliopolis, Giza and two in town. Offer the usual fast food service of hamburgers, cheeseburgers, fried chicken, milkshakes, sundaes, etc. Popular with residents, crowded in the evenings; carry-out service. Open late.

Tea Houses/Pastry Shops/Snack Bars

Many hotels and sporting clubs have tearooms or outside gardens where you may enjoy afternoon tea or coffee. Some of the most pleasant are the Mena House veranda, the rest house at the Pyramids, and the café at the foot of the Sphinx. Each of these has a view of the Pyramids and is particularly pleasant at sunset. Also, the Lido of the Gezira Sporting Club is usually lively at teatime.

L'Americaine, corner of Sharia Talaat Harb and Sharia 26 July. Stand-up counter serves juices, ice cream, cakes and sodas. Open until midnight.

Arcade, behind the Continental Hotel. Several shops selling the famous sweetmeats of the Levant are located in the shopping arcade.

Brazilian Coffee Shop, 38 Sharia Talaat Harb and 12 Sharia 26 July. Variety of coffee—expresso, au lait, capuccino from Brazilian coffee beans. Also sells roasted beans. Open from 7:00 A.M. to 12:00 midnight.

Excelsior, 35 Sharia Talaat Harb, beside Cinema Metro. Tea room offering snacks and beverages.

Fishawi's, perhaps the most famous tea and coffee house in Cairo, is located in the Mouski. Its atmosphere transports one centuries into the past. Fishawi's has had a tradition of being especially popular during the month of Ramadan, around midnight, when it is full and lively. There is now a new one, across from the old one, and both are located near the El Hussein Hotel within the shadow of the minaret of the El Hussein Mosque.

Groppi's, Kasr el Nil at Midan Talaat Harb. Phone: 46194. (Another with a garden at Sharia Abdel Khaled Sarwat and a third in Heliopolis.) Groppi's is a landmark in Cairo and its location and ambience have always made it a great rendezvous spot. Recently refurbished, good food and service. Even more famous for its patisserie than its restaurant, the former serves sandwiches, pastries and ice cream and the candy shop sells the best chocolates in town. The restaurant is open for lunch and dinner. Prices are moderate.

Indian Tea House, 23 Sharia Talaat Harb. Serves imported Indian tea and pastries and other Indian specialties.

Lappas, 17 Sharia Kasr el Nil. Like Groppi's, though smaller; popular rendezvous for midtown. Has a bar which serves food. Moderate prices.

New Kursal, 12 Elfi Bey Street (buffet-restaurant). Snack bar.

Shepheards, the romance of tea at Shepheards might be planted permanently in the minds of Westerners, especially Americans, who have read turn-of-the-century travel books and whodunits set in Cairo. We hate to disappoint them, but it is not the same. There is no Edwardian parlor or palm court orchestra or even a veranda overlooking the Nile.

Tower of Cairo, Gezira Island. Located on top of Cairo's modern version of the obelisk, the restaurant is meant to revolve slowly, enabling guests to view the fabulous panorama of the city while they eat. A full revolution takes half an hour (if it's working). A British paper once described its revolution as being like Nasser's: it turned once and stopped working. Not all Egyptians saw the humor. The restaurant revolves again! The elevator ride to the top of the tower costs 40 pts. Best time to go is for afternoon tea.

BARS. There are dozens of bars around town, mainly in hotels. Cocktail time in Egypt is approximately from 7:00–9:00 P.M. Among the nicest where women can go unescorted and feel comfortable are:

Baccara (Meridien), small, pleasant. Background piano music.

Mena House, where you can enjoy a view of the Pyramids with your cocktails.

Ramses Hilton, the new lobby bar with its towering columns resembling the Temple of Karnak, and the rooftop lounge has lovely panorama of Cairo. Ask the bartender, George, for a "Georgie"—it's a delicious cocktail.

Safari Bar (Hilton), lively, a favorite meeting place for Americans, Europeans and prosperous Egyptians.

Sheraton, small, lively and popular meeting place for Egyptians as well as foreign visitors.

There are many other bars. Leading sporting clubs also have them—often outdoors by a pool or on a terrace overlooking the Nile and Cairo.

ENTERTAINMENT. Cairo has a wide range of entertainment and cultural activities. It is one of the centers of the movie industry in the Arab world, and its air-conditioned cinemas show the best American and European films as well as Arabic ones. Nightclubs are numerous and the entertainment varied. The highlight of the evening's performance is one of the famous belly dancers, of whom Egypt has the best. There are three gambling casinos and horseracing in Zamalek and Heliopolis during the winter season.

Egyptians are fond of walking or lingering outdoors, which they do frequently in the many parks and public gardens throughout Cairo.

One of the most pleasant ways to pass an evening is a moonlit sail in a felucca on the Nile or at a desert party near the Pyramids. Either of these may be arranged through your hotel or a travel agent.

Top priority during your visit should be the Son et Lumière show at the Pyramids. This Sound and Light show was one of the first ever created by the French firm that developed the concept, and it is still one of the best. The show is presented in English, Arabic, French and German. (See Chapter V, the Pyramids, for schedule and cost.)

Cairo by Night is a brochure distributed by hotels and travel agents. It isn't very good, but it, along with *Cairo Today,* a monthly, and the daily newspapers are the best quick references available.

GAMBLING. In Cairo there are casinos at the Hilton, Shepheards and Sheraton Hotels, and at the Cecil Hotel in Alexandria. Egyptian citizens are not allowed in the gambling rooms and a foreign visitor must show a passport to enter. Roulette, twenty-one, chemin de fer and baccarat are played. Only foreign currency can be used.

THE NATIONAL CIRCUS. Initiated by the Egyptian Ministry of Culture in 1960 and trained by Soviet experts, the circus was inaugurated in 1966. Since then, the Big Top in Agouza, a Nile-side district of Cairo across the bridge from Zamalek, has been popular with old and young, residents and tourists. It has a seating capacity of 2,500, and its team of 200 performs nightly a classical repertoire of circus entertainment plus showstoppers by Arabian thoroughbred horses that prance and display their acrobatic skills to the beat of Arabic music.

On days of folkloric festivals or national holidays, the circus mounts shows in the different provinces of Egypt, and in July and August it takes up headquarters in Alexandria.

NIGHTCLUBS AND DISCOTHEQUES. Cairo has a variety of nightclubs from which to choose. Many have romantic settings in outdoor gardens or terraces where you dance under swaying palms against a moonlight sky. Some of the best nightspots are the nightclubs and discotheques of hotels. Large cabarets, mostly for men, are located on the road to the Pyramids.

Nightclub shows do not start before 11:00 P.M. Some clubs have both local and European floorshows; others have none. Orchestras play all the latest international hits and Latin American or European music for dancing.

One could say that Cairo is the new R and R center of the Middle East—especially for men working in the surrounding countries where the deserts are dry in more ways than climatically. As a result, Cairo has a large number of cabarets, and they are to be distinguished from the nightclubs and discotheques.

Also, in Cairo, the term discotheque has a slightly different meaning from that in most other countries. It is actually a small nightclub with stereo music rather than a live band, but there frequently is a show, usually a performance by an Oriental dancer, which will last 30 to 45 minutes. Prices are less than at nightclubs or cabarets. At some of the discos you can watch the show if you plan to stay at the bar only. At all the better nightclubs in the city you are required to reserve a table for dinner and dancing. This feature seems to separate the men from the boys, so to speak. In cabarets, men can go for the show without having dinner and are joined by the ladies of the house, for whom they must buy champagne. Perhaps the major distinction between a discotheque and a cabaret is that in a disco no one will try to pick up a women when her escort goes to the men's room.

Contrary to what you might imagine, the age group at discotheques runs the gamut. It appears to be related directly to the decibel level of the music—the higher the count, the lower the age.

If you have the opportunity, be sure to see a performance by a leading Oriental dancer, or belly dancer, as they are known. When performed by a first-rate artist, the dance is one of tremendous beauty and artistic skill, and is not the bumps-and-grinds version too often passed off by third-rate dancers as the real thing.

Visitors might be interested to know that the standards for dancers are changing. In the last few years the impact of rock and other modern beats can be seen in the movements and heard in the music of the dancer, particularly in the tempo. The classic form is slower with movements more elongated. There is an interplay and subtle flirtation between the dancer and the music. It is graceful and sophisticated. The form that is popular now is noisier and more detached. There is a frenzy to the movement that is not part of the old classical form.

The following are Cairo's major night spots. All are most crowded on

Thursday and Saturday nights, therefore reservations are generally necessary—particularly in those nightspots where dinner is required.

Abu Nawas, Mena House Hotel. The hotel's indoor winter nightclub.

Aladin, Sheraton Hotel (second floor). Summer nightclub (next to swimming pool); Oriental dancer, European chanteuse, good food, dancing; reservations essential.

Arizona, Pyramids Road (Sharia el Haram), Giza. Cabaret, recommended for men.

Auberge des Pyramids, 325 Pyramids Road. Big and brassy. The long European cabaret show usually includes a good Egyptian dancer. After the show, the action moves into a smaller part of the establishment and it becomes a late night cabaret. Dinner from 9:30 P.M.; show at 11:00 P.M. Expensive by Cairo standards.

La Belle Epoque, Meridien Hotel. The rooftop dining room becomes a supper club in the evening with a combo for dancing; entertainment is short—a European chanteuse and an Egyptian dancer; excellent food and view; reasonably priced by international standards; reservations essential. In summer the nightclub moves outside as the *Bab el Sama*. It has a great panoramic view; Oriental dancer; international attractions (mainly French); buffet dinner. The hotel plans to change the decor and ambience this year, so don't be surprised if it has a new name and a new look.

Belvedere, Nile Hilton Hotel. Winter (October through May) supper club on the roof of the hotel; dancing; panoramic view; decor represents Egypt in the nineteenth century; Oriental dancer and show. French and Oriental cuisine, buffet nights Tuesday and Friday; reservations essential. One may sit at the bar to watch the show without having dinner. Nightclub moves outdoors near swimming pool in summer as the *Tropicana*.

Caravan, Holiday Inn Pyramids, features show that currently includes Egypt's best belly dancer.

Casino Granada, Opera Square. Definitely for men.

Chateau de Versailles, 12 Sharia Mohamed Sakeb, Zamalek. The restaurant becomes a supper club with dance floor and band in the evening. Patronized by local residents.

Geisha (Atlas Hotel), Opera Square. Late afternoon teenagers' discotheque, *Sweet Sixteen*; older crowd takes over after 10:00 P.M.

Goha, on the Nile in Gezira facing the bridge. Popular discotheque with the college set. Stays open late and often gathers a late, late crowd after other nightclub shows close.

Good Shot, Corniche el Nil, next to Maadi Yacht Club. Restaurant on Nile with live music in summer on weekends and juke box music in winter.

Al Hambra, Sheraton Hotel (top floor). Panoramic view of Cairo; Western entertainers and a belly dancer. Reservations recommended.

Jackie's, Nile Hilton. Continues to be the most popular spot of disco chic. It might be called Regine's-by-the-Nile as it's very reminiscent. To all non-Hilton guests, Jackie's is a private membership club for L.E. 30 per year. With liquor prices having doubled, boozing here is not recommended for budget-conscious travelers, but the music and dancing are great, if you like discotheques. It's a chance to see how Cairo's smart set swings.

Merryland, Sharia el Lewa Ahmed Fouad Sadek, Roxy, Heliopolis. Spacious tea garden with restaurant and nightclub with show. Very popular with Heliopolis residents and worth the 20-minute drive from Cairo on Sunday evenings. Family oriented. Men alone not allowed.

New Arizona, 6 Elfi Bey Street. Suggested for men only.

Nile Garden, Maadi Road by the Nile. Pleasant garden restaurant by the Nile; has live music and show in summer.

The Oasis, Mena House Oberoi Hotel. In warm weather you dine and dance at the poolside nightclub on an outdoor patio set in a garden of bougainvillea and geraniums under the moonlit silhouette of swaying palms and the Pyramids of Giza. Show has western and Oriental attractions; reservations recommended. Expensive by Cairo standards. Indoors in winter as *Abu Nawas.*

Omar Khayyam, Saray Gezira, Zamalek, at entrance to Gezira Sporting Club. Oriental setting on a yacht. At one time, this was Cairo's best nightclub, but it's lost favor now with so many new ones available. Show is brief and usually features a belly dancer. The food is good but selections are limited. Moderate.

Palmyra, 16, 26 July Street. Suggested for men only.

Ramses, Pyramids Road, Giza. Cabaret, suggested for men only.

Red Carpet, 51 Sharia Studio Misr, off the Pyramids Road (neon sign posted at turn). Situated in the house that once belonged to a Saudi prince and has been converted into a hotel. Dinner, dancing, Oriental dancer. Nightclub moves to the swimming-pool area in summer.

La Ronde, on Alexandria desert road behind Mena House Oberoi. Popular Egyptian singer and Oriental show. Dance band. Go late. Cairo's answer to the Village Vanguard in New York.

The Saddle, Mena House Oberoi Hotel. One of the most popular discotheques in town; music is by stereo but kept at a low enough volume for conversation. Western, ranch-style decor; so is the menu. Moderate.

Sahara City, Alexandria Desert Road. A nightclub in a fancy tent that boasts having the most belly dancers in town and no one disputes the claim. Show starts at 10:00 P.M., and you are expected to have dinner, too. (It's included in the price.) Expensive.

Salt and Pepper, Sharia Abou el Fedda, at north tip of Zamalek. Has lost some of its earlier popularity. Hard rock and psychedellic lights, live and loud music; show has Oriental dancer.

Sweet Sixteen, Atlas Hotel. Early evening discotheque for teenagers, from 5:00–9:00 P.M. It becomes the *Geisha* in the evening for the older crowd.

Tamerina, 417 Sharia Gamal el Din el Alghany, off the Pyramids Road (sign posted). Pleasant and quiet in comparison to some others; small dance floor, garden. Limited menu but good. Opens at 9:00 P.M., but it will be almost empty until 10:00.

Tropicana, Nile Hilton Hotel. Poolside summer supper club. As the name suggests, decor is tropical with bamboo umbrellas, dancing under stars. Barbecue and Oriental cuisine, open hors d'oeuvres and dessert buffet; good dance orchestra, belly dancer; reservations recommended. Open from 9:30 P.M. but does not get rolling until 10:30.

Venus, off Sharia el Haram (Pyramids Road) at Tereit el Maryutia. New cabaret, western and Oriental attractions. Mostly for men.

MODERN EGYPTIAN ART is an interesting fusion of the country's art history—Pharaonic, Coptic and Islamic. Of all the country's modern cultural activities, art is the most outstanding in quality, quantity and originality. Although many of the outstanding artists have trained or been trained by those who studied in Europe, the works of Egyptian artists reflect the influence, faith and inspiration of their native land. In general, Egyptian artists have been influenced by their native art heritage more than those of other Middle Eastern countries—a characteristic that may be particularly Egyptian.

For those interested in more specific information, *Contemporary Art in Egypt,* Ministry of Culture, 1964, covers the history of the development of Egyptian art with details on outstanding painters and beautiful colored plates of the best art works.

Exhibits of local artists are held throughout the year, and several shops on or near Kasr el Nil Street in Zamalek and at leading hotels, particularly the Meridien Hotel, show local artists. The long entrance passage to the Arabesque Restaurant, 4 Kasr el Nil, serves as an exhibition hall for paintings by Egyptian artists, and art is changed on a regular basis.

Galerie des Beaux Arts, 4 Midan el Falaki, Bab al-Luc, has regular shows of foreign as well as Egyptian artists. It is maintained by the Ministry of Culture and is open 10:00 A.M.–2:00 P.M.; 5:00–9:00 P.M. Unfortunately, there is no commercial gallery specializing in Egyptian art, only gift shops that maintain a stock of paintings. One must visit the artists in their studios or get to know which of the gift shops deal in art. Even those, however, have a limited selection and no proper facilities for display. A list of artists/addresses is available in the *Practical Guide to Cairo.*

Cultural centers such as the **Goethe Institute,** the **French Cultural Center,** and the **Egyptian Center for International Cultural Cooperation** sponsor shows from time to time. For the dates and times of periodic exhibits check the daily newspapers.

Society of the Friends of Art, 3 Sharia Ahmed Pasha, Garden City, sponsors an annual competition for contemporary artists and also holds shows periodically.

Teachers of art and others who want to have greater knowledge of art activity in Egypt might visit the **Art and Life Center, Beit Sennari** and **Wekalet el Ghouri,** all three of which have workshops attached to them. (See *Cairo Sightseeing* for addresses and description.)

One of the best places to visit is **Musaferkhana** (near El Hussein Mosque in the Al Azhar area) and **Harraniya** village on the Sakkara Road. The former is an historic building where several artists have studios. The caretaker will show visitors each studio and you may purchase paintings from him. Or you can phone in advance for an appointment with the artists.

The village of Harraniya is quite a different story. Thirty years ago an architect, Ramses Wissa Wassif, and his art teacher wife put a theory into practice that has turned out to be one of the country's best artistic expressions.

Wassif believed that children, especially Egyptian village children, when unencumbered by the restraints, restrictions or inhibitions of adults, could find their own innate artistic ability if given the atmosphere, encouragement and freedom for self-expression. He tried first with one orphan child and then another and another and, to his delight, found that the results exceeded his expectations. He and his wife taught the children to weave (a village craft from ancient times in Egypt) and put them to work on hand-driven looms, allowing their imaginations to run free and giving them only a minimum amount of direction and advice.

Over the years the tapestries they created found an audience and attracted the attention of collectors and critics. With the profits from their sales, which Wassif shared with the weavers, the group expanded from a handful of people to a small village, where today the families grow their own vegetables from which they make natural dyes. They live in a village Wassif designed, based on the old village architecture.

Today, many of the artists are veteran weavers who have been with the settlement from the beginning, and a new generation of children are working at their side. To understand how the value of their work has grown, a tapestry a meter square that might have sold for $50 two decades ago is now $500. A small tapestry by a young student apprentice might be under $50, and the price climbs to $4,000 for large wall hangings of several meters, depending on the artist, intricacy of the design, and the dyes. For the most part, the motifs are taken from daily life and picture the birds, animals, plants and trees of the Egyptian countryside, in beautiful colors and shadings and often with great whimsy, which is so much a part of the native Egyptian character. Ramses Wissa Wassif died in 1975, but the work of the village is being continued by his wife, who lives there.

We regret to report that fame seems to have distorted the perspective in this village somewhat. On a recent visit, Mrs. Wassif demanded that we remove our information regarding prices, claiming that it was misleading and made the endeavor appear "too commercial" for a school and that each piece is priced according to its artistic value and quality. However, since the tapestries are expensive and there are now so many tapestries being sold elsewhere for lower prices, we believe it is important for readers to know what to expect and to understand the differences. In our judgment, this knowledge in no way detracts from the beauty or quality of the Harraniya tapestries and, in fact, helps newcomers to evaluate better their worth. A recent innovation at the school is the making of batik with beautiful free-flow designs and colors. They are available in small squares for pillow covers or larger pieces for wall hangings and other uses, and range in price from $15 up.

Visitors should be aware that others claim to be selling the Harraniya tapestries to the extent that some have set up shop near the Wassif village and labeled their tapestries "Harraniya," but the only other place in town where the tapestries and batiks can be purchased is at **Senouhi,** 54 Abdul Khalek Sarwat Street.

A visit to Harraniya can easily be combined with a trip to Sakkara or to the Pyramids.

There is no question that the tapestries made by Harraniya are the best from an artistic point of view. However, we do not want to give the impression that they are the only ones. Weaving is an art of many villages in Egypt and several have weavers whose skill and imagination are on par with the many of those at Harraniya. Assiut and Beni Suef are two of the best-known areas. Tapestries from Assiut are available from *Mousky Chic,* a shop in the Nile Hilton Arcade. Owner Louis Fanous does not have these on display but will bring them out of storage for serious buyers. Those we saw on our most recent visit were wonderful. In the Khan al-Khalil, there is a shop that specializes in tapestries from Beni Suef. In both cases the prices are half those of Harraniya.

Another place that is very much frequented by tour groups is the village of **Kerdassa,** near the Pyramid, on a back road two miles beyond Andrea's restaurant. Most of what is made here is junk. Good traditional designs have been badly distorted and cheapened, but there are some good craftsmen among the weavers, if one is willing to persevere and is not after museum quality. On a recent visit, we were pleased to see a marked improvement in the weaving. Tapestries are good buys at L.E. 15–30 per square meter, provided one understands the nature of the works and does not take them to be great works of art. The best buy of all is handwoven stoles for only L.E. 2. They are wonderful gifts to take home.

At the shops of *Abdel Hamid el Issa* and *Golden Bazaar,* one can watch and photograph workers at their looms. Weaving has been a tradition for these families for generations.

The Sakkara/Harraniya road is becoming something of a center for Egyptian artists. Mohie el-Din Hussein, one of the country's leading ceramic artists, lives near Harraniya village in a house designed by Wissa. Here, he creates modern pieces inspired by Egyptian designs from Islamic, Coptic and pharaonic history, carrying forward an ancient tradition of the country. The artist uses clay from Aswan and mixes his own glazes, which often results in a luminescent, metallic finish. Pieces are on display and for purchase at his home; prices are moderate.

Farther along the road, a house on the west, marked by two large ceramic scarabs, belongs to Zakaria el Konani and his wife, Aida Abd al-Kerim, artists who work in glass and ceramics. El Konani, a chemical engineer by training, has created a brillantly toned turquoise paste, known as *faience,* which has a glazed finish when fired and therefore does not need glazing. At higher temperature it turns to glass—a substance believed to have been first discovered by the ancient Egyptians. From these materials, his wife, a professor of art at Helwan University, makes wonderful pieces of jewelry and objets d'art. El Konani concentrates on creating glass plates and sculpture with lovely modern designs inspired from his Egyptian heritage. Each piece is a true work of art; one of them is on display at the Corning Glass Museum in the U.S. The couple receive visitors in their country house on Sundays, from 12 noon to 5 P.M., and their works are on display and for sale at moderate prices. Phone: 982926. Cairo address: 21 A Amin Elradie St., Dokki, Apt. 104.

MUSIC. In the winter season there are symphony concerts and ballets by visiting European and other artists at the newly enlarged **Sayed Darwish Concert Hall.** Other concerts by visiting and local musicians are also held at various cultural centers throughout the city. The United States Information Service sponsors American artists and performers from time to time, as do other foreign cultural missions.

The **National Ballet** (Bolshoi-trained) is of recent origin. It and several folklore and television dance groups give frequent performances. The best-known dance troupe, the Reda Group, is seen often on television and cinema and frequently performs at the Baloon Theatre in Agouza.

The **Cairo Symphony Orchestra** gives concerts weekly during the season. The **National Conservatory of Music,** the **National Ballet** and the **Cinegraphic Institute** are located in a complex of buildings just off the Pyramids Road.

The most famous singer of this century in the Arab world was an Egyptian woman by the name of Um Kalthum. Although she is no longer living, during the day or evening you might hear her voice on the radio in a shop, a local coffee house or an apartment building. The Egyptians love her and are ecstatic listening to her singing. When Um Kalthum gave public performances, she could draw crowds numbering in the tens of thousands. When she died, the entire nation went into mourning.

In recent years, the best-known classical musician in the Arab world has been Muhammad Abd-al-Wahab, also an Egyptian. In addition to his singing and composing of classical Arabic music, Abd-al-Wahab has written a number of interesting pieces adapting western forms to the five-tone minor scale of eastern music.

It is important for a newcomer to Egypt to understand that cultural activity of a western nature extends as far as western influence has penetrated Egyptian society. In other words, those attending and participating in such activities are mainly western-educated Egyptians from the middle and upper classes—these being the strata of Egyptian society on which western culture has had an impact. The bulk of Egyptians spend their leisure time enjoying the fruits of their own cultural heritage. Unfortunately for the visitor, these usually require a knowledge of Arabic for understanding and appreciation.

LITERATURE. The greatest vehicle for artistic expression throughout the Arab world has been the Arabic language, which is richest and most highly developed in poetry. Even classical Arabic music is poetry set to music—the music being incidental to the verse.

Egypt has produced many of the leading philosophers and political and social thinkers of the Arab world in this century. The most famous is Taha Hussein, who, blind from the age of six, writes with a sensitivity and depth equal to the best in world literature. Several of his works have been translated into English. The best known are *From an Egyptian Childhood* and *Stream of Days*. English translations of these and other popular literature are available in Cairo bookstores.

THEATERS. Cairo has been the center of theater and film in the Arab world, staging high-quality productions regularly throughout the year. These productions have included original Arabic plays, as well as translations of American and European ones. Unfortunately, the last year or so has seen an exodus of talent to higher-paying jobs in the Gulf and Tunisia, where much of the film industry has shifted. People in the industry cite bureaucracy, wages and artistic freedom as points of concern. Another factor contributing to Cairo's decline as a leader in the arts has been Egypt's isolation from the other Arab countries following the Camp David accords.

The following is a list of leading Cairo theaters, but do not be surprised to find many of them closed. Presentations are usually in Arabic. Performances are advertised in the local daily newspapers. Shows usually start at 9:30 P.M. unless otherwise indicated.

American University at Cairo, Eward Hall, Sharia el Sheikh Rihan and New Theatre, Sharia Mohamed Mahmoud, New Campus. Occasional performances by local and visiting foreign artists.

Cairo Puppet Theater, Ezbekia Garden. Performances nightly from October through May at 6:30 P.M. and Fri. and Sun. at 11:00 A.M.

The building for the Cairo Puppet Theatre was completed in 1964. Performances are in Arabic, but they can be followed by non-Arabic-speaking audiences and enjoyed by adults as well as children. Occasionally, visiting puppet troupes perform.

Cairo University Theater, Cairo University, Giza. Occasional performances by local and foreign artists.

Um Kulthum Theater (formerly Balloon Theater); Sharia el Nil, Agouza. Performances in Arabic by local folklore groups nightly from October to March.

Sayed Darwish Concert Hall, Sharia Gamal el Din el Afghany, off the Pyramids Road, same street as that of Tamerina Night Club. Recently enlarged to replace the famous Cairo Opera House destroyed by fire a few years ago. Alternate weekly performances are given on Thursdays by the Arabic Music Troupe and on Saturdays by the Cairo Symphony Orchestra, with occasional performances by visiting foreign troupes, as well as local ballet, music or dance troupes.

Sphinx Theater, at the foot of the Sphinx. On special occasions, plays, ballets and musical concerts and shows are performed during summer in this open-air theater under the sponsorship of the Ministry of Culture.

Wekalet el Ghouri, 3 Sharia el Sheikh Mohamed Abdu (Al Azhar area). A restored caravanserai, which has been made into a handicrafts and folkloric arts center, is sometimes used for visiting foreign troupes. The courtyard serves as an arena or concert hall.

Zaki Tolaimat Theater (formerly known as Pocket Theater); Midan el Ataba and Sharia 26 July. Avant garde productions in Arabic and translations of western writers are performed during the season from October to May. The theater is named for a famous Egyptian actor who was also a director and producer.

SPORTS. Egypt's climate makes it ideal for playing tennis, badminton, golf and squash, or for sailing, fishing, riding horseback and water-skiing the year round. Most sporting activity centers at clubs in the city. Deluxe hotels have swimming pools, some have tennis courts and, ordinarily, there is a club attached to the hotel that allows Cairo residents to use the hotel's facilities.

CAMPING. The Mediterranean coast offers camping on white sand beaches near Alexandria, Alamein and Mersa Matruh. Camping trips to the Red Sea are great fun if you have the necessary equipment and do not mind roughing it. Campers must take all provisions, including drinking water. The area is excellent for fishing and skin-diving. The sea is crystal clear and the beaches are good.

The best camping of all is in the desert near the Pyramids or at Sakkara. Local travel agents will make all arrangements; costs will depend on how simple or elaborate the provisions.

FISHING. On the Mediterranean (April–Nov.) and the Red Sea (Nov.–April). The Red Sea is one of the most famous bodies of water in the world for its variety of fish. The Sheraton Hotel at Hurghada has become the nucleus of the Red Sea area's development and a center for fishing, scuba diving and snorkeling.

GOLF. Two 9-hole golf courses—at the Gezira Sporting Club and at the Mena House Oberoi Hotel (with the Pyramids as a backdrop)—are open all year. The Mena House Oberoi's annual membership is L.E. 290 per couple with golf, L.E. 240 without, plus L.E. 45 tax. Green fees are L.E. 3 for members, 5 for guests.

Equipment and instruction are available at the Gezira Sporting Club.

Fees are part of the club's dues for membership and use of facilities, which are detailed in the next section under *Sporting Clubs*.

In Alexandria, there is an 18-hole course at the Alexandria Sporting Club.

HORSEBACK RIDING. Good horses—with or without guides—can be hired from the stables near the Pyramids. Fee: approximately L.E. 3 per hour. A moonlit ride across the desert is great sport in Egypt, but it is not suggested for a novice. Desert riding is difficult and the terrain deceiving. Arabian horses are spirited, and in the desert nothing holds them back but the rider. The most comfortable gait for an Arabian horse is a canter or gallop. Only English saddles are used. Jodhpurs and English riding boots can be made locally at very reasonable prices.

Overnight or longer camping trips in the desert may be arranged through local travel agents. Cost depends on the degree of luxury desired, but it is generally moderate.

The five-hour ride from Giza across the desert to Sakkara and back is a popular excursion of Cairo residents and experienced riders. It would be very tiring for a beginner and is not recommended for an inexperienced rider. Reservations can be made directly with the stables.

The Ferrosia Riding Club is located at the south edge of the Gezira Sporting Club. Phone: 800692. The club boards private horses and also has several horses for instruction. Visitors may obtain a three-month membership. There is another riding club in Heliopolis; stables are next to El Shams Club and the Hyatt El Salam Hotel.

HORSE RACING. Saturday and Sunday from mid-October to mid-May. Horse racing is available on alternating weekends at the tracks at the Gezira Sporting Club in Zamalek and the Nadi Etehad el Gomhuriyat (and formerly El Shams Club) in Heliopolis. The racing form appears in the Saturday edition of the *Egyptian Mail* newspaper. Races begin about 1:30 P.M. Pari-mutuel betting.

Many people enjoy going to the races for the pleasure of watching the beautiful Arabian horses. In Egypt, famous for its breeding of pure Arabian stock, racing is a sport. Purses are small.

The Egyptian Agricultural Society owns a famous stud, Al Zahraa, and breeds pure Arabian horses at Ein Shams. Visitors are welcome. For an appointment, contact Dr. Khalil Soliman.

HUNTING AND SHOOTING. Hunting is excellent, in Egypt, but there are few wild or nonprivate hunting areas. The Shooting Club at Dokki offers the best introduction, as it owns and maintains duck, snipe and pigeon camps in Cairo and Delta areas, shooting ranges and a clubhouse. There are no set bag limits; licenses for guns and hunting are required. Most hunters use 12-gauge guns. Birds are plentiful and there are some gazelles. There is little game for rifle. Fayoum is a popular hunting area.

Duck season begins toward the end of November and lasts through January. It is supervised by the Shooting Club of Egypt. The quail and wild dove season comes twice a year: April and May in the Delta and Lower Egypt, late August and September along the Mediterranean coast.

Information is available from the Egyptian Shooting Federation, 37 Abdel Khalik Sarwat Street, Cairo.

BOATING. Rowing: The Egyptian Rowing Club is located on a boat moored near the Sheraton Hotel. Rowing is a popular sport in Egypt, and a visit by a U.S. team such as Harvard University is an annual event.

Sailing: You may enjoy sailing in Cairo on the Nile the year round, and in Alexandria on the Mediterranean in all months except January and February, when the sea is rough. Alexandria, Cairo and Maadi yacht clubs have their own boats. In Cairo, the 14 ft. Lightning class is excellent for Nile sailing.

At the Cairo Yacht Club, members and guests may rent sailboats by the hour.

At Alexandria, the favored classes are the Dinghy and the Fairey (an English class boat of approximately 25 ft. with built-in center board). Club membership is open to foreign residents and visitors are welcome. Members and guests must pass a sailing test to man a boat.

Sailing on the Nile in a felucca, the graceful sailboat often pictured in scenes of Egypt, is a delightful experience that no visitor should miss. These boats with crew may be rented at the dock near the Meridien and Shepheard Hotels. Be sure to bargain for the price. Cost for a small boat should be about L.E. 5 per hour. The best time to go is about an hour before sunset. An evening cruise in summer is also fun.

THE BEACH. Scuba, skin-diving and snorkeling: The Red Sea is famous for the variety and colors of its fish. Underwater photography here is among the best in the world. (See final chapter under *Hurghada* for details.)

Swimming: In Cairo from April to November one can swim in a pool at one of the sporting clubs or deluxe hotels. In summer, the beaches along the Mediterranean at Alexandria or Mersa Matruh are popular swimming resorts for Egyptians as well as visitors, and they are crowded.

The strong sun and highly chlorinated water in pools are extremely wearing on bathing suits and rubber caps. Be sure to bring several changes if you plan an extended visit.

Swimming is one of Egypt's favorite sports, in which her native sons consistently win international competitions.

WARNING: Do NOT swim in the Nile. Its waters are heavily polluted.

Water Skiing: It is possible to water ski in Cairo, but since the Nile isn't the cleanest body of water in the world, the sport is more popular in Alexandria and other seaside resorts on the Mediterranean.

TENNIS. Only clay courts are used in Egypt, and there are many in Cairo. The Gezira Sporting Club has 20 courts, and instruction is available at reasonable prices. (Don't forget to tip the ball boys.) Regulation white is generally required for both men and women on most courts.

Tennis is one of Egypt's most popular competitive sports. Tournaments by local participants, as well as visiting international groups, are held often throughout the year. The Annual Tennis Open is held in March.

SPORTING CLUBS. Cairo has excellent sporting clubs, similar to our country clubs, that offer facilities for outdoor and indoor sport, all within a few minutes' drive from the city center. Tourists and other transient visitors may obtain temporary membership. All clubs have increased or are planning to increase prices for foreigners using facilities on a temporary basis. If you want to use the facilities of a particular club ask your hotel to inquire.

Cairo Yacht Club, 3 Sharia el Nil Street, Giza. Phone: 984415. The club has facilities for sailing, water skiing and rowing, and holds weekly regattas in which guests who qualify are welcome to participate.

Gezira Sporting Club, Zamalek. Phone: 806000. Established in 1882 and covering 67 acres, this club derives its name from the island in the Nile on which it is situated. Once the epitome of British colonial snobbery when Egyptians were not even allowed to enter, the club is now open to all. It has two swimming pools, a 9-hole golf course, 20 tennis courts, croquet lawns, volleyball, basketball and polo grounds, squash courts, boxing and judo rings, a riding school and horse racing on weekends throughout the winter season. Indoors, there are bridge, billiards and table tennis rooms in addition to lounges, salons, restaurants and bar. There is a children's playground, a gymnasium, sauna and barber shop. Tourist membership for one week is L.E. 22.50 per couple, L.E. 15 single. Annual membership fees per year are L.E. 210 per couple, L.E. 180 single. The business office is open daily from 9:00 A.M. to 2:00 P.M., except Friday and Sunday afternoons.

Heliolido Sporting Club, Sharia Galal, Heliopolis. The club includes eight tennis courts, two swimming pools, squash, volleyball and basketball courts, a football field and a gymnasium.

Heliopolis Sporting Club, Sharia Mirghany, Heliopolis. Phone: 601814. Business office hours 10:00 A.M. to 2:00 P.M.; closed Tuesdays. One of the largest and oldest clubs, situated in the lovely suburb of Heliopolis. Its facilities include 18 tennis courts, 8 squash courts, 3 swimming pools, billiards, croquet and soccer grounds, basketball and volleyball, judo and gymnastics. Temporary membership is L.E. 68 per couple for one month; L.E. 45 single.

Maadi Sporting Club/Yacht Club, 8 Sharia Damashk, Midan El Nadi, Maadi. Phone: 35091. Located a few miles south of Cairo in the residential suburb of Maadi, the club has a wide range of facilities for indoor and outdoor sports, including its own sailboats moored on the Nile less than a mile away at the Maadi Yacht Club. Facilities include swimming pool, sauna, barbershop, beauty salon, and dining and bar facilities. There are tennis and squash courts and horses for riding. Films are shown five nights a week. Temporary membership, open to nonresidents only, is available for one month at L.E. 18 single and L.E. 28 for a couple, for three months at L.E. 25 single and L.E. 54 per couple. One year is L.E. 250 single and L.E. 300 per couple.

Nadi Etehad El Gomhuriyat (El Shams), Heliopolis (next to the Hyatt El Salam Hotel and available for use by hotel guests). Phone: 871278. Facilities for tennis, swimming, basketball, volleyball, handball and squash are available. There is a racetrack and restaurant. Membership L.E. 300 for six months; 500 per year per person.

National Sporting Club, Gezira Island, adjacent to the Gezira Club and Botanical Gardens. Phone: 806626. The club includes tennis courts, swimming pool, gymnasium and playing fields for other sports. Membership fee per year is L.E. 75 per couple; no temporary membership.

Shooting Club, Dokki. Specializes in trap shooting, but has tennis courts, swimming pool, children's playground and restaurant. Temporary membership (three months) available at L.E. 400 per couple. The club also has facilities on the Red Sea at Mersa Allam. Business office in Dokki, phone: 704333.

Tewfikia Tennis Club, Medinet El Awkaf, Agouza. Phone: 801930. The club has eight tennis courts, two swimming pools, squash and basketball courts, table tennis, children's playground, restaurant and a summer open-air cinema. The annual open tennis championship of Cairo is held here in January.

SOCIAL CLUBS. In addition to sporting clubs, several social clubs might be of interest to visitors.

Automobile Club, 10 Sharia Kasr el Nil. The club has no sporting facilities in Cairo but its dining room serves some of the best food in town. Members of this club automatically become members of the Automobile Club of Alexandria, which has a seaside location in a convenient area of the city. The club can secure international driving licenses only for holders of Egyptian driving licenses. Membership fees are L.E. 500 for initial admission and L.E. 20 for annual dues.

Egyptian Cultural Club, 1 Sharia Osiris, Tagar Building, Garden City. Phone: 27530; 26030. A social and cultural club with a restaurant offering good food at reasonable prices. Prospective members must be recommended by two members.

Rotary International, 3 Ali Labib Gabr, (Kasr el Nil and Talaat Harb). Phone: 741737. Cairo Rotary meets for lunch at 1:45 P.M. on Tuesday at the Nile Hilton Hotel; the Giza Club at 2:00 P.M. on Wednesdays at the Sheraton Hotel; Heliopolis at 2:00 P.M. on Mondays at the Heliopolis Sporting Club.

OPENING AND CLOSING HOURS. *Modern Districts:* 9:00 or 10:00 A.M.–1:00 P.M.; 4:00 or 4:30 to 7:30 or 8:00 P.M. summer hours; 9:00 or 10:00 A.M. to 5:00 or 6:00 P.M. winter hours. Most shops close Saturday evening and Sundays, some close Thursday afternoon and Friday.

The Mouski (Khan Khalil): 9:00 A.M.–1:00 P.M.; 3:00 to 8:00 P.M. Some shops do not close for lunch, but the owner will probably not be around from 1:00–3:00, and his helper won't be much help. Some shops close on Friday, some Saturday, others Sunday. During Ramadan, stores often close all afternoon and do not reopen or reopen only after sundown.

SHOPPING. Cairo's modern shopping districts have a wide selection of clothing, shoes, accessories and furniture made in Egypt, but for tourists the biggest attraction remains the old bazaar known as the Mouski—one of the best in the world. Here is where you will want to spend your time leisurely—watching the craftsmen, sipping coffee with the shopkeepers and examining the array of handicrafts, so enticing it will be difficult to resist a wild buying spree.

Shopping Districts

City Center: The main shopping streets are Kasr al Nil, 26 July, Talaat Harb, Sherif, Adly, Abdel Khalek Sarwat, Midan Mustapha Kamel and the area encompassed by these streets. Cairo's modern district, unlike many Eastern cities, does not have well defined areas for specific goods. Rather, it is like a European city where several types of shop are found on any one street.

Residential Districts: Garden City, Zamalek, Dokki, Giza, Maadi, Mohandiseen and Heliopolis have neighborhood shopping areas. Those planning an extended stay or residence in Egypt should patronize neighborhood shops for everyday needs. Also, you might consult the *Practical Guide to Cairo,* American University in Cairo Press, which lists services and shops by commodities and is particularly useful for someone setting up housekeeping or opening an office.

Mouski: The old bazaars are situated in or near the street called the Mouski, the oldest commercial street in Cairo. Its narrow, picturesque lanes are lined with tiny shops sheltered from the sun by wooden awnings, and teem with milling crowds and mingled scents. You may watch a craftsman work in the same manner as his predecessors did five centuries earlier and wander through the bazaars full of copperware, ivory works, gold and silver jewelry, perfume, gems, spices and silk. The owner of each tiny shop will invite you to enter and will offer you coffee or tea while you browse.

The Mouski is made up of several souqs or bazaars. About a half mile up Mouski Street is the *Souq al Nahassin,* where coppersmiths squatting on the ground hammer at pots, pans, vases and trays. Nearby in the *Souq al Siyagh* are the booths of the goldsmiths.

On the street leading to Bab al Zuweileh are the perfume bazaars in *Souq al Attarin* and various shops selling native fabrics in *Souq Ghouriyeh.*

Walking southeast along Mouski Street one finds *Souq Khayamia,* the tentmakers. Here, one also finds the tiny shops where the applique, often seen in tapestries of Egyptian motifs, is made. *Bazaar Shop,* No. 18, has different types of the work, including calligraphy, and will make items to order. Another stall, *Hanafi Mohamed Ibrahim,* has tote bags of brightly colored canvas on which he does the applique. *Farahat Sosdy* has a catalogue of his designs. Farther along, another covered lane leads to *Souq Saramatiyeh,* where leather shops make camel saddles, ottomans, native sandals and other leatherwork. Close by is *Souq Kariyeh,* where Turkish delight and other Oriental sweets are sold.

About 200 yards from this area and in front of Al Azhar University is the entrance to *Khan al Khalili*—the best of all the bazaars and the one in which you are likely to spend most of your time. Its narrow, devious paths lead past shops—jewelry, carpets, amber, brass, copper, antiquities, glass, leather, silver, to name a few.

Some shops in the Mouski also have shops or displays in leading hotels, but to buy at hotels is to miss half the fun and is usually more expensive.

Because of the labyrinth of streets and alleyways, a newcomer can easily become confused. It is wise to go with a guide or friend who knows the way. On the other hand, if you should want to strike out on your own, you need not hesitate. Egyptians are enormously helpful to visitors. They will stop their work to help you and it is not unusual to have someone walk several blocks out of his way to show you directions.

Bargaining: Bargaining is an accepted pattern in Egypt. No one pays the original asking price—at least, not in the bazaars. Your skill at the practice will determine the price. Egyptian merchants expect customers to bargain and enjoy it. If you end up at half the price originally asked, you deserve a blue ribbon. One third off is the usual settlement. Remember, no one in Egypt is in a hurry—least of all in the Mouski. If you browse in a shop for several hours, yet buy nothing, the shopowner will not object. In true Middle Eastern fashion, he will philosophize that if he does not sell it today, he will sell it tomorrow—if Allah is willing.

In Egypt, as in most countries of the world, guides are likely to take you to their favorite shops—those from which they get a commission. Look around first and do not feel under any pressure to buy. Incidentally, one of the best ways to bring the price down in bargaining is to leave! Because most tourists do not enjoy bargaining nor have the time for it, more and more merchants are posting fixed prices. Even though they do not bargain, when you buy a lot from one shop, you can ask for a discount. It usually works.

Egyptian Crafts

The Mouski overflows with items made strictly for tourists. These do not need describing as they will be obvious immediately. The shopping guide here is intended to point out the more unusual items and the best buys in Cairo. Much, of course, will depend on individual taste.

Alabaster: Inexpensive vases, ashtrays, lamp bases and figurines are available in Cairo at gift and souvenir shops or you may buy from the factory in Luxor. Be sure to have your purchase packed carefully. It is more fragile than it looks.

Antiquities: Although several stores in the Mouski and in downtown Cairo are authorized to sell Egyptian antiquities, a new batch of regulations has made it virtually impossible for them to sell them and for you to buy them. Furthermore, customs authorities have become so difficult (they have even been known to search visitors on departure), it apparently is not worth the risk. As a further warning, there are more fakes than real antiquities in the market—none but the trained eye can tell the difference—and even the experts sometimes get fooled. So, unless you are prepared to be taken for a ride and to run the risk of big, big trouble with Egyptian authorities, do not buy antiquities.

As a matter of interest, small amulets are frequently used in designs for jewelry or, as amulets, are sometimes encased or mounted in gold to be worn as charms. There are several types:

The *Ushabtiu* was the name given by the ancient Egyptians to representations in stone, alabaster, wood, clay and glazed faience of the god Osiris made in the form of mummies. These were placed in wooden boxes or on the floor of the tombs. They were intended to do manual labor for the deceased.

Udjat or Uzait Horu, or the sacred eye of Horus, represents the human eye. This amulet was a divinity in itself and enjoyed independent existence. It was perhaps the most popular of all Egyptian amulets. It was meant to ward off the evil eye—a belief that pervades Africa and the Middle East to the present day. Those who wore it were supposed to be safe and happy under the protection of the eye of Re. The *udjat* was the principal design in the bracelet found on the right arm of the mummy of Tutankhamun. It is now seen frequently on the new jewelry and fabrics that have copied ancient Egyptian motifs.

The *Scarab,* an Egyptian desert insect, was worshipped by the ancient Egyptians as being a living representative of a god. *Xepera,* father of the gods, was the hieroglyphic name given by the pharaohs to the scarab. He was creator of all things in heaven and on earth, and he made himself out of matter that he produced himself. In time, the scarab came into common use. People wore it as an act of homage to the creator of the world. Also, it served as a seal.

Nassar Brothers, Khan Khalili, is one of the best and most reliable dealers. They have amulets made into charms, cuff links or tiepins. Prices might be higher than in other places, but workmanship is outstanding. (See *Gold Jewelry* for more information.)

For Islamic antiquities and copies of pharaonic and Islamic furniture, *Hatoun and Sons,* Mouski Street, is the best. You may also visit their workshop. Even if you have little intention of buying such items, you will find a visit to the store worthwhile to see the displays.

Brass and Copper: The Mouski is filled with tempting objects of brass, copper and copper washed with tin. The new ones with pharaonic designs are popular, but the old ones with arabesque are more artistic. Copper plates encrusted with metal or silver (used for hanging or as trivets), tall pitchers and vases (excellent for making lamps), candlesticks, samovars and braziers are among the best selections.

Although the products are similar in most shops, there is a great difference in the quality of the workmanship. You must shop around if you are looking for anything more valuable than trinkets and inexpensive souvenirs. And you must bargain. Try *Farag Ali Abou Taleb* and *Mohamed El Gameel,* both in Khan El Khalili.

Carpets: The Egyptians make a plain beige carpet known as a western desert rug. It is sold by the square meter and the thickness of the pile determines the price. These rugs are made to order for reasonable prices at the *Egyptian State Industries Store* near Mustapha Kamel Square.

Stores in the Mouski also have Oriental rugs from other Middle East countries for sale. *El Fatarani, Sharia Kasr el Nil, Ismail Ali* and *El Kahal* in Khan El Khalili have carpets and rugs.

Ceramics/Glass: Charms, cuff links, brooches and earrings are made from old pieces of mosaic glass. The lovely patterns run through the entire thickness of the piece and resemble abstract designs of modern ceramics. Two types were made in ancient days: the mosaic bowls produced primarily at Alexandria and small, decorative plaques of high technical and artistic skill. The latter, mostly Ptolemaic, were used to inlay jewelry boxes and furniture or as ornaments to be admired at close range. This glass was one of the most amazing achievements in the history of glassmaking. Apparently experts are still not sure how the ancient Egyptians made it. (See *Modern Egyptian Art* earlier in this chapter for more details.)

Egyptian Accessories and Objets d'Art: Some of the most interesting and reasonably priced jewelry in Cairo is found in the boutique of *Senouhi,* 54 Abdul Khalek Sarwat. Owners Leila and Omar Rachad have a great love for good Egyptian crafts and a good eye for bits and pieces that can be worked into contemporary conversation pieces.

This unassuming atelier, where five people make a crowd, is located on the fifth floor; there is a name plaque at the building's entrance. The tiny elevator, to the left on entering, offers the ride up; customers, usually satisfied, walk down. Hours are 9:00 A.M. to 5:00 P.M. Shop is closed on Sat. afternoon and Sun. and during September.

Senouhi is also the only shop in Cairo where one can buy the tapestries and batiks from Harraniya Village. The selection may vary considerably because the stock is small. If you are there when a new batch has arrived you will have trouble deciding which one to buy. Senouhi also handles works by other leading artists and will have on hand representative examples of each. Prices are fixed. Also available are handwoven fabrics that can be used for bedspreads, table covers or decorating accents. Some, too, are made into shirts and dresses. Everything in the shop is different from the usual items you will see around town. Most are one of a kind or an artist's creation. Both Leila and Omar Rashad are designers. *Al Ain Gallery,* 73 El Houssein St., Mohandesseen, is a Cairo insider's favorite.

For more traditional selections, *Onnig's,* the gift shop at the Antiquities Museum, is perhaps the most reliable store in Egypt. Prices are reasonable and fixed. Onnig is a well-known jewelry designer and one of the leading gemologists in the Middle East. The popular and often copied wide gold band with multicolored stones, known as Cleopatra's bracelet, is his design. He is frequently called upon by the Egyptian government and others for his expertise and to participate in shows and exhibits.

Fabrics: Cotton is the best fabric to buy in Egypt. Material for shirts and ready-made shirts are inexpensive. Reliable stores are *Swelam,* Adly Street; *George,* Talaat Harb Street; and *Adel,* Sherif Street. A man's tailor-made shirt costs about L.E. 10 to 151—tailoring takes a month or more.

A variety of dress materials is available. The best and most expensive selections are at *Salon Vert.* There are several smaller stores across the street, such as *Miss Paris* and *La Poupée,* which have cheaper fabrics. Good selections of all types of fabrics are available at *Hannaux* and *Cicurel.* On Kasr el Nil, Talaat Harb and 26 July Streets there are dozens of fabric stores where at least one clerk or the owner speaks enough English to be able to communicate.

At *Eid,* 35 Talaat Harb, cotton shirt fabric of the best quality is L.E. 4 per meter (2.5 meters for a shirt). Wide variety of ready to wear shirts range from L.E. 8 to L.E. 10. Good selection of cotton pajamas, underwear, jackets and trousers, and dress fabrics—all at reasonable prices.

One of the best of all buys in Egypt is *galabiyah* cloth. As the name implies, the fabric is used to make the *galabiyah,* the long outer robe worn by native-dressed Egyptian men. It is usually striped in soft colors, very sturdy, excellent for draperies and upholstering, and is inexpensive. You should buy it in the Mouski where selections are unlimited. L.E. 2 to 3 per meter is the average price. *Abas Hegazi,* Khan Khalili, has a wide assortment of top quality galabiyahs and will make them to order. Costs range from L.E. 10 to 25, depending on the quality and amount of fabric.

Among the most attractive kaftans (which Egyptians call *galabiyah,* too) are those being made by local artists with block prints and other methods using Pharaonic and Islamic designs. At the handicraft centers in the Manteserli Art and Life Center and Sennari they cost L.E. 25 and up. One of the best collections is at *Mousky Chic,* a shop in the Nile Hilton. Prices are a little more expensive, ranging from L.E. 40, but the selection is excellent.

At *Elle,* a kaftan of unpolished cotton is L.E. 2 and those of traditional polished cotton are L.E. 15, while the fancier acetate fabrics are L.E. 30. *Shahire Mehrez,* 12 Sharia Abi Emana, sixth floor, in Dokki, within walking distance of the Cairo Sheraton, is a shop owned by seven Egyptian women from well-known families, and open 10-1 P.M.; 4-7 P.M. Tel. 988182. Here you will find modern and old dresses from different areas of Egypt at very reasonable prices.

Atlas, Khan Khalili, has a stock of kaftans for ladies and men or will make them to order. Prices start at L.E. 14 and go up to L.E. 50 for the fancy ones with pearl applique. *Oriental Bazaar,* Khan El Khalili, also has a large selection for similar prices. They are available in hotel shops but are more expensive. The best selection and price for inexpensive cotton kaftans are in Luxor. Prices range from L.E. 12 to 40, depending on the quality of the cotton and the extent of design or applique. Kaftans can be made to order and completed in one day at no extra charge from shops in major hotels and along the main street near Luxor hotels.

Gold Jewelry: Gold is sold by weight and is one of the best buys in Egypt for its workmanship. Charms of the Pyramids and Sphinx are available, but the most popular is a cartouche with one's name in hieroglyphics. The price is determined by the weight, carat of gold and the nature of the writing—engraved or applied. The cheap ones are very thin and have the hieroglyphics glued on. Those properly made are soldered and cost L.E. 90 to 170. Engraving is usually the most expensive. Deal only with reliable stores, such as *Onnig's* at the Antiquities Museum.

A more unusual item is cuff links with one's name inscribed in Arabic or in hieroglyphics. Another popular product is the thin, plain, solid gold bracelet used by native Egyptian women as their dowry. For an interesting experience, buy in the *Gold Souq;* for jewelry made to order, *Nassar Bros.,* Khan Khalili, is excellent. The owners have their own workshop where artisans train under the watchful eye of Mr. Nassar, who creates all his own designs. Nassar is expensive by Egyptian standards but the quality is unexcelled, and similar models in Europe or the States would be three times the price.

In a completely different vein, but no less outstanding is *Nakhla,* 10 El Nil St. (in front of the boat Happi Joe), Giza, a new jewelry boutique owned by two designers who use masses of pearls, lapis, topaz and other stones with gold to create fabulous necklaces and bracelets. The work is high style, original, handsome and expensive—from L.E. 700 and up. Phone: 720938.

Inlaid Wood: Trays, jewelry and cigarette boxes inlaid with ivory and ebony are attractive. Also, mother-of-pearl mosaic inlay is available.

Mushrabbiyah and other woodwork: At the Mena House and on tours of old mosques, houses, churches and palaces you will see examples of beautiful woodwork called *mushrabbiya* (sometimes identified as harem screens). The woodwork from demolished old buildings is rare. The new, unfortunately, does not have the same grace and excellent workmanship as the old, but it is available. In the Mouski, you can watch the intricate pieces emerge from a raw stick of wood under the dexterous hands of a skilled Egyptian craftsman at any of the workshops specializing in wood.

Exquisitely carved wood to make tables and screens is also available. Copies of pharaonic furniture are interesting buys, especially the mahogany stool with a string woven seat. These are available from *Zaki & Boutros,* Khan Khalili, or *Hatoun,* Mouski Street, both of whom will ship to the States. *Mushrabiya* is a new shop on a country lane near Felafel Restaurant in the Pyramids area, where lattice-work wood is sold by the meter.

Leather Work: Egypt is the place to buy the camel saddle you always wanted. Many decorative kinds are made for the tourist market, but the old type, free of brass design, is nicer. *Mustapha Soliman,* Khan Khalili, is one of the few shops selling the old type of camel saddles; the new models are available in any Oriental shop. Mustapha also has a good assortment of poufs or ottomans, sandals and inexpensive leather suitcases. Near the entrance to Khan Khalili there is a small alleyway with several leather shops. Browse awhile before buying.

Another large assortment of inexpensive leather goods is available in the arcade in front of the Continental Hotel and the shops surrounding it, and in another arcade at the entrance of the Tourist Administration's headquarters, 5 Adly Street.

Not to be overlooked in leather is the new line of shoes for about L.E. 15–20 and handbags for about L.E. 20–30. They are important fashions for export and are continuously being improved in quality and design in order to compete in the international market. Every other store on Kasr el Nil and Talaat Harb seems to be a handbag and shoe shop with fashionable ladies shoes; stores selling leather coats and jackets are not yet quite as numerous. At *Abbassi & Co.*, 25 Adly Street, men's and women's jackets range from L.E. 35 and up. There is also a showroom for export. Its trade name is Formax. Another is *Lumbroso,* 19 Talaat Harb, which has leather coats for L.E. 50 and up. *Mohamed Gadallah,* 5 Sayed el Baky, Zamalek, carries high-fashion shoes. *K.M.,* 1103 Isis Street, two blocks from Shepheard's Hotel, specializes in top quality leather, snakeskin, lizard handbags, shoes and belts.

If you are planning to live in Egypt, bring the books in your library that need rebinding. An average-size book costs less than L.E. 2 or 3 for combination leather and cloth binding, and the workmanship is good. (Three shops are listed in *A Practical Guide to Cairo* under *Bookbinders*.)

Mouski Glass: Inexpensive but fragile hand-blown glasses and dishes are made from melted-down glass of broken soda and beer bottles. A drinking glass costs 20 pt. The glass must be carefully packed for shipping as it is very fragile. *Ismail Hassan Mahmoud,* Khan Khalili, has a good selection. Any Tuesday or Friday you may visit the factory where the glass is made. Hurricane lamps are especially attractive and inexpensive.

Perfumes: There are several perfume shops on Mouski Street. Scents are heavy and sweet, but their novelty is appealing, and they make inexpensive gifts to take home. Any of the perfume shops will give you an array of scents to sample, but the place that makes the biggest show of it is *Scharazad,* Midan Tahrir (across from the Antiquities Museum). The owner claims to be one of the major suppliers of oils to many famous perfume houses in France.

Semiprecious Stones: Alexandrites, aquamarines, topaz and pearls are made into earrings, rings, pins or bracelets at reasonable prices. Many jewelers offer designs inspired by pharaonic design. Workmanship is good. Amber, too, is a good buy. *Onnig's* has a wide selection.

Silver: Egypt is a good place to buy silver, also sold by weight. Almost any type of dish, ashtray, tray and candelabrum is available. A plain, sterling silver cigarette or jewelry box engraved with one's initials or name in Arabic (or English) is a lovely gift. Try the *Egyptian Silver Work Factory* and *Saad,* both in Khan Khalili.

Stamps: Egypt has interesting stamps, old and new, and it is a good place for collectors to fill in Middle East countries issues missing from their collection. A hundred commemorative stamps of Egypt costing L.E. 1.20, and 50 stamps of pharaonic design, L.E. 1 are among those in the selection. A well established shop is *Oriental Philatelic House,* Continental Arcade. It has a U.S. counterpart in New York, and you can deal with the Cairo store by mail. The shop also has slides and unusual postcards.

Facilitating Export of Local Items: Oriental stores in the Mouski and in hotels will ship goods to the States. They are reliable, but it can take six months or longer to receive parcels. Do not attempt to mail a parcel on your own from Egypt. An export license is necessary and the red tape is stupefying.

WARNING. One of the most constant complaints of visitors is the long delays in receiving goods shipped from Egypt. There are two reasons for the problem: First, Egyptian bureaucracy is so layered that merchants can waste days and weeks getting the paperwork through; and second, there is no direct sea-freight service from Egypt to the U.S., so this creates delay. Further, the backlog at the port of Alexandria is unbelievable. No matter what a merchant tells you, parcels shipped by sea will take six months or more; those sent by air can take up to three months.

Sending Gifts to Egypt: Persons living in Egypt may receive gifts from outside, but to save them a great deal of trouble, give them your gift in person. Gifts are subject to customs duties and clearing a package through customs is a long, difficult and exasperating process.

Modern Stores and Goods

Department Stores: Even in the modern shopping districts, stores tend to specialize in one item—shoes, fabrics, sportswear, etc. There are a few department stores, but they are small in scale by comparison with ours.

Chemla, 11, 26th July Street. Cheap quality. *Cicurel,* 3, 26th July Street. Expensive. *Egyptian Products Sales Co.,* 2, 26th July Street. Household fabrics. *Hannaux,* Kasr el Nil Street. Good fabrics and linens. *Omar Effendi,* Moderately priced. *Salon Vert,* Kasr el Nil Street. Largest selection of highest-quality Egyptian fabrics.

Bookshops: Downtown Cairo and most residential areas have many bookshops. For books in English, our favorite is *Reader's Corner,* 33 Sharia Abdel Khalek Sarwat, which also has bookstores in the Nile Hilton, Holiday Inns and Hilton cruise boats and art shops at the Ramses Hilton and Meridien. The store carries originals and copies of the famous Robert's prints as well. Also recommended is *Anglo-Egyptian,* 165 Sharia Mohamed Farid, where you must be prepared to browse, as old and new books are stacked floor to extra-high ceiling. The shop's Middle East selection is one of the best in town. *Lehnert and Landrock,* 44 Sharif Pasha Street, is probably the largest. At *Menzozzi,* 19 Sharia 26 July, the two ladies running the store are absolutely charming and eager to help. *Libraire Hachette,* Talaat Harb Square, has French selections. For old and rare editions, *Orientalist Print Shop,* 13 Kasr el Nil Street (next to American Express) is the best. This store also sells old maps and the famous Robert's prints of old Egyptian scenes. Once available for a few dollars each, they now sell for L.E. 300 to 500 per print! Magazines and newspapers are sold by vendors, but shops in major hotels have better selections, especially the Meridien, Sheraton and Hilton.

Across the street from the Continental and around the fence of the Ezbekia Gardens there are outdoor stalls where, if you have the time and inclination, you can spend hours browsing through old books. Most are junk, but you never know when you might happen on a rare one.

Clothing: Many urban Egyptians and those of the younger generation have adopted western dress. Ladies are smartly dressed and influenced mainly by French and Italian styles, which their dressmakers and tailors copy easily from a picture. The prices are reasonable.

There are also a large number of shops on Kasr El Nil, Talaat Harb and the side streets between the two, as well as many neighborhood boutiques in Zamalek and in Heliopolis that have ready to wear items. Imported clothes and accessories are expensive, locally made ones are not.

The best buy of all is children's and baby's clothes. Dresses with pretty embroidery, playsuits and other items are very inexpensive when compared to U.S. prices for similar products. *Bamco* and *Papillon,* Kasr el Nil, have clothing and toys, as do others along same street.

Cosmetics and Toiletries: If you have a favorite brand, bring supplies sufficient for your visit. Some American products are packaged locally or imported from Europe and Britain. Leading European makes are available and all are expensive.

Egypt is the land of mascara (called *kohl* in Arabic), as is evident in the ancient tomb drawings and wall paintings. Some gift shops sell *kohl,* and the salesgirl will show you how to use it.

Florists: Cairo has a year-round profusion of flowers. They are inexpensive, especially when bought from vendors. Egyptians give and send flowers on the slightest occasion. If you have been entertained at dinner in an Egyptian home, sending flowers in advance or the following day is a popular way to say thank you. Bouquets average L.E. 10 to L.E. 15, depending upon the kind of flowers and time of year, and can be delivered. A box of candy is also an appropriate gift for a visit to someone's home or for a hospital visit.

Among the leading florists are *Fresh Flowers,* Garden City (across from the American Embassy); *Hilton Hotel Florist; May Flowers,* 116 Sharia 26 July, Zamalek; *Meridien Hotel Florist;* and *Sheraton Hotel Florist.*

Food Products: Few American and European food products can be purchased in Egypt. When they are available, they are expensive. Local fruits and vegetables are good, inexpensive but seasonal, although canning is one of Egypt's fastest growing industries. Refrigerated meats are limited.

Meat is usually sold the day it is slaughtered and can be purchased only on Thursday, Friday, Saturday and Sunday. Although Moslems do not eat pork, one can buy it in Cairo. Cairo has no equivalent of the American supermarket. However, several Zamalek stores, where language is not a problem, have good selections. With only a few words of Arabic you can manage surprisingly well in food markets and it is fun to try.

Linens: Bed and table linens of fine-quality Egyptian cotton with embroidery are reasonable in price. Try the department stores and specialty shops on Kasr el Nil and Talaat Harb streets. Fine cotton table cloths and ten napkins with lovely applique run about L.E. 20; bed sheets and pillowcases with embroidery and applique are also very reasonable in price.

Tobacco and Cigarettes: Popular American and English brands cost up to 85 pts. per pack. Buy a carton on the plane before arriving and carry a lighter. Matches are not given away; they are bought, and you'll never have enough. The best Egyptian filters, *Cleopatra* and *Nefertiti,* cost about 50 pts. There are also nonfiltered cigarettes.

Toys and Dolls: Locally made toys and dolls are available at department stores and at specialty shops, especially in the shopping arcade between Sharia Adly and Sharia 26 July.

BABY-SITTERS. The old English term "nanny" was imported to Egypt by the British and is still used. Inquire at your hotel—otherwise you will need to rely on friends to locate a nanny. There is no established baby-sitting service in Cairo, but the Maadi Women's Club telephone book lists three names with phone numbers. Deluxe hotels can also provide this service.

For those planning a longer stay, nannies or American teenagers willing to babysit frequently advertise on the bulletin board next to the accommodation exchange cashier at the American Embassy.

BARBER SHOPS AND BEAUTY SALONS. What was once the best bargain in Egypt has vanished with inflation, and in places catering to tourists, such as deluxe hotels, prices are comparable to those in the U.S. An unfortunate practice that has developed at hotels in only the past few years is charging foreigners double or more than Egyptians.

A man's haircut is L.E. 8–10 but can be as little as L.E. 4 in neighborhood shops, plus tips to all who attend you. Most barber shops close on Mondays.

There are many good beauty shops. At salons in deluxe hotels, a wash and set is L.E. 15–25; cut, L.E. 8–10; manicure, L.E. 3–5; and pedicure, L.E. 8–10. But a wash and blow-dry is only L.E. 6–10 in downtown shops and less in the suburbs.

Most shops open from 9 A.M. to 7 P.M. and do not schedule appointments. Hairdressers close on Mondays, except those in hotels, but they are open on Fridays and Sundays.

You should tip the boy or girl who washes your hair and the one who helps the hairdresser (50 pt. is appropriate). A tip of a similar amount should be given to the manicurist and pedicurist. If the owner prepares the set, you need not tip him, although most clients do.

Service tends to be slow, as Cairo ladies consider their salon a meeting place for coffee and gossip—only foreign tourists are ever in a hurry. Expect to spend two hours or more with the hairdresser.

Gharib, 15 Sharia Kasr el Nil, across from Middle East Airlines. Phone: 750950. Open daily including Sunday and Friday; closed Monday. Gharib himself gives the best haircut in town. Mrs. Sadat must think so, too, as he has been her hairdresser for more than 20 years and traveled with her on important state visits. Gharib is always busy and juggles five or six customers at a time. There are several people around who speak enough English to manage. Wash and blow-dry is L.E. 10; cut, L.E. 5; manicure, L.E. 3; pedicure, L.E. 3. Facial L.E. 20; makeup, L.E. 20.

Nile Hilton Salon. This shop has been patronized by foreign residents and many of Cairo's most fashionable women since the hotel opened 25 years ago. It is good, but expensive by Cairo standards. The shop is not up to its high fashion or cleanliness standard of the past, but it is still good and it takes customers by appointment. If you go when the shop is busy, you will still have to wait, even with an appointment.

Socrate, 25 Sharia Kasr el Nil, across from Lappas. An old-time favorite of leading ladies in Cairo. Wash and blow-dry, L.E. 6. Open Mondays.

Other Cairo favorites are: *Francois,* 12 Sharia Kasr el Nil; *Myrabel,* 8 Sharia Talaat Harb, west of the Midan; *Romance,* 157 Sharia 26 July, Zamalek; and *Sheraton Hotel,* Giza.

LAUNDRIES AND DRY CLEANERS. Cairo has many laundry and dry-cleaning plants that are adequate for normal needs, but few cope well with difficult fabrics. You are best off with 100-percent cotton clothes, which are handled beautifully and inexpensively. All hotels usually have speedy service at reasonable prices. Average rates: shirt, L.E. 1.50; suit washed and pressed, L.E. 4.50. Dry cleaning is more expensive: a suit cleaned and pressed is about L.E. 6.

Some residents hire a washerwoman and ironing man to come to their home weekly; others make an agreement with a neighborhood shop to pay a flat rate per month. The price depends on the amount of work, but it is very little compared to prices for similar service in the States.

Egypt has much longer periods of hot weather than most parts of the States or Europe. And that ever-present sand dust is hard on clothes. Summer clothing is used longer and washed more often. Good quality, sturdy fabrics for clothing and linens are recommended. Bed and table linens of fine Egyptian cotton are readily available in Cairo at reasonable prices.

PHARMACIES. Many pharmacies are located in or near leading hotels and in the neighborhood districts of Maadi, Zamalek, Garden City, Dokki and Heliopolis. Prices are set by the government. Many pharmaceuticals are medicines produces by leading American and European companies, bottled and packaged in Egypt. Most pharmaceuticals are available, but local packaging and labeling may make them difficult for a newcomer to recognize. If you have special health problems, bring your required medicines and prescriptions with you.

Pharmacies open daily and with day and night service: *Gumhuria,* Sharia Shagaret el Dor, Zamalek; *Isaaf,* Sharia 26 July; *New Universal,* Sharia Hassan Sabri, Zamalek; *Riad,* across from American Embassy. Pharmacies stay open until 10:00 P.M. In town: *Windsor,* Midan el Tahrir, and *Zarif,* 1 Midan Talaat Harb. These stores may have medicines that are hard to find elsewhere.

REPAIRS. At many hotels, shoes left outside the hotel room at night will be shined by morning. For special repairs, consult your hall porter or the concierge.

Watch Repair: Jewelers in leading hotels and downtown shopping areas as well as in the Mouski either have repair service or will know where to have such work done quickly and at reasonable prices.

BUSINESS SERVICES. The Meridien has a full scale Business Service Center with telex, copying machine, secretarial services and private office space for rent. It is conveniently located in the lobby corridor and accessible to outsiders as well as hotel guests. Typing is L.E. 3 per page. Office rates range from L.E. 15–25 for half-day; L.E. 20–30 for full day. Conference room for up to 20 is L.E. 30 for half-day; L.E. 50 for full day.

Executive Business Services, 7 Lazoghli St. (near American Embassy). Phone: 31824. Contact: Ann Wolfe. Two partners, one American and the other Egyptian, offer instant office space, secretarial services, and conference management. They also handle the Business Service Center at the Marriott Hotel. Another client is the newly created *American Chamber of Commerce,* which is also headquartered at the Marriott. Ex. Dir: Pat Brown.

Egyptian Business Services, 13 A. Marashly St., Zamalek, Phone: 809346. Telex: 93060 GIFAM. Provides wide range of support and promotional services for individual or corporation, including meetings, public relations, marketing, translating and trade shows. Contact Mona Korashy. Owner has installed an art gallery of about 40 contemporary Egyptian artists, some of whom are on hand on Fridays.

International Business Associates. 1079 Corniche el Nil, Garden City, second floor, has the most comprehensive office service in Egypt ranging from instant, temporary office space with messenger, courier, telex, phone, etc., for $50 a day, $500 a month, or $1800 a year as a complete turn-key operation. Also can undertake specific assignments throughout the Middle East, such as recruitment, training, car and van leasing, conferences and catering; consultants, project managers; apartment rental and renovation. Company's American owner, William Harrison, is publisher of *Cairo Today*.

Office Space: Arabian-American Real Estate Co., 1079 Corniche el Nil, Garden City, phone: 25465. Telex: 92548 WWH UN. Full service real estate company that can handle all negotiations with owners, write contracts, etc. for offices and apartments to accommodate individuals or an entire company in Cairo and Alexandria. Fees negotiated; references available; staff speaks six languages.

Photocopying: Several downtown photo and camera stores have photocopying service at 20–30 pts. per page.

Arabic Language Courses: *Berlitz,* 165 Moh.Bey Farid St., phone: 915096; *International Language Institute, Arabic Language Center,* Mahmoud Azmi Street, Mohandiseen, phone: 803087; *Egyptian Center for International Cultural Cooperation,* 11 Shagaret El Dor, Zamalek, phone: 815419; and *American University in Cairo,* phone: 24110.

USEFUL ADDRESSES. Emergency Numbers: *Ambulance:* Emergency calls 44554/743251. *Hospitals:* Anglo-American, Gezira Island, tel. 806163; Dar El Shifa, 375 Ramsis, Abbassiya, tel. 820255. *Information:* tel. 16/180. *Pharmacies* (night and day service): Gumhuria, Sharia Shagaret El Dor, Zamalek, tel. 866434; Isaaf, Sharia 26 July, tel. 40369. *Police:* Emergency, tel. 122; Tourist, tel. 912644. *Radio and International Calls:* tel. 903120.

Travel Agencies. *American Express,* 15 Kasr El Nil St.; *Thomas Cook & Son,* 4 Champolion St. Other leading agencies are: *Cairo Transport,* 28 Talaat Harb St.; *Eastmar,* 13 Kasr El Nil St.; *Gabry Travel,* 1 Talaat Harb Sq. *Misr Travel,* 1 Talaat Harb, is the autonomous, government-owned agency and the largest one with offices throughout Cairo and the country.

Airlines. Air France, 2 Talaat Harb Sq. Tel. 743300, 743235 office: 66102 airport.

Air India, 1 Talaat Harb St. Tel. 742592 office; 966756 airport.

ALIA-Royal Jordanian, 6 Kasr El Nil St. Tel. 750905 office; 963903 airport.

British Airways, 1 Abdel Salam Aref St. Tel. 759977 office; 963456 airport.

EgyptAir, 6 Adly St., 12 Kasr El Nil St.; 9 Talaat Harb St. Tel. 920999 office, 747444 reservations; 694400 airport.

Japan Airways, 4 Kamal El Din Salah Sq. Tel. 740809, 740845 office; 963843 airport.

KLM, 11 Kasr El Nil St. Tel. 740999 office; 965226 airport.

Kuwait Airways, 4 Talaat Harb St. Tel. 759874 office; 963130 airport.

Lufthansa, 9 Talaat Harb St. Tel. 750366 office; 873149 airport.

Nile Delta Air Service, 1 Talaat Harb St. Tel. 40935 office; 746197 airport.

Olympic Airways, 23 Kasr El Nil St. Tel. 751277 office; 963270 airport.

Pan American (Emeco Travel), 2 Talaat Harb St. Tel. 747302 office.

Royal Air Maroc, 9 Talaat Harb St. Tel. 740378 office.

Sabena, 2 Mariette St. Tel. 753694 office; 965144 airport.

Swissair, 22 Kasr El Nil St. Tel. 757955 office; 966746 airport.

Trans World Airlines, 1 Kasr El Nil St. Tel. 965310 office; 871050 airport.

Shipping Agencies. Adriatica (De Castro), 12 Talaat Harb. Tel. 743144.

Cairo Shipping Agency, 7 Abdel Khalek Sarwat. Tel. 745755.

Egyptian Navigation Co., 20 Talaat Harb.

Eyres Travel & Shipping, 52 Abdel Khalek Sarwat.

North African Shipping Co., 171 Mohamed Farid (S. G. Cottakis & Co., Hellenic Mediterranean Lines, Spanish Line, Typaldos Brothers Steamship Co.). Tel. 914682.

United Arab Maritime, 26 Sherif. Tel. 46322.

Embassies. Australian, 1097 Corniche El Nil, Garden City, tel. 28197.

British, Latin America St., Garden City, tel. 20850/9.

Canadian, 6 Mohamed Fahmy El Sayed St., Garden City, tel. 23119, 23110.

United States, 5 Latin America St., Garden City, tel. 28211/9.

Banks. American Express, 15 Kasr El Nil; Hilton Hotel Branch; Meridien Hotel Branch. American Express International Banking Corp., 15 El Nabatat, Garden City.

Bank of America, 15 Brazil St., Zamalek.

Bank Misr, 151 Mohamed Farid; Hilton Hotel Branch; Sheraton Hotel.

Bank of Nova Scotia, 3 Ahmed Nassim St., Giza.

Cairo Barclays International, 12 Sheikh Yousef Sq.

Central Bank of Egypt, 31 Kasr El Nil.

Chase National Bank, 12 El Birgas, Garden City.

First National City Bank, 4 Ahmed Pasha St., Garden City.

RADIO AND TELEVISION. Egyptian broadcasting is government controlled. Radio Cairo has regular programs of classical and popular Western music, in the morning and late evening, with news broadcasts daily in English. Voice of America and BBC are received in Cairo; reception is best in the early morning or late evening.

Cairo and Alexandria have two television channels. Most programs are in Arabic. They usually operate five hours a day and telecast in color. Some American serials are shown with Arabic subtitles. A new satellite ground station permits live local coverage of significant world events. There are newscasts daily in English and French.

NEWSPAPERS. Cairo has one English daily, *The Egyptian Gazette*. *The International Herald Tribune* may be purchased at newsstands, as well as the *Arab News,* published in English in Saudi Arabia. A monthly magazine in English, *Cairo Today* can be found at newsstands for 75 pts.

Amun, Patron God of Thebes

UPPER EGYPT

Luxor, Karnak and the High Dam

A visit to the Egyptian Museum, or to Memphis and Sakkara, is only an introduction to the antiquities of Egypt. Not until you have made a trip to Luxor, Aswan and the other sites of Upper Egypt does the magnitude of ancient Egypt's civilization become apparent. The 534 miles from Cairo to Aswan are dotted with ancient monuments and temples, with more being discovered all the time.

Strictly speaking, Upper Egypt is that narrow strip of green which stretches from the apex of the Delta 14 miles north of Cairo to the first Cataract at Shellal, about six miles south of Aswan. It resembles the long stem of the lotus of which the Delta, or Lower Egypt, is the flower.

Only the most important sites are described in this section, but those who have the time will find dozens of lesser known places with fabulous monuments and ruins to explore.

Over 700 tombs have been discovered on the West Bank of the Nile at Luxor. If you were to visit only 15 of the best you would be exhausted and probably saturated with Egyptian art for a long time to come. Do not overdo your sightseeing. If your time is limited, visit only a few tombs. You should not attempt to see all those listed below unless you are staying at least four days in Luxor.

If you rely only on a guide to explain the drawings, you will miss a great deal of their artistic value. For maximum benefit, familiarize yourself in advance with the names of the gods, the important Pharaohs and their representations in wall paintings. You should read, if you have not already done so, or reread "The Egyptian Scene" chapter of this book prior to a visit to Upper Egypt. If you plan an extensive visit to the tombs, you will benefit immensely by carrying with you a book that details the drawings with pictures and explanations.

Other useful items for the trip to Upper Egypt are a flashlight, premoistened face cloths and moisturizing cream. At sites of antiquity, on trains or in cars, dust from the sand will collect on your skin. Cleanse your face quickly with a moistened cloth, follow it with a moisturizer and you can feel refreshed quickly and easily. Also, bring fresh lemons, lemon drops or mints, a collapsible drinking cup, a small thermos for water on sightseeing rounds in the open, and a flash attachment for your camera for picture-taking inside tombs. Keep cameras, films, and lenses in plastic bags when not in use as protection against the sand and dust.

Only art specialists and professional photographers are given permission to photograph in the tomb of Tutankhamun, but in the others, everyone is permitted to take pictures if the crowds of sightseers permits.

And last of all, you will need a strong pair of legs, comfortable shoes and a zeal for tomb exploring—no matter what!

LUXOR

The present-day town of Luxor on the east bank of the Nile is situated 400 miles south of Cairo on the site of ancient Thebes, the capital of Egypt at its zenith during the Middle and New Kingdoms. The actual site of Thebes is said to have occupied all the area between Luxor and Karnak, a village a few miles north of Luxor. Today the area contains the ruins of the most gigantic monuments, statues and temples in all Egypt. These represent the greatest artistic accomplishments of the ancient Egyptians from the XIII to the XXX Dynasties.

When viewing the monuments of Luxor and Karnak, you should remember that these marvels were once profusely decorated. The walls were overlaid with gold, silver, alabaster and marble, the gates plated with gold and the temples connected with each other by pillars, courtyards and gardens.

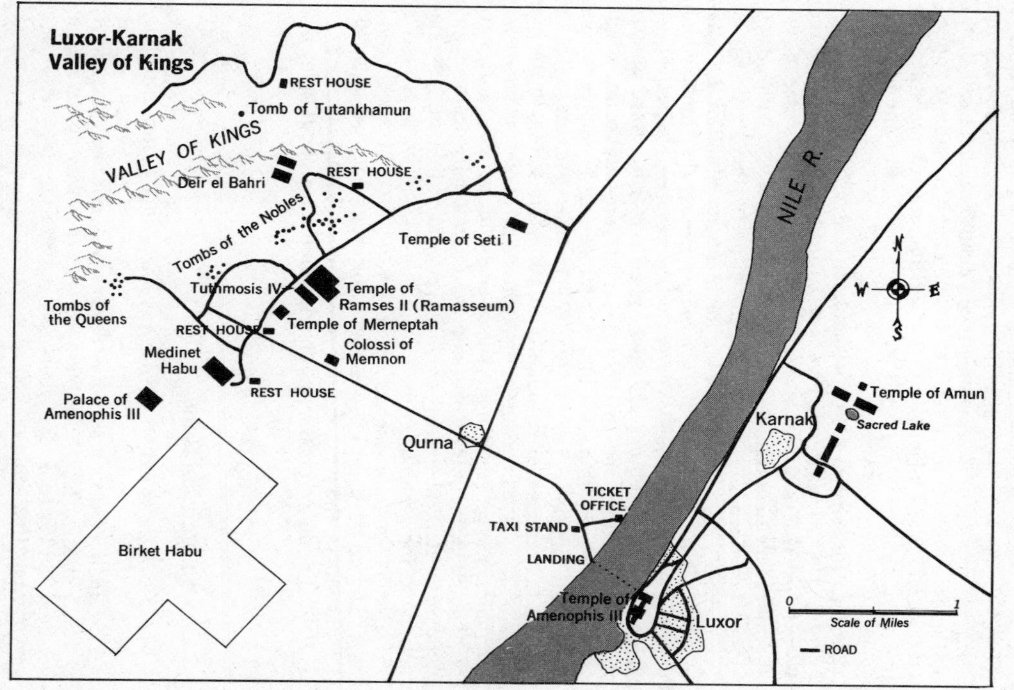
Luxor-Karnak
Valley of Kings
REST HOUSE
Tomb of Tutankhamun
VALLEY OF KINGS
Deir el Bahri
REST HOUSE
Tombs of the Nobles
Temple of Seti I
NILE R.
N
W
E
S
Tombs of the Queens
Tuthmosis IV
Temple of Ramses II (Ramasseum)
Temple of Merneptah
REST HOUSE
Colossi of Memnon
Medinet Habu
REST HOUSE
Palace of Amenophis III
Temple of Amun
Karnak
Sacred Lake
Qurna
TICKET OFFICE
TAXI STAND
Birket Habu
LANDING
Temple of Amenophis III
Luxor
0
1
Scale of Miles
ROAD

On the west bank of the Nile is the world-famed Valley of the Kings, the burial grounds of the great pharaohs of the Empire. In the cliffs nearby are the Tombs of the Nobles. The inside walls and ceiling of these tombs are painted with beautifully detailed scenes and inscriptions in colors so vivid they could have been applied yesterday. On the plain at the foot of the monuments stand the mortuary temples of Deir al Bahri, the Ramesseum and Medinet Habu.

A guide for the day at Luxor should cost about L.E. 15–20. On one's first visit a guide is necessary, especially for a visit to the West Bank. In Luxor, horse-drawn carriages are a popular means of conveyance to antiquity sites. A ride around town costs L.E. 1.

South of Karnak Temple, an excavation by the University of Pennsylvania has revealed the outline of a temple built by Akhenaten. Scholars, using computers to piece together the stones which have been found in other parts of the Karnak Temple bearing the likeness of the pharaoh and his queen, Nefertiti, were able to locate the temple and to reconstruct the position of its walls. Akhenaten is said to have built eight temples in Thebes before he moved his capital to Tell al Amarna. The new discovery was the first of his temples ever found, although stones from them had been found as it was common throughout the history of Egypt for the builders to reuse the materials of an earlier period. In the case of Akhenaten, the priests of Amon had intentionally destroyed his temples to Aten. Therefore, the discovery of any remains from this period are remarkable.

Luxor, A Guide to Ancient Thebes by Jill Kamel is an excellent paperback to have with you as a guide during your visit in Luxor, Karnak and on the west bank. It is available in local bookstores for L.E. 4. It contains good maps and descriptions without being academic.

Sites on the East Bank

Temple of Luxor: By the Nile, near the Luxor Hotel. Entrance: L.E. 2.

Less than a century ago, the Temple of Luxor was completely covered under a hill of rubble and hovels. It was discovered by accident, and it took two years to excavate the excellently preserved ruins that are now visible.

The original temple was built during the reign of Amenhotep III and was dedicated to the trinity of the Theban gods: Amen-Re, his wife Mut and their son Khonsu. From the North Gate an impres-

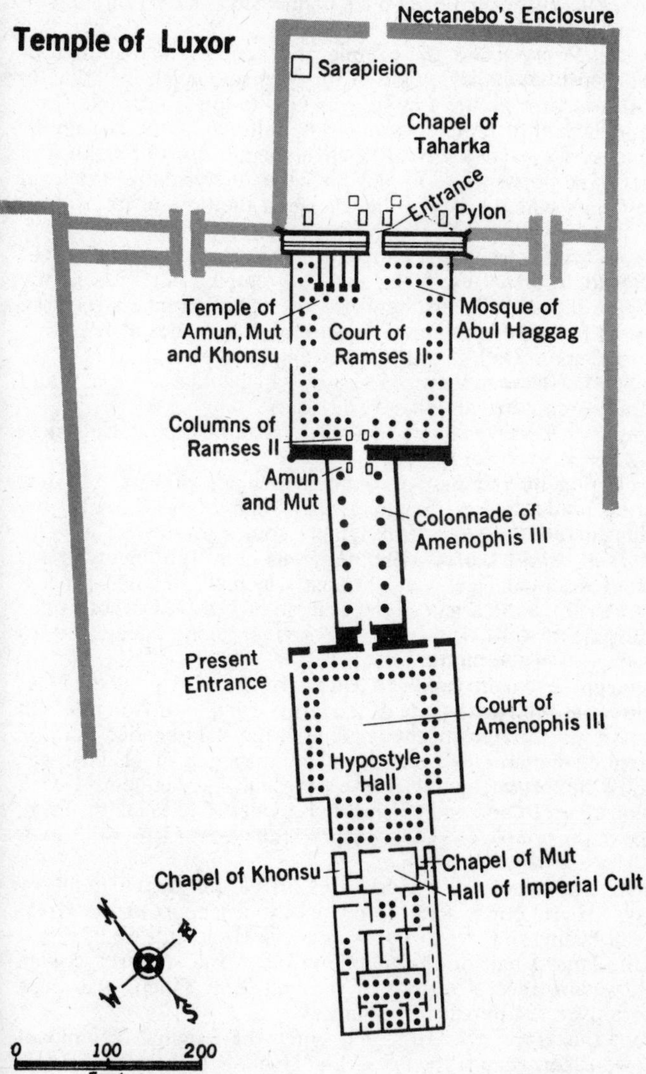
Temple of Luxor
Nectanebo's Enclosure
Sarapieion
Chapel of Taharka
Entrance
Pylon
Temple of Amun, Mut and Khonsu
Court of Ramses II
Mosque of Abul Haggag
Columns of Ramses II
Amun and Mut
Colonnade of Amenophis III
Present Entrance
Court of Amenophis III
Hypostyle Hall
Chapel of Khonsu
Chapel of Mut
Hall of Imperial Cult
N
E
W
S
0
100
200
Feet

sive Avenue of the Sphinxes once connected Luxor Temple with the Temple of Karnak.

Ramses II expanded the temple and added many statues of himself and two obelisks. One of the obelisks, given by Muhammad Ali to Louis Philippe in 1831, is now in the Place de la Concorde in Paris. The temple was also later altered by the Ptolemies.

Immediately inside the North Gate is the mosque of Sheikh Abu Haggag. The position of the mosque helps one visualize the level of the debris which covered the temple at the time of its excavation.

The best time to visit the temple is in the afternoon. The light of the afternoon sun softens the color of the temple's surface, and the reliefs are more easily distinguished. For photographers too, the colors are deeper and richer. A visit to the colonnades at full moon is also recommended. A tour of the Temple takes an hour. On the other hand, a detailed view of its many halls, columns, statues and inscriptions could easily fill several hours.

Temple of Karnak: About two miles north of Luxor. Entrance: L.E. 2.

Proceeding by the road through the village of Luxor, a few hundred yards before reaching the Temple of Karnak, the magnificent South Gate of the temple comes in view. The gate, which is in almost perfect condition, was built by Ptolemy III. It was the ceremonial gateway through which the festival processions passed from Karnak to the Temple of Luxor. On both sides of the gate a wall originally enclosed a temple dedicated to Khonsu, god of the moon.

If you proceed from Luxor to Karnak by the road along the Nile, you arrive at the North Gate of the Great Temple of Amen-Re. In front of it are the ruins of the Avenue of the Ram-headed Sphinx. The temple dedicted to Amen-Re, the patron god of Thebes, was the most important temple in the kingdom. Consequently, each pharaoh enlarged and embellished it as evidence of his faith. From the top of the temple entrance you get a full view of Karnak, Luxor and the west bank of the Nile.

Inside the temple of Amen-Re is an earlier temple built by Ramses III. Its construction predates the forecourt of the Great Temple. From the forecourt you enter the Hypostyle Hall, reputedly the largest hall of any temple in the world. Its area covers 50,000 square feet. The roof of the hall (now fallen) was once supported by 134 immense columns.

From the Hypostyle Hall you enter the original Temple of Amen-Re. Here stands the Obelisk of Queen Hatshepsut—97 feet tall, cut from one piece of pink Aswan granite. At the end of the

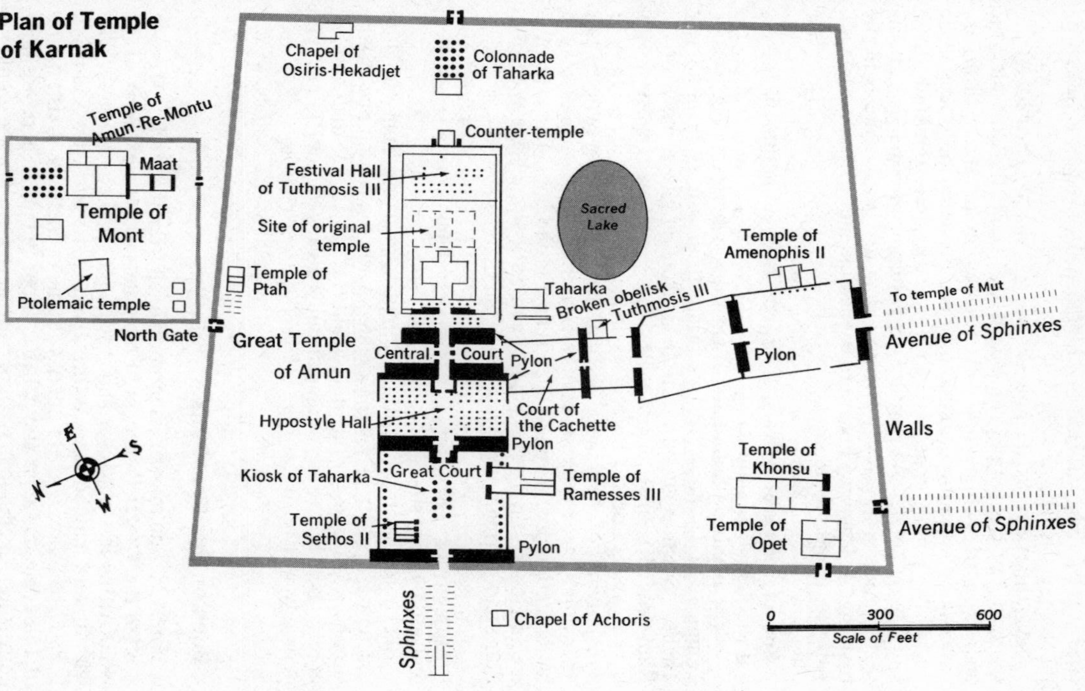
Plan of Temple of Karnak
Chapel of Osiris-Hekadjet
Colonnade of Taharka
Temple of Amun-Re-Montu
Maat
Temple of Mont
Ptolemaic temple
North Gate
Counter-temple
Festival Hall of Tuthmosis III
Site of original temple
Temple of Ptah
Sacred Lake
Temple of Amenophis II
Taharka
Broken obelisk Tuthmosis III
To temple of Mut
Avenue of Sphinxes
Great Temple of Amun
Central Court
Pylon
Pylon
Court of the Cachette
Hypostyle Hall
Pylon
Walls
Temple of Khonsu
Great Court
Kiosk of Taharka
Temple of Ramesses III
Avenue of Sphinxes
Temple of Sethos II
Temple of Opet
Pylon
E
S
N
W
Sphinxes
Chapel of Achoris
0
300
600
Scale of Feet

temple is the Festival Hall of Thutmose III, used as a church by the early Christians.

Near the Amen-Re Temple are several smaller shrines. At the south end of the temple complex is the Sacred Lake, which the ancients used in connection with religious ceremonies. At Karnak, extensive restoration of the temple has been and continues to be made. The temple may be reached by carriage in 20 minutes from any Luxor hotel. The carriage and waiting time fee is L.E. 1. (Settle price in advance.) The best time to visit the site is in the morning. At least two hours are needed but allow a full morning to view the temple in detail.

Son et Lumière at Karnak. Price: L.E. 4; hours: 6:30 P.M. winter, 7:30 P.M. summer.

Every evening a Sound and Light show is performed at Karnak Temple. The 1½ hour program brings to life the story of ancient Thebes. Starting at the entrance in front of the Avenue of the Ram-headed Sphinx, guests walk along the Great Hypostyle Hall to the Central Court, while voices and lights play on the great walls and drawings of the temple. Then at the Sacred Lake (where seats are available) the program continues with an impressive display of lights on the monuments, which reflect in the pool. Performances are in English on Tues., Thurs., and Sat.; French on Wed. and Sun.; and German and Arabic on Thurs.

Museum of Luxor, L.E. 2; hours: 4:00–9:00 P.M. winter; 5:00–10:00 P.M. summer.

Between Luxor and Karnak Temples, near the Etap Hotel, is the new Museum of Luxor created with the assistance of the Brooklyn Museum for the municipality. It has only a small number of displays, but these are beautifully arranged and lighted and definitely worth a visit.

Sites on the West Bank

For 25 pt. you may ride a motor launch from the landing stage in front of the Winter Palace and Etap hotels to the west bank of the Nile. At the landing stage and rest house on the west bank, cars with drivers may be hired to drive you to the sites. Cost is about L.E. 12 half day; L.E. 15 full day. Some of the large taxis hold up to 10 people and cost about L.E. 10 per person. There are donkeys, too, for about L.E. 1 per hr. plus a tip for the donkey's owner. Hearty visitors can make the excursions on bicycles, but distances between the sites are too great to attempt the excursions on foot. Cars drive over a good asphalt road, well marked with direction signs. Visitors usually go first to the Valley of the Kings where a rest house is located.

Our favorite driver is Gahlan Hassan Ahmed, taxi driver No. 94. You can contact him in advance by writing to him in Luxor, West Side, El Qorna. Give him the date of your arrival and the hotel where you will be staying.

In recent years, sightseeing on the west bank has been greatly facilitated. Nonetheless, it is very tiring. Be prepared to do a great deal of climbing, especially up and down stairs inside the tombs. Do not try to do it all in one day. There is too much to see. Furthermore, if you see too much at one time, it will begin to blur and you will not enjoy any of it.

Tombs of the Kings: In the Valley of the Kings at the extreme west of the necropolis. Entrance: L.E. 3.

Sixty-four pharaohs' tombs have been found in the Valley of the Kings. The safest and most interesting are open to the public. Only the best preserved or those with the most interesting and elaborate wall paintings are described here, and are listed in their order of priority.

If you are not in the company of a guide, you should tip the gatekeeper at each tomb about 25 or 30 pts. and ask him to use his aluminum paper reflector to illuminate the drawings inside the tombs. A battery flashlight is also very useful.

Tomb 17: Seti I (XIX Dynasty, 13th century B.C.).

Many experts consider Seti's tomb to be the most interesting one in the necropolis. It is the largest and certainly the most impressive. The wall decorations begin at the entrance and continue all the way to the bottom of the tomb. The drawings and reliefs are exquisite and in excellent condition.

Note especially the drawing of the kneeling Isis with outstretched winged arms, and one of Seti I in the presence of the gods Osiris, Isis, Horus and Nephtys. An important feature of this tomb is the zodiac on the ceiling of the inner chamber.

Tomb 283: Tutankhamun (XVIII Dynasty, 14th century B.C.). Separate entrance fee: L.E. 2.

The tomb is the first one on your right after the entrance to the Valley of the Kings. It is the only one so far discovered which escaped the tomb robbers of ancient times. The chambers are small in comparison to other tombs, but the colors of the fine drawings are remarkably well preserved.

The golden mummy of King Tut lies *in situ* encased in the middle of the three coffins which originally held the mummy. You should take time to examine carefully the detail work on this world-famous masterpiece.

Tomb 35: Amenhotep (Amenophis II, XVIII Dynasty, 15th century B.C.).

The tomb is called the Tomb of Safety because several coffins, moved there by the high priests for safekeeping against the tomb robbers, were found in it. The wall drawings are completely different from those in the tombs of Seti I and Tutankhamun. Note especially the painting of the goddess Isis kneeling on the emblem of gold, asking the god Gheb to protect the dead king.

Tomb 9: Ramses VI (XX Dynasty, 12th century B.C.).

The excellent wall drawings, especially on the ceiling and sidewalls of the last chamber, are an interesting variation from the other tombs.

Tomb 33: Haremheb (XIX Dynasty, 14th century B.C.).

In the small room of the inner chamber the colors of the drawings are excellent, but some are unfinished. Visit the tomb only if you have plenty of time.

Tomb 34: Thutmose III (XVIII Dynasty, 15th century B.C.).

The climb up to the tomb is very steep and the descent into it is long. Further, you need an explanation of the line drawings, or some knowledge of hieroglyphics, to appreciate them. There are no painted drawings like those in other tombs, and parts appear to be unfinished. The tomb is listed by many experts as one of the major ones in the necropolis, but for a novice it is hardly worth a visit.

Tomb 11: Ramses III (XX Dynasty, 13th century B.C.).

The drawings are badly damaged and smoked. Visit it if your time permits. Only about half of the tomb is lighted and accessible to visitors.

Tombs of the Queen and Princes: In the Valley of the Queens at the extreme south of the necropolis. Entrance: L.E. 1.

More than 57 tombs have been discovered in the Valley of the Queens, but very few are open and only two are worth a visit. No. 66, the tomb of Nefertari (wife of Ramses II), is the most outstanding tomb in all Egypt for its art-work. Unfortunately, it is considered unsafe and can be visited only by special permission.

Tomb 55: Prince Amenherkhepshef (son of Ramses III).

The wall paintings are quite different from those in other tombs, as pastel colors were used. The well-preserved decorations are definitely worth examining. Note the drawing of Ramses III leading the goddess Isis by the hand, and another of the king introducing his son to the god Ptah.

Tomb 52: Queen Thyti (Tyti, c. XX Dynasty).

Parts of the drawings in the tomb are in bad condition, but you should visit it if you have time. Queen Thyti was the wife of one of the Ramseses.

Tombs of the Nobles: In various groups along the edge of the desert. Entrance: L.E. 1 for each group. Visitors are allowed to photograph; flash attachment required.

The private tombs of the priests and nobles in the courts of the pharaohs are famous for their fine wall decorations and drawings, which depict scenes from the daily life of the ancient Egyptians. The nobles' tombs are very small in comparison to those of the kings. After viewing the wall drawings in the Valley of Kings, those in the nobles' tombs appear as miniatures. The important tombs are located in the hills between the Ramesseum, Deir al Medinah and the Temple of Hatshepsut. The best belong to the XVIII Dynasty between the 15th and 14th centuries B.C.

It is from these drawings that Egyptologists and historians have been able to piece together much of the information found in popular writing on the daily life of the ancient Egyptians, their government, customs and beliefs.

Tomb 52: Nakht, Scribe of the Granaries.

In this tomb is the famous drawing of the dancing girls (located on the left after entering). The banquet scenes are especially good. Note the detail in the drawing of the three seated ladies, one of whom is smelling a lotus blossom. The details of the hunting scene with Nakht are also lovely (located on the wall right of the entrance). The drawings in this tomb are among the most frequently reproduced ones in art books on ancient Egypt.

Tomb 55: Ramose, viser or prime minister of Ikhnaton.

Although the tomb is damaged, it has some of the most beautiful drawings from antiquity and is definitely worth a visit. On the right and left walls immediately upon entering are the reliefs of Ramose and his wife. These are exquisite: be sure to study the detail. On the left wall, the upper panel is one of the most famous murals in ancient Egyptian art and the only painted one in this tomb. It shows the funeral procession and the wailing women, carrying the mummy of Ramose to the tomb. On the back wall on the right side are the badly damaged remains of the symbol of Aten, created during the time of Ikhnaton, which is the sun disc with rays that end in cupped hands.

Tomb 69: Menna, Chief of the King's Estate.

The details of the hunting scene, especially the beautiful birds, should be noted. The harvest scenes are interesting. In the first row, the land is being measured; in the second, the quantity of grain is being recorded; and in the third, grain is being harvested.

On the back wall there is a well-preserved drawing of the scale of balance, weighing the heart against a feather, to judge the truth of the deceased's account of his life before Osiris.

Tomb 96: Sennefer, Prince of Thebes, Superintendent of the Granaries and Cattle of Amon (under Amenhotep II).

This is one of the best of the nobles' tombs. The ceiling decoration and formation are meant to represent grapevines. Be sure to visit this tomb, even though you will need to climb down many steep stairs. The tomb has two rooms and some of the best preserved drawings in the necropolis, although the quality is inferior to others.

Tomb 100: Rekhmire, minister of Queen Hatshepsut.

The tomb has good drawings of the daily life.

Other Tombs. *Tomb 1* (also listed as No. 36 in some references): Sennezen (Sennutem), minister to Tutankhamen.

Located near the French Archeological Expedition. Guides will not take visitors here unless requested to do so. This tomb is small, but from my experience it has the best preserved drawings in all the west bank. The tomb must have escaped the centuries of robbers, religious fanatics and curiosity seekers because none of the drawings are damaged and the colors are so bright and fresh they could have been applied this morning. The walls are covered on all sides with drawings, as is the ceiling. Note especially the panel of Anubis, god of embalming, preparing the mummy; another complete panel at one end describes paradise. All the panels are wonderful, and photographers, particularly, will have a field day.

Tomb 359: Mennakhouey.

Located near the tomb of Sennezen. The tomb is small and so are the drawings, but they are very good and unusual, although parts are badly damaged.

The Temples. *Deir al-Bahri:* At the foot of the Theban Hills. Entrance: L.E. 2.

The mortuary temple built by Queen Hatshepsut (XVIII Dynasty, 15th century B.C.) is one of the most handsome monuments in Egypt. It is often pictured in books on Egyptian antiquities. Its plan—terraced and colonnaded—is unusual in ancient Egyptian architecture. Its location at the foot of towering cliffs enhances its majesty.

Upon the death of the powerful Queen Hatshepsut, her nephew and stepson, Thutmose III, attempted to obliterate all traces of her. As a consequence, many of the wall drawings at Deir al-Bahri were destroyed. The chapel dedicated to the goddess Hathor is the best preserved section of the temple. You should allow yourself an hour to view it.

Ramesseum: South of the Valley of the Kings. Entrance: L.E. 1.

A mortuary temple built by Ramses II (XIX Dynasty, 13th century B.C.), this is one of the largest temples in Egypt. At the front on the east is the fallen head of Ramses' statue—the largest in Egypt, cut from a solid piece of stone. You should allow one or two hours to view the temple adequately. The colonnaded courts and wall drawings deserve close attention. The caretaker of the temple is very knowledgeable and can explain the drawings on the walls, the statues, etc. It is worth taking the time to study these carefully as they will help you to understand similar carvings in other temples in Upper Egypt.

Medinet Habu: South of the Valley of the Kings. Entrance: L.E. 2.

A mortuary temple built by Ramses III (XX Dynasty, 12th century B.C.), this is one of the most colossal monuments in the world and is considered second only to Karnak in architectural importance. The well-preserved temple is actually a complex of four temples—two built by Ramses III, one by Amenhotep I, and another by Queen Amenartas (700 B.C.).

From the top of the front pylon on the right, ascending by the original stairway, you get a magnificent view of Luxor and the Nile Valley. Throughout the temple the wall drawings are good and deserve careful attention. To view the temple complex thoroughly, you need half a day.

Deir el-Medineh: South of the Valley of the Kings. Entrance: L.E. 1.

A temple dedicated to the goddesses Hathor and Maat, built by Ptolemy IV about 210 B.C. As it is similar but inferior to other Ptolemaic temples in Upper Egypt, you should plan to visit it only if you have ample time.

Colossi of Memnon: South of the Valley of the Kings.

Twin statues representing Amenhotep III in the classical sitting position are located on the edge of the desert, facing the Nile. Each statue is 64 ft. in height. They apparently formed the entrance to a temple complex that no longer exists. In ancient times many legends were created about the statues because of a sound which was said to emanate from them each dawn.

Temple of Seti I: Located on the left of the road en route to the Valley of the Kings. Entrance: L.E.1.

By comparison with other temples in the vicinity, the ruins and reliefs are in bad condition. Only if you are spending a week at Luxor would you find it worth a visit.

HOTELS IN LUXOR. Akhenaton (Bella Donna), on the Nile south of town, 144 rooms. Booked as tour through Club Med. One night is L.E. 39 with dinner, show and breakfast; full board L.E. 62. Non-guests may have lunch and use swimming facilities, L.E. 10, or dinner and show, L.E. 15. Phone: 777575. Attractive four-star hotel operated by Club Mediterranee opened last year. Rooms on two floors are grouped around swimming pool and central courtyard in the style of a caravanserai. Accepts individual bookings when not fully booked by Club Med tours.

Beau Soleil, on south edge of town, 22 rooms. L.E. 11.50 dwb.

New, small, very simple, clean. No elevator; all rooms with bath, but shower only; restaurant; air conditioning extra. L.E. 1.50.

Etap Luxor, on the Nile, 188 rooms. L.E. 32.20 swb; L.E. 37.15 dwb. The lovely hotel opened in 1977 and is managed by Etap, the French company owned by Wagon-Lits. It is air conditioned, and has a swimming pool and garden, coffee shop, bank and telex facilities. The larger public rooms are richly decorated with marble and wood—more elaborate than one would expect from its exterior. Guest rooms are attractive and very comfortable. All have bath & a/c. The dining room has one seating with a fixed and a la carte menu. There is a bar, discotheque and shopping arcade.

Isis, on Nile south of town, 256 rooms. L.E. 26 swb; L.E. 29 dwb. Phone: 749381; 82750. A four-star, modern hotel, opened in 1981. Rooms simple, nicely furnished, but maintenance appears to be poor. Rooms have air conditioning, phone, radio, balcony overlooking river. Swimming pool (heated in winter), tennis, bus service to town, hair salon, shop, exchange facilities. Dining room, Swiss restaurant, poolside snacks; bar, nightclub; room service.

Luxor, opposite the Temple of Luxor, 86 rooms. L.E. 22 dwb.

Mina Palace, on Nile in town. L.E. 14 swb; 15 dwb. Small, modest three-star hotel, appears to be well run; reports are good. Air conditioning, restaurant, bar.

Movenpick Hotel Jolie Ville Luxor, situated on Crocodile Island, about 2.5 miles from Luxor. 350 rooms. L.E. 50 swb; L.E. 70 dwb with half-board, service and taxes. Single story bungalows in a garden setting. All rooms have air conditioning, mini-bar, phone, bath/shower, and terrace. Two restaurants, bar and garden snack bar. Tennis, pool, and jogging.

Ramoza, located in town, 48 rooms. L.E. 14 swb; L.E. 15 dwb with breakfast. Phone: 82270. All with air conditioning, phone; baths with shower only. Roof garden, bar, and restaurant with music.

Santa Maria, on edge of town, 24 rooms. L.E. 13 swb; L.E. 14 dwb. Air-conditioned rooms with bathroom, showers only, phone; restaurant, bar.

Savoy Hotel, El Nil Street, 246 rooms. L.E. 13 swb; L.E. 14 dwb. Tourist-class. Set in nice garden. Rooms and furnishings adequate.

Winter Palace, El Nil Street, by the Nile, 268 rooms. L.E. 31 swb; L.E. 34 dwb. A grand hotel of 19th century charm and elegance, surrounded by beautiful and extensive gardens. The newer part of the building, adjacent to the old Winter Palace, is modern. The large rooms have a view of either the

Nile or the gardens. The hotel is air-conditioned and open all year. There is a swimming pool.

Several hotel chains have announced their intention to build here in Luxor. These include a 300-room Sheraton, 350-room Marriott, and a 250-room Hilton to be built near Karnak Temple. It will have extensive recreational facilities and private dock and is scheduled to be completed in 1984.

On the West Bank, there are three hotels. None can be recommended unless you are ready to accept very basic accommodations and share bath facilities. *Habou Hotel* in Qorna can house up to 50 people.

SHOPPING. Shops in and near hotels have the usual array of Egyptian crafts. Luxor is best place to buy inexpensive cotton kaftans. *A. A. Gaddis* in Winter Palace shopping arcade and *Oriental Jewellers* are long-established stores, but shop around before you buy and bargain hard. Kaftans cost L.E. 12–40 depending on quality of fabric and design.

RESTAURANTS. *Chez Farouk,* on the Nile, has fresh fish; otherwise, only hotel restaurants are recommended.

Sites Near Luxor

Nile steamers which cruise between Luxor and Aswan stop at sites mentioned below, enabling passengers to visit the monuments. Or you may travel by train from Luxor or Aswan to towns near the ancient sites. From the train station, you either walk, ride a donkey or hire a carriage, car or boat to the site as the situation requires. Another way to go is to hire a car in Luxor or Aswan for the journey between the two points. This works very well for a party of two or more, but for only one person it can be expensive. Should you hire a car for a day's excursion, be sure to take along a box lunch.

An alternative is by motorcoach from Cairo to Luxor, taken in two 200-mile sectors, or about 200 miles per day. This allows travelers to visit the site of Tell al Amarna near Minya, Assuit and Abydos, among the most interesting in Upper Egypt but less visited because of the difficulty of access. Fortunately, most of the longer (but more costly) tours now offered by U.S. operators include several of these sites, especially Denderah and Abydos.

North of Luxor

Denderah: 40 miles north of Luxor at Qena. Entrance fee: L.E. 2.

The train ride from Luxor to Qena (Keneh) is about one-and-a-half hours. A half-hour carriage ride from the station takes you to the river where you cross the Nile by bridge to the west bank. From there you ride a donkey or walk to the site in a half hour.

Nile steamers stop on the west bank near the site, and waiting buses take passengers to the temple in 5 minutes, or it is a pleasant 20-minute walk along a country road where one may have a close-up glimpse of rural life. By car or motorcoach from Luxor to Qena is one hour. Here one crosses a bridge for a short drive to the site.

Denderah was the capital of the sixth district of Upper Egypt under the Ptolemies. Here you may visit the Temple of Hathor, one of the best preserved monuments in Egypt, built in the 1st Century B.C. near the end of the Ptolemaic rule. The temple was dedicated to Hathor, goddess of heaven, joy and love, and patron deity of Denderah. It took about a hundred years to build, and some parts were never completed.

The temple is elaborately decorated, although the reliefs are not as fine as Egyptian art of earlier periods. Many of the drawings were defaced by early Christian and Moslem zealots.

On the roof of the temple are two chapels, one of which contains a reproduction of the zodiac (the original is in the Louvre). On the back wall are drawings of the last and most famous Queen Cleopatra (there were seven Cleopatras in ancient Egyptian history). From the side of the main chambers, steps lead to the crypts below. The drawings in the lower chambers are better preserved than those on the upper floors. The mud brick wall surrounding the temple also dates from the 1st century B.C. Be sure to climb the stairs to the roof to enjoy the view of the Nile Valley.

Abydos: 90 miles north of Luxor at Balianeh. Entrance: L.E. 1.

From Luxor, you can take a modern motorcoach or the early morning train. The latter arrives at Balianeh about 11:00 A.M. You can return by evening train, reaching Luxor about 10:30 P.M. The temple lies seven miles west of the Nile. Donkeys, carriages and early vintage autos are available to take you to the site. Another way is to hire a car for the day in Luxor and drive to Balianeh. It is a pleasant trip over a good road and takes three hours. The trip will cost at least L.E. 30 to L.E. 40. Nile steamers from Luxor on long itineraries stop on the second day at Nag Hamadi, 19 miles south of Balianeh, from where visitors proceed by bus to the site (an hour's drive). The road from Luxor along the west side of the Nile crosses by bridge at Nag Hamadi to the east side. This bridge has locks on the east side, which are opened twice daily—morning and afternoon—to allow the river traffic to pass through. From the bridge to the temples is about a 40 minute drive. There is also a good road along the east bank, but it is desolate as it passes through the desert rather than the valley.

For centuries Abydos was a place of pilgrimage; the tomb of Osiris was supposedly located in the area. Abydos is situated on the site of the ancient city of This (Thinis), which was one of the earliest settlements of man in the Nile Valley. Tombs of the Pharaohs from the first Dynasty have been discovered here.

The most important monument here is the Temple of Seti I, built on the site of an earlier temple. It was later enlarged and completed by Ramses II, son of Seti I. The Temple of Seti I, dedicated to Osiris, is considered one of the most important monuments in Egypt for its art work. The art of Egypt during this period reached its peak and is unequalled for its beauty and delicacy. You should allow yourself enough time to examine carefully the wall drawings and reliefs; they are truly magnificent. It contains seven sanctuaries, each dedicated to a different god. Around the wall of the first hall a border of symbols represent the 42 provinces of ancient Egypt.

The most important feature in the temple is the group of some seventy cartouches of the pharaohs of Egypt arranged in chronological order. Upon discovery of these cartouches, Egyptologists, correlating them with information from other sources, established a definite timetable of the ancient dynasties for the first time.

Unfortunately, the location of Abydos is not convenient for the modern traveler. Nonetheless, a visit is very rewarding. Many experts consider the temple to be the most outstanding in all Egypt. A short distance from the ruins is a new restaurant, *Abydos Tourist Rest House,* which offers sheikh kabab and simple meals.

South of Luxor

All the Nile steamers for tourists that sail between Luxor and Aswan or vice versa stop at the locations described below. The journey takes three nights/four days and is sold as a four-night/five-day package. An alternate method, which is rapidly growing in popularity, is to travel by car or motorcoach the 250 miles between Luxor and Aswan. It is a long and tiring trip, but it enables one to see more of the village life of Nubia and to take in other lesser known sites. The journey by car takes approximately four hours.

Esna: 30 miles south of Luxor. Entrance: L.E. 1.

By car from Luxor the drive takes less than an hour. By early morning train, you arrive at Esna in about one hour. The temple is small and may be seen in 30 minutes, enabling you to return to Luxor by the morning train. By steamer departure from Luxor will probably be late at night, arriving early the next morning at Esna.

The Temple of Khnum is Ptolemaic in origin. From other evidence, however, it appears an earlier temple was constructed by Thutmose III (1500 B.C.) on the same site. Work on the Ptolemaic temple probably began about 180 B.C. and ended in 250 A.D., as the Emperor Decius is mentioned in a relief. The drawings in this temple were the latest representations of a pharaoh found in Egypt. The temple is well preserved and restored.

Edfu (Idfu): 70 miles south of Luxor, about halfway to Aswan on the west bank. Entrance: L.E. 2.

The morning train from Luxor arrives in Edfu about 10:00 A.M., and you may return on the afternoon train to Luxor. The steamers from Luxor stop here on the second day.

The ancient Greeks called the site Apollonopolis, after Apollo (or Horus), whose representation here is in the form of an eagle. The Temple of Horus is practically intact and is one of the finest examples of Ptolemaic art in Egypt. Its foundation was laid in 237 B.C. under the reign of Ptolemy III, but the temple was not completed until two centuries later.

On the side walls of the stairway to the roof are fine representations of the ceremonial procession of New Year's Day.

Kom Ombo: About 105 miles south of Luxor and 30 miles north of Aswan. Entrance: L.E. 1.

By train the one hour trip is usually made from Aswan. From Luxor, the trip by road is long and duration will depend upon how much time is spent in Esna and Edfu.

Kom Ombo is situated on a hill overlooking the Nile at a point where the river makes a wide bend to the west. In ancient times it was a strategic location on the desert route to Nubia and Ethiopia.

The principal deities of the ancient town were Harwar, a hawk-headed god, and Sobek, represented in the form of a crocodile. The Temple of Kom Ombo is dedicated to the two deities and is unlike any other monument in Egypt. To avoid offending either god, a twin temple was constructed, the left half dedicated to Hathor, the right half to Sobek. Although only the bases of the columns and the back walls remain, the temple's majestic proportions and grace are impressive. The fine reliefs throughout the temple are worth your careful attention. At the side of the temple is a small sanctuary containing dozens of mummified crocodiles.

ASWAN

From its beginning, Aswan, located 534 miles south of Cairo, was the gateway to the south and the trade route from Egypt to Central Africa. Today, it combines the Oriental and African influences of its history.

Before construction on the new Aswan Dam began, the population of Aswan was about 50,000. Today its numbers have swollen to 500,000. If you have time, stroll through the town. Along the way you may stop in a carpet weaving shop to watch the owner and his small boys at work. This craft is performed similarly in hundreds of villages on the Nile in Upper Egypt. The market, too, is lively. It is one street in from the main street along the Nile.

By train and steamer you arrive in Aswan on the east side of the Nile. By plane you land at the airport on the west side of the river, and cross from east to west by a road over the Dam. The major hotels, travel offices and shops are located on the east side.

If you are not careful, Aswan cabdrivers will overcharge you. Settle the price before you start out. Quoted fares are for the taxi ride, no matter whether there are one or five passengers.

If time allows, a sail in a felucca (feluka) around the islands at Aswan is delightful. Boats can be hired at the landing dock by the Cataract Hotel or the docking stations of the Nile steamers in town, and cost about L.E. 5 for a sail around the island. Some feluccas hold up to 20 people; the price has to be negotiated, depending on the number. Stops can be made at Kitchener's Island to visit the Botanical Gardens, and at the foot of the Aga Khan's Mausoleum, which is open to visitors. The walk up to the hilltop where the tomb is located takes about 10–15 minutes. There are donkeys and camels for those who prefer to ride. The trip around the islands takes about two hours—depending upon the wind, of course.

A felucca ride or cruise is often included in the sightseeing tour of Aswan on packaged tours. It should not be confused with the Nile cruise by steamer, which is an entirely different matter.

Sightseeing in Aswan

Aswan has long been a favorite winter resort because of its dry climate and beautiful location. The late Aga Khan maintained a villa in Aswan and asked to be buried there upon his death. His handsome mausoleum facing the Minarets of Bilal stands out on a hill behind his villa. His widow continues to winter at the villa.

In the desert behind the Aga Khan's mausoleum are the ruins of the Monastery of St. Simon, built by Coptic monks in the 6th century A.D. It is one of the largest and best preserved Coptic buildings in existence.

From a hilltop on the west bank of the Nile, you get an excellent view of the old Aswan Dam, completed in 1902, the lovely landscape around Aswan, and the graceful white sails of feluccas on the Nile carrying visitors to Kitchener's Island and Elephantine Island, the ancient frontier fortress of Egypt. Elephantine Island also has an interesting museum and ancient tombs of the princesses of Aswan. Kitchener's Island, so named because it was presented to Lord Kitchener when he was Consul-General in Egypt, has botanical gardens created by him, with exotic plants from all over the Middle and Far East. (Another good view is from the top floor of the Oberoi Hotel.)

On the east bank of the Nile south of Aswan are the granite quarries where stones were cut for use in ancient monuments throughout Egypt. You should visit the quarries to see the partially completed giant obelisk. This will help you appreciate the colossal task that was involved in transporting the granite from Aswan to Luxor and even to Baalbek in Lebanon. There is an unfinished one, *in situ,* which measures 125 feet in length and is estimated to weigh 1,170 tons.

On the west bank of the Nile overlooking the new High Dam is the reconstructed Temple of Kalabsha. Entrance fee: L.E. 2. In 1962–63, a German group dismantled the structure at its original site and moved it to its present location in order to save the temple from future inundation. The work has been done so well that only a trained eye can detect the reconstruction.

The Temple, one of the best examples of Egyptian art from the Roman period, was devoted to the Nubian god Mandulis. It is the second largest standing temple in Nubia after Philae. The temple is near the airport road about 11 miles from the Cataract Hotel.

The Kiosk of Qertassi: A small Roman temple with many Greek inscriptions. It resembles Trajan's Kiosk on the island of Philae.

The Tombs of the Nobles: Tombs carved in the cliff's face on the west bank of the Nile are opposite the northern tip of the island of Elephantine. These tombs were constructed by nobles and princes of the region about 2300 B.C. Important among them are the tombs of Mekhu, Si-Renpowet, Pepi-Nakht and Khuf Har.

Temple of Isis: South of town. This temple was the work of Ptolemy III and Ptolemy IV but was not completed.

The High Dam: Building projects of great magnitude—the Pyramids, the Suez Canal and now the Aswan Dam—have been milestones in Egyptian history. All gained international attention, but to present-day Egyptians the new High Dam at Aswan represents the most important undertaking in their history.

Every year since ancient times, the flooding of the Nile has been the Egyptians' main concern. The necessity to cope with the inundation led the ancient Egyptians to acquire mathematical, astronomical and engineering knowledge far in advance of other civilizations. Planning for the lean years during the years of plenty established law and order. This continuity of purpose for 6,000 years of Egypt's history is unique among nations. Now, with the building of the High Dam, the unpredictable behavior of the Nile is a thing of the past.

The new dam is located four miles south of the old one at

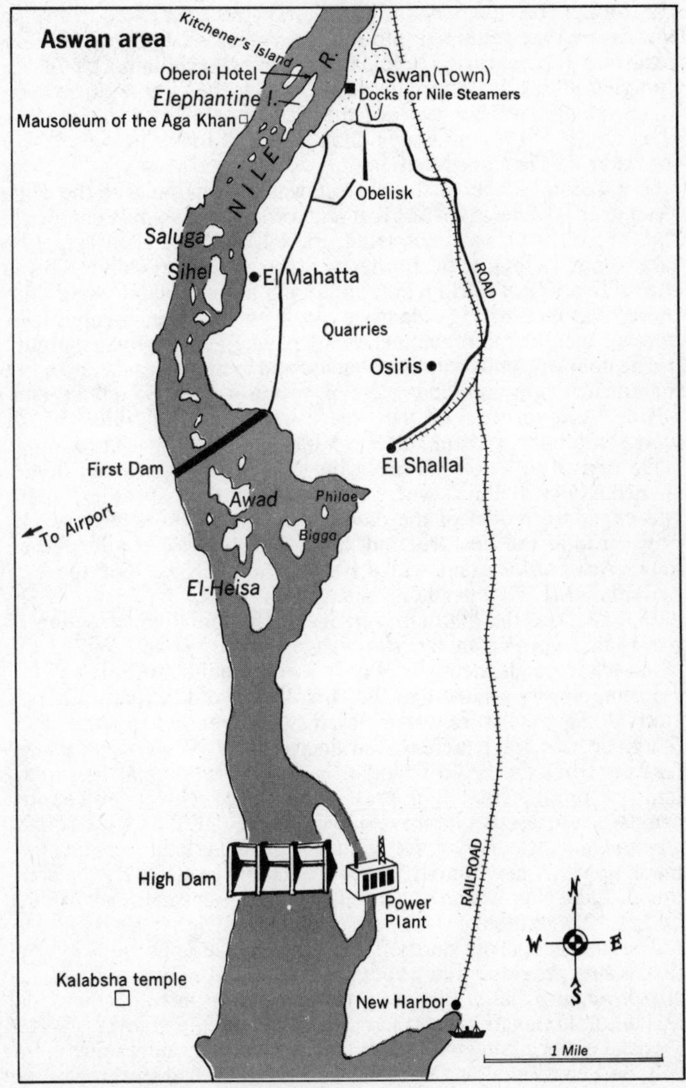
Aswan area
Kitchener's Island
Oberoi Hotel
Elephantine I.
Mausoleum of the Aga Khan
NILE R.
Aswan (Town)
Docks for Nile Steamers
Obelisk
Saluga
Sihel
El Mahatta
ROAD
Quarries
Osiris
First Dam
El Shallal
Awad
Philae
Bigga
To Airport
El-Heisa
High Dam
Power Plant
RAILROAD
N
W
E
S
Kalabsha temple
New Harbor
1 Mile

Aswan. In the first stage of construction, a diversion channel was cut through the east bank of the Nile. The rock removed in cutting the channel was dumped into the main riverbed to form a cofferdam and to create the foundation of the new dam. Upon the completion of this cofferdam in May 1964, the course of the Nile River was altered by man for the first time in history. Now the river spills into the diversion channel and through tunnels where its water can be controlled.

The second stage of the project was the building of the High Dam itself to a height of 364 feet and a width of two miles across at the top. When it was completed, the billion-dollar dam created a lake 300 miles long to the border of Sudan. Its waters have allowed the cultivation of two million additional acres of land—one-third more than in 1965. The dam's hydro-electric plant, located halfway up the diversion channel, has tripled Egypt's power output.

The dam was built with Russian aid and technical assistance, but the construction and labor were Egyptian—about 35,000 in manpower. As one watched the orderly movement of thousands of workers, a similar scene at Giza 5,000 years ago sprang to mind.

On arrival at the dam site, you should go first to the dome-shaped exhibit building where competent English-speaking guides will explain a model of the dam, maps and pictures. Afterward, drive around the construction site. A hurried look will take an hour. Any Aswan taxi will drive you to the site. Set the fare beforehand. L.E. 3 per hour is adequate.

1980 marked the 20th anniversary of the initial construction of the High Dam. From the start it was controversial. Would the benefits outweigh the cost? What were the hidden problems?

Its supporters argued that the High Dam would expand Egypt's cultivated area, ensure water for irrigation even in the years when the river was low, increase productivity by converting 700,000 feddans from the basin irrigation system to perennial irrigation, improve productivity by improving drainage, protect the country against high floods, improve navigation conditions year-round, generate electric power for industrial and agricultural development, spawn a new tourist area and a fishing industry by the creation of Lake Nasser and increase the annual gross national product by L.E. 234 million.

The jury is still out on the High Dam. There is no question but that is has provided new productive land and new power. It has also brought a batch of new problems—many are technical and agricultural ones to which there are no immediate answers. Water seepage undermining buildings and foundations, salt residue in the soil, and erosion along the Nile banks, which had in the past received new layers of top soil annually from the mud carried by the river, are already creating problems at an alarming rate.

The Temple of Philae, on an island situated between the old and the new dams, is the most interesting of Aswan's antiquities. Most of the temple was under water except during the flood months from August to December when the old dam was open. When the dam was closed, only the cornices of the two pylons were visible.

With the building of the new dam, provision was made to save the temple by dismantling, crating and moving it to another location where it has been reassembled. Here, it is free from inundation and visible year-round. The rescue operation took three years.

The oldest part of the Philae Temple dates from the XXX Dynasty (4th century B.C.); the rest was completed during the Ptolemaic and Roman periods. The goddess Isis reigned here, and her cult continued to be followed even after Christianity had become the official religion of the Roman Empire.

Philae has several important temples. The largest was built by Nectanebo I, for the worship of Isis and her son Horus. This temple was renovated by Ptolemy II.

The approach is made by an outer courtyard, flanked by western and eastern colonnades, each of whose 26 columns has a different design, topped with a distinctive capital. The columns combine pharaonic, Greek and Roman motifs, revealing how much the cultures had, by this time, become mingled. Behind the eastern colonnade is the *Temple of Imhotep*.

The *Outer Court* leads up to steps flanked by two lions carved out of granite, and to the terrace of the First Pylon. On the walls, drawings show the ruler offering sacrifices to the gods Isis, Osiris, Khum and others. In the temple's old location, when the waters were highest only the top portion of the pylon was visible. Water marks left by centuries of inundation are clearly distinguishable. An entranceway known as the *Portal of Nectanebos* leads to the forecourt of the temple and to the back pylon, which is the entrance to the *Temple of Isis*. At the back was the Holy of Holies, and a small chamber on the right, marked by a Greek cross, was at one time used as a church. There are other Christian drawings covering the ancient inscriptions.

West of the Isis Temple stands *Hadrian's Gate* and the *Temple of Harendotes,* and at the very north end of the complex, the *Temple of Augustus*.

About 50 yards east of the large temple lies the *Temple of Hathor*. On one of the pillars, there is a drawing of a fluteplayer with Bes, the god of happiness, playing the lute and dancing.

The building that has come to symbolize the island is Trajan's Kiosk of 14 pillars. It is among the most beautiful relics on the island.

There was considerable disagreement among scholars as to whether or not Philae should have been preserved, as it never ranked high on the list of artistic achievements of the ancient Egyptians. Indeed, its construction was long after the period of decline had begun. But there has always been a sentimentality attached to the temple, perhaps because of its dedication to Isis; others would say because of its location. The architecture and drawings represent a fusion of three great civilizations: Egyptian, Greek and Roman.

Plans are underway for installing a Son et Lumière show at the island. To reach Philae, one still must take a boat from a landing stage on the east bank at Shellal, several miles south of the old dam. Entrance tickets, L.E. 3, should be purchased at the booth at the boat landing. The boat round-trip is about L.E. 2 per person, depending upon how many people there are. Because of its difficult accessibility, visitors would be wise to buy a tour of Philae that includes transportation, boat and guide from a travel agency in Aswan or to have the tour included in a complete program for Upper Egypt.

HOTELS IN ASWAN. Aswan Oberoi, Elephantine Island, 160 rooms. L.E. 39 swb; L.E. 44 dwb. Phone: 762835.

Large deluxe hotel and one of the best in Egypt; wonderful location in the middle of Nile with view of Aswan and Nile Valley all around. Facilities include swimming pool, restaurant, gardens, bar and nightclub, and fully equipped health spa with sauna, steam room, whirlpools, open-air sand baths and other facilities. Aswan sand has long been known for its medicinal and healing properties. Hotel's guests include dignitaries and celebrities from around the world.

Cataract Hotel, Aqtal al Tahrir St., one mile south of Aswan on a hill overlooking the Nile, 73 rooms. L.E. 23 swb; L.E. 23 dwb.

For half a century this hotel has been a famous wintering spot for European aristocrats. It has an Old World elegance and a completely relaxing atmosphere. Its rooms are large and comfortable and most have a beautiful view of the Nile. Open from December 15 to March 31.

New Cataract Hotel, next to the Cataract Hotel, 144 rooms, L.E. 33 swb; L.E. 41 dwb.

An exact duplicate of the new Winter Palace in Luxor. Air-conditioned and open all year.

Kalabsha, 120 rooms. L.E. 18 swb; L.E. 24 dwb.

Hotel Amun, Amun Island, 36 rooms. L.E. 15 swb; L.E. 20 dwb.

On its own little island in the Nile, reached by boat from the west bank; pleasant and adequate.

Abu Simbel, on the Corniche in town, 66 rooms. L.E. 12.50 swb; L.E. 16 dwb. Phone: 2888.

An overrated three-star hotel. All rooms face the river and have bath, but most with shower only. Air conditioning is extra. There is a restaurant, bar; elevator. The hotel is located next to the public swimming pool and in front of the docks for the Sheraton and Hilton Nile steamers.

Ramsis, in town two blocks east of river, 112 rooms. L.E. 9–11 dwb.

It is the newest but would be overrated at two stars. All rooms have bath with shower. There is a restaurant, bar, elevator.

Grand Hotel, on the Corniche at south end of town, 90 rooms. L.E. 7 swb; L.E. 10 dwb. Phone: 3266.

It's the oldest hotel in Aswan, but it is still in better shape than some of the new ones. Rooms are simple but large; management is very pleasant and obliging. There is a restaurant, bar, shops, snack bar. 30 rooms have air conditioning, which is extra; only half have private bath and phone. There is an outside garden. Hotel is conveniently located next to shops, EgyptAir offices and within walking distance of New Cataract Hotel.

Misr Travel, which has a village with Club Mediterranee at Hurgada, is developing a village in Aswan near the Kalabsha Temple.

ABU SIMBEL

On the edge of the Nile, 768 miles south of Cairo and 168 miles from Aswan, stands the *Temple of Abu Simbel,* the most colossal temple in all of Egypt and one of the best preserved. Situated on the western bank of the river, it was carved out of the side of a sandstone rock cliff and faces east to let the light of the rising sun penetrate the innermost sanctuary. Entrance fee: L.E. 3.

The huge complex was built between 1300–1233 B.C. by one of the greatest Pharaohs, Ramses II, and dedicated to the three principal gods of ancient Egypt whose combined spheres of influence covered the entire land: Ptah, god of the underworld as he was worshiped in Memphis, the first capital of Egypt; Amen-Ra, patron god of Thebes; and Ha-Rakhte, a form of the sun god Horus, worshipped at Heliopolis.

At the entrance to the Great Temple are four colossal statues of Ramses II in a seated position. Each is over 65 feet high. To the right and left of each statue are smaller statues of the royal family. On the left of the second colossus is Ramses' mother, Queen Ti, and on the right stands Queen Nefertari, his favorite wife. On the facade of the temple are representations of Amen-Ra and Ra-Harakhte. On the south wall outside the temple is an inscription of a treaty of peace between the Egyptians and the Hittites. It is believed to be the first treaty of its kind in history.

From the facade to its innermost chamber, the temple measures 200 feet. The first room, the Great Hypostyle Hall, has a ceiling supported by eight columns faced with huge statues of Ramses II in the pose of the god Osiris. The ceiling and walls throughout the temple are beautifully decorated. The color in many places is in excellent condition. Note particularly the exquisite details of these wall carvings. To the side of Hypostyle Hall are several small storage rooms that also have wall decorations.

The second hall measures 36 by 25 feet and is supported by four pillars. The reliefs on the walls show Ramses II and Nefertari burning incense before the sacred ship of Amen-Ra. The reliefs of Ramses, his horses and chariots are exceptionally good.

The third hall is the innermost chamber and sanctuary. Four seated figures, Ramses II flanked by the gods to whom the temple was dedicated, keep watch in the Holy of Holies, which only the Pharaoh and the High Priests were allowed to enter. Twice a year at the equinox the sun rises directly in front of the temple, and its rays are meant to penetrate the innermost chamber, casting its light on the statues. This feature of the Abu Simbel temple is considered one of the greatest engineering feats of all time.

Near the Great Temple stands the *Temple of Hathor,* also carved out of solid rock. This smaller temple was built by Ramses II for his wife Nefertari and dedicated to the goddess Hathor. Outside the temple are six large statues, four of Ramses II and two of his wife, as well as smaller ones of their children. Inside, the Hypostyle Hall has a roof supported by six pillars topped with the head and face of the goddess Hathor, and reliefs similar to those in the Great Temple. The reliefs at the back of the temple that picture the Queen and the goddess are particularly lovely.

Photographing Abu Simbel: The best time to take pictures of the temples is in the morning, soon after sunrise. You should be careful not to overexpose film, as the sun and its reflection on the temples are deceptively bright. You will need a flash for the temple interiors.

Preserving the Antiquities of Upper Egypt

The temple of Abu Simbel was a place of worship as long as the ancient cults lasted—that is, well into the Christian era. In the centuries which followed, sands piled up around the temples until they were finally buried and forgotten. Then in 1813 the Swiss explorer Burckhardt discovered them. He was soon followed by other explorers and archaeologists who excitedly wrote about them, and by the turn of the century the great parade of Egyptologists had tourists at their heels. It was not, however, until the building of the Aswan Dam and the publicity to save the monuments of Nubia that an avalanche of visitors fell on this desolate spot. One of the best and most vivid descriptions of the trip to Abu Simbel, written before the salvage operation began, is given in Alan Moorehead's *The Blue Nile*.

Upon the completion of the new Aswan Dam, the area between Aswan and the Sudan border was inundated by the Nile waters. In anticipation, the Egyptian Government, through UNESCO, sent a worldwide appeal to governments, schools, archaeological foundations and cultural organizations for assistance in exploring the area and saving the most important ancient monuments, which would otherwise be lost forever. The response to this appeal was tremendous. About twenty groups worked in the area and made many important finds. In addition, some thirty monuments and temples were dismantled and transported to other areas.

The most difficult of all the projects was saving the temples at Abu Simbel. Hundreds of proposals were submitted, but the one finally adopted seemed the most practical, certain and perhaps least costly.

The salvage project began in 1965, first by building a wall around the temple to protect it from the rising waters of the Nile. The temples were then dismantled (all 400,000 tons of them) by cutting them into parts which were crated and reassembled in the exact position as before at the top of the mountain cliff, ninety feet above the old site. The project was executed with such precision that only an inch by inch examination of the stones can detect the salvage work. It is truly a remarkable achievement and one in which the world can take pride. About fifty nations helped in the rescue operations, and millions of people around the globe who have never been to Egypt, and may never have the chance to go, sent contributions to help defray the cost.

The project is completed and the water of the lake has risen almost to the same level in relationship to the temples as it was at the old site.

After you have visited Egypt's monuments from Memphis to Abu Simbel, many of which were built by Ramses II and adorned with his colossal statues and wall paintings, you might have the impression—religious considerations aside—that Ramses II was the greatest egomaniac of all time! Yet, whether it was religious fervor or egomania, when you have seen Abu Simbel you are grateful that time has preserved such a masterpiece, and that the efforts to preserve it for future generations were so successful. You may pass this way only once in a lifetime, but certainly, when you have seen Abu Simbel, you know that you have seen one of the great wonders of the world.

HOTELS IN ABU SIMBEL. The 20-room, 32-bed *Nefertari* is the only hotel in Abu Simbel. It is about halfway between the airport and the antiquity site. It is overrated at two stars, but will have to do until something else comes along. At no time should you go to Abu Simbel with the idea of remaining overnight without first obtaining a confirmed reservation. Misr Travel is developing a hotel village at Abu Simbel.

NOTE: The excursion to Abu Simbel is generally made as a one-day trip from either Cairo (via New Valley or Aswan) or from Aswan. Be sure you have confirmed reservations and be at the airport early to claim your seat. Because of the limited number of flights, especially in high season, these flights have become notorious for overbooking and leaving passengers stranded en route.

SUGGESTED ITINERARY FOR UPPER EGYPT

The following itinerary covers the most important sites in the shortest possible time. It is not, however, the ideal way to see Upper Egypt and is suggested only for those who are pressed for time. By adding another day or two in Luxor, one is able to see more and at a slower pace.

First Day. *Morning:* Depart Cairo by air for Luxor, arriving in time for lunch.

Afternoon: Visit Karnak and Luxor Temples (start early). Depending on time of arrival in Luxor, it might be possible to visit one of these temples in the morning. However, remember that the sun is very hot by midday and sightseeing should be avoided if possible at this time.

Evening: Enjoy the Sound and Light Show at the temples.

Second Day. *Full Day Tour:* Cross river and visit the Valley of the Kings. Ramesseum, Colossi of Memnon, Deir el Bahri (Queen Hatshepsut's temple) and, if time permits, visit at least one or two of the Tombs of the Nobles.

Third Day. *Full Day:* Depart by morning plane to Aswan. In Aswan, visit the new High Dam, the granite quarries and the temples of Philae. Enjoy a felucca ride to Kitchener and Elephantine Islands or visit the local market.

Fourth Day. *Full Day:* Fly to Abu Simbel by early morning plane. Two hours of sightseeing are provided at Abu Simbel before returning to Cairo.

As an alternative, one may eliminate Aswan altogether. Or one can fly directly from Cairo to Abu Simbel and pick up this itinerary in reverse order.

Hathor, Goddess of Joy and Love

ALEXANDRIA

Ancient Queen of the Mediterranean

Egypt's second largest city and chief port, Alexandria (in Arabic *Iskandariyah*), is 110 miles northwest of Cairo on the Mediterranean. Its excellent beaches, climate and lively atmosphere have long made it the country's major summer resort.

When Alexander the Great conquered Egypt in 332 B.C., he founded a city bearing his name on the site of the tiny fishing village of Rakotis, facing the rocky island of Pharos. Under the Ptolemies, the city grew rapidly and remained the capital of the Empire throughout their reign.

The city also became a great cultural center and attracted the most famous scientists, scholars, philosophers, poets and artists of the time. It had two celebrated royal libraries, said to contain 490,000 different scrolls. Around the museum housing one of the libraries rose what is considered one of the first universities in history. Under Ptolemy II, the great Tower of Pharos, one of the

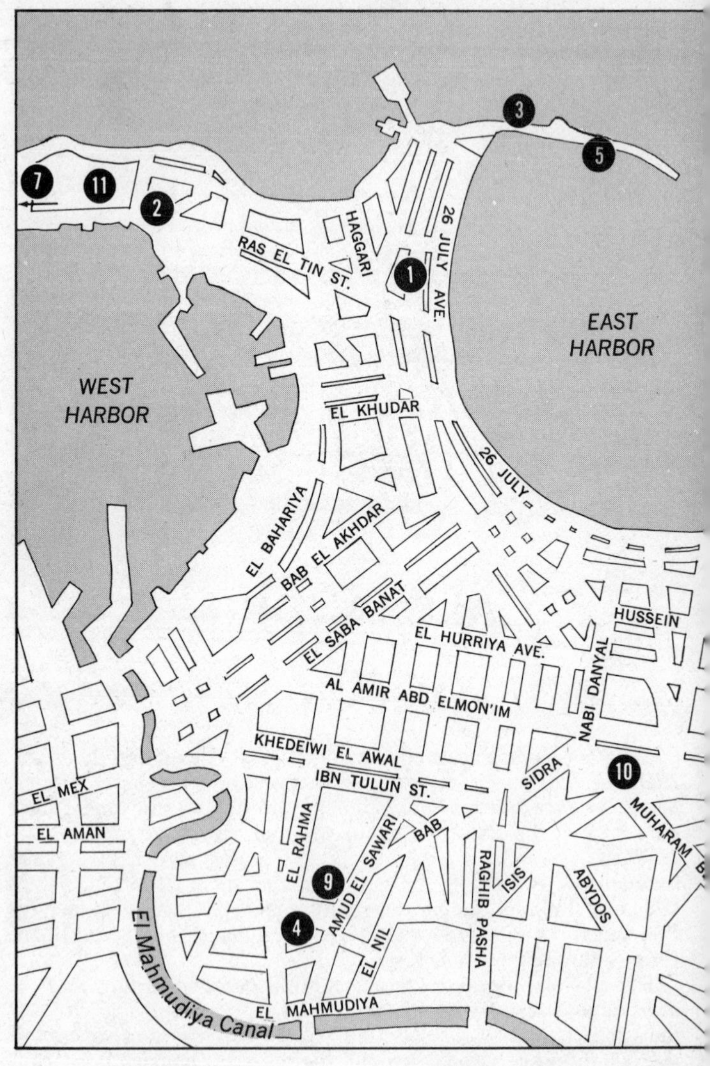

Alexandria Points of Interest

1) Abu el Abbas Mosque
2) Anfushy Necropolis
3) Aquarium
4) Catacombs of Kom-esh-Shuqafa
5) Fort Qait Bai
6) Greco-Roman Museum

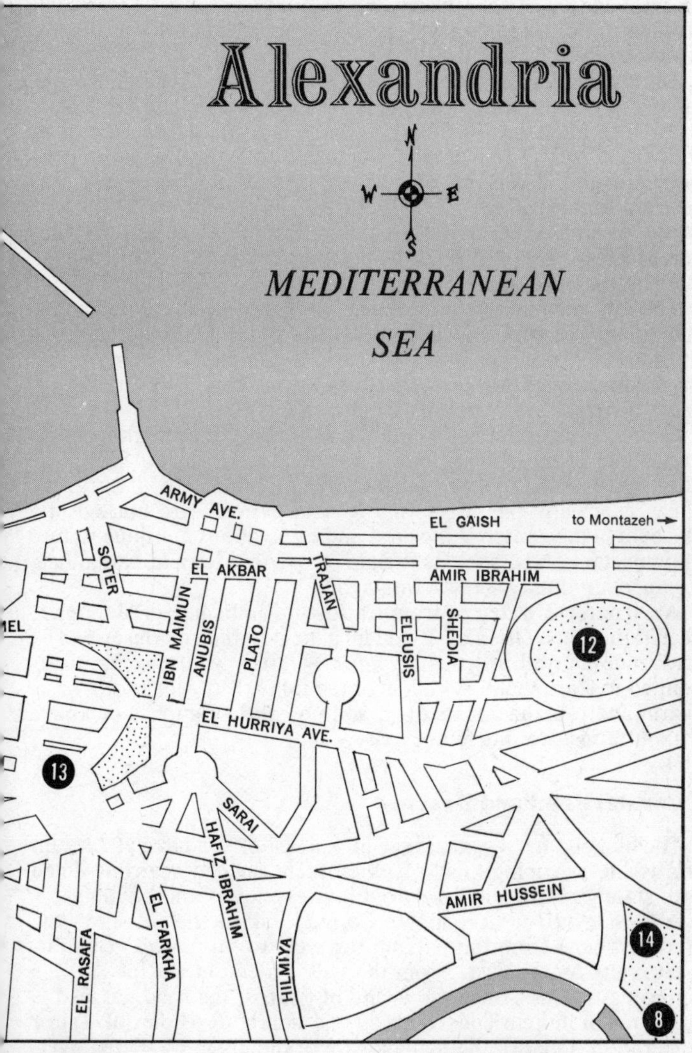

7) Lighthouse
8) Nuzha and Antoniadis Gardens
9) Pompey's Pillar
10) Railway Station
11) Ras-el-Tin Palace
12) Sporting Club
13) Stadium
14) Zoo

seven wonders of the ancient world, was built. The Tower, 220 feet high and lighted by night, is said to have been the world's first lighthouse.

During the time of Julius Caesar, Alexandria became the second largest city of the Roman Empire. When Octavian entered the city in 30 B.C., after the suicide of Anthony and Cleopatra, it became formally a part of the Roman domain. Under the Byzantine Empire, Alexandria was one of the great centers of Christendom and see of a patriarchate.

By the time the city fell to the Arabs in 642 it had declined considerably. In 1798 when Napoleon's troops landed in Egypt, Alexandria was a mere village.

The city regained its importance once more under Muhammad Ali. In 1819 he ordered the construction of the Mahmudiya Canal to the Nile, thus bringing large areas in the city's vicinity under irrigation. Under Muhammad Ali's successors, Alexandria became the traditional summer capital of Egypt.

Today, Alexandria has a population of about four million people and is one of the chief seaports on the Mediterranean Sea. Very little remains of the city's ancient past. Remnants of its onetime glory, especially the Greek and Roman periods, are housed in a museum in the center of the city, and excavations continue to turn up important finds, such as the almost perfect Roman amphitheater uncovered only a few years ago.

Alexandria is different from Cairo—its ambience is Mediterranean rather than Oriental. If you imagine it as the city described by Lawrence Durrell in his *Alexandria Quartet,* you may be disappointed to learn that it is no longer the same. But Alexandria has a charm and romance of its own, and no trip to Egypt is complete without a visit to this famous city.

Coastal Road and Beaches

The first and most remarkable look a visitor can have at Alexandria is the sweeping view of its crescent shaped seafront, lined with stately palms and lovely old houses, hotels and buildings.

A 15-mile east-west road, the Corniche, skirts the city along the Mediterranean from the port on the west to Montazah at its farthest limits on the east. From the western end at Ras el Tin, the peninsula that was once the Island of Pharos, the road passes the city's major hotels and cafes on the south to Midan al Tahrir (Liberation Square), the main square of the downtown area overlooking the eastern harbor, and Ramleh, the main tram station. On the far side of the harbor, the road continues along the Mediterranean to the city's most beautiful residential sections on the south and a series of beaches on the north. Many of the beaches have the same names as the city districts behind them: Chatby, Cleopatra, Sidi Gabr, Rushdi, Stanley, Glymenopoulo, San Stefano, Sidi Bishr, Mandara, Montazeh.

Here cabins may be rented for the summer season. On both sides of the Corniche Drive, hotels, nightclubs, sidewalk cafes and restaurants are the center of activity for the thousands of Egyptians who spend the summer here.

In bygone days the entire government moved from Cairo to Alexandria for the summer, and the diplomatic corps gladly moved with it. Now the country no longer indulges in this extravagance.

Sites of Antiquity

Pompey's Pillar: Entrance: 50 pt. A column 84 feet high and about seven feet thick, made of polished Aswan rose granite, was erroneously called Pompey's Pillar by the Crusaders. In fact, it had nothing to do with Pompey. It was erected by the Roman prefect Posthumus in honor of the emperor Diocletian and was part of the splendid Temple of Serapis. Some historians contend that it was originally within a portico surrounded by 400 columns, on the spot where tradition places the famous library of Alexandria. An entrance on the west of the pillar leads down a flight of stairs into long subterranean chambers which may have been part of the Temple of Serapis. Some claim the chambers were part of the famous library, but this is doubtful.

Roman Amphitheatre: Entrance: 50 pt. Not far from the site of Pompey's Pillar an enormous area is now being excavated. To date the most important find has been an amphitheater in almost perfect condition. It is the first one of the Roman era to be found in Egypt. Carvings of the cross and other Christian symbols indicate that it was used long after the last Roman departed. The entire complex was discovered in the course of digging the foundation for a new building.

Catacombs of Kom el-Shuqafa (*Chogaga*): Entrance: 50 pt. The funerary construction of the Kom el-Shuqafa dates from the 2nd century A.D. (Some authorities date it as early as the 2nd century B.C.) The dead were lowered through a shaft into the catacombs, which are three stories high. A winding staircase leads into the chambers of the first floor. The catacombs are unique both for their plan and decoration, which are a curious blend of Greco-Roman and Egyptian designs. They were discovered only in 1900. After one has visited the temples and tombs of Upper Egypt, it is easy to see how the nation's art had sadly deteriorated by the late Ptolemaic period.

Anfushi Necropolis: In a park near the entrance to Ras-al-Tin Palace is a necropolis dating from the 2nd century B.C. Although it is older than the catacombs of Kom el-Shuqafa, it is less important because of its inferior decorations. All the tombs are carved out of rock and contain no other building material. A visit is recommended only if you have plenty of time.

Fort Kait Bey: On the spot where the Pharos Lighthouse once stood, a fortress and mosque were built by Sultan Kait Bey in the 15th century. These structures have recently been restored. The site is especially worth visiting for the view of Alexandria from the harbor. However, at the present time visitors are allowed only in the part of the fort which contains the museum. *Alexandria,* by E. M. Forster (see reading list), has an interesting description of the history of the Pharos and the development of the island. The description of Pompey's Pillar, the catacombs and the necropolis are useful for visits to these sites.

Museums and Royal Palaces

Greco-Roman Museum, hours: winter 9 A.M. to 4 P.M. Closed Fridays from 11:30 A.M. to 1:30 P.M. Entrance: L.E. 1.

The museum, founded in 1891, gives a visitor some idea of the grandeur of Alexandria under the Greeks and Romans. Further, it provides the link between the Egyptian Antiquities Museum and the Coptic Museum in Cairo.

The collection includes statues, bas-reliefs, capitals, earthenware, jewelry and amulets of mingled Egyptian, Greek and Roman design. The museum has a large collection of coins minted in Alexandria during the Greco-Roman period and an excellent display of Tanagra figurines. Note especially the exhibits of iridescent and fused glass and the fragments of Coptic fabrics.

Hydrobiological Museum, hours: winter and summer 9 A.M. to 2 P.M. daily. Fee: 10 pt.

Located on the south side of the street immediately before Fort Kait Bey, the museum houses a collection of colorful and interesting fish from the Mediterranean, Red Sea and the Nile River.

Ras el Tin Palace: Begun by Muhammad Ali in 1834 and completed in 1845, it was the official summer headquarters of the rulers of Egypt down through the mid-20th century. Its eastern gate is made up of six tall granite columns topped by the royal crown of Egypt and bearing inscriptions from the Koran.

Inside, the rooms to visit are the Throne Room, the Gothic Hall and the Marble Hall. The room in which King Farouk signed his abdication is on the ground floor. After signing the document, Farouk descended the stairs leading to the wharf below, boarded his yacht, and sailed to Italy. The palace is not open to the public now but is being used as a guest house for official guests and visiting dignitaries.

Montazah Palace: Built by Khedive Abbas in 1892, the palace is made up of several separate buildings. The estate is located east of Alexandria on the Mediterranean shore and is surrounded by 350 acres of beautiful parks and gardens. The main building is not open to the public at present. The Salamek (women's quarters) is a hotel. Visitors may swim at its beach or relax in the Palace gardens, which are open daily from 7 A.M. to sunset. Entrance fee to gardens and beach: 75 pt.

Sites East of Alexandria

Abukir, 18 miles: On the site of ancient Canopus stands a small fishing port. Here Nelson's fleet defeated the French in 1798, thereby crushing France's attempt to gain a foothold in the eastern Mediterranean. The area contains the remains of ancient public baths, a temple dedicated to Serapis and relics of Napoleon's expedition to Egypt. *Zephyron,* a seafood restaurant well known to Alexandrian residents, is located in town by the sea. It is considered one of the best seafood restaurants in Egypt. Patrons select their own fresh fish, which is weighed before them to determine the price.

Rosetta, 35 miles: The town, founded in the 9th century on the site of ancient Bolbitine, was once important as a center for commerce with the Orient. In 1799, near Rosetta at Fort St. Julien, one of Napoleon's soldiers found the now famous Rosetta Stone, a basalt tablet inscribed by the priests of Ptolemy V in hieroglyphics, demotic characters and Greek. From this stone, Champollion found the key to deciphering Egyptian hieroglyphics, thus enabling scholars to unravel the mysteries of ancient Egypt. The stone, captured by the British in 1801, is now in the British Museum.

Ras al Barr: The narrow extension of land between the Mediterranean Sea and the Damietta Branch of the Nile is a popular fishing area. Temporary bungalows of wood and dry reeds, put up each spring and removed in autumn, may be rented for the summer season. It is about a three-hour drive from Alexandria and is easier to reach from Port Said.

Sites West of Alexandria

The road west of Alexandria passes through Meks, the main industrial center of Alexandria, and skirts the sea. Another road slightly further inland bypasses some of the town. The North

Coast Highway is being widened to a four-lane carriageway from Alexandria to Mersa Matruh, and the infrastructure is being laid for further resort development of the Mediterranean coast.

Al Agami, 12 miles: The beach at Agami is one of the best in the vicinity of Alexandria and has become the most popular beach on the coast. Houses are available for rent during the summer season, and there are several hotels on the beach. Many Alexandrian and Cairo families own cottages in the area and spend their summers here.

Burg al-Arab and Bahig, 27 miles: Near Abusir are the remains of a 3rd century B.C. temple dedicated to Osiris, later turned into a fortress by the Arabs. Also in the area are the ruins of a Ptolemaic lighthouse believed to be one in a chain that stretched from the Pharos at Alexandria across the North African coast to Cyrene. Seven and a half miles south of Bahig, St. Menas is the site of a once great Christian city. Its ruins include several churches, monastery buildings, the sacred baths and a cemetery.

Burg El Arab was formerly on a caravan route, and the village and the dress of its people are especially colorful, retaining a flavor of their Bedouin origins. From this village to El Alamein, the road overlooks the white sand dunes bordering the Mediterranean's blue and green waters. The way is lined with fig groves. Camels, sheep and goat herds wander about the white desert, and tents of the Bedouin can be seen in the distance. It is exactly as one imagines the North African coast.

Wadi el Natrun, 63 miles southwest of Alexandria: Near the Natrun oasis is a complex of monasteries dating from the second century A.D. (Descriptions are available in Dorothea Russel's *Medieval Cairo and the Monasteries of Wadi Natrun.*) The monasteries can most easily be reached off the desert road halfway between Cairo and Alexandria. You must telephone the Patriarchate in Cairo (822256) for an appointment to visit Wadi El Natrun.

A thousand years ago there were as many as 50 monasteries here, but now there are only four still occupied by monks. These may also be seen in the distance from the desert road just before the resthouse situated at the halfway point between Cairo and Alexandria. A sign on the west side of the road designates the track to the monasteries.

Al Alamein, 64 miles on the Mediterranean: At this location one of the decisive battles of World War II was fought between the German Afrika Corps led by Rommel and the British 8th Army commanded by Montgomery. As you enter the village itself, the first monument on the south side of the road is the Greek monument, followed by the British Memorial, cemetery and garden. A pavillion at the cemetery bears this inscription:

> Within this cloister are inscribed the names of soldiers and airmen of the British Commonwealth and Empire who died fighting on land or in the air where two continents meet and to whom the fortune of war denied a known and honoured grave. With their fellows who rest in this cemetery, with their comrades in arms of the Royal Navy and with the seamen of the Merchant Marine, they preserved for the West the link with the East and turned the tide of war.

In the village of El Alamein is a military museum, directly on the north side of the coastal road. It contains material from the World War II battle as well as Egyptian military displays.

Nine miles beyond the village is the German monument, on a bluff overlooking the sea. After you leave the main road, at the fork in the sand track, bear to the right, and this will take you there. The caretaker, who speaks English, lives in the little house at the base of the memorial. Inside the enormous stone structure, in addition to the ashes of the known dead, is the grave of 31 unknown soldiers of undetermined nationality, bearing the inscription "Death knows no country."

Beyond the German cemetery (2.4 miles) is the Italian memorial, cemetery and a small museum. The caretaker lives in the house to the east of the monument. Sound your car horn and he will appear with the key. Beyond this memorial, on the coastal road, are markers designating the Axis and British minefields.

Sidi Abdel Rahman, 92 miles west of Alexandria: The small village has a shrine mosque to Abdel Rahman, a venerated Moslem holy man, especially popular among the Bedouin.

Between El Alamein and Mersa Matruh there is only one gas station, located on the south side of the road about halfway into the village of El Dabah.

Mersa Matruh, 170 miles on the Mediterranean: The small port of Mersa Matruh is situated on a lagoon cut off from the sea by a chain of rocks. Its superb beach and crystal clear waters have made it a favorite off-the-beaten-track vacation spot. It may be reached by car and train from Cairo and Alexandria. The train, however, is not recommended at this time. There are no first class coaches, and the journey from Alexandria may take six hours. Car travel from Alexandria is about three hours and from Cairo about seven hours.

Even before the Ptolemies, Mersa Matruh was a lively trading center. At the time of Alexander the Great the city was named Amonia, probably because it was the entrance to the desert route to the Siwa Oasis where Amon was worshiped. Later, beautiful palaces were built at Matruh by Cleopatra, who chose to settle here with Caesar. In the hills north of the town is a church dating from the early Christian period.

A large lagoon west of the main harbor, formed by a tall rock with a natural hollow center, is called Cleopatra's Bath. Legend says that two tunnels leading into the rock were carved on the seaside and shoreside to let fresh seawater in and out. Local tradition claims that Cleopatra actually bathed here. Because of its proximity to a military area, the rock and Cleopatra's beach cannot be reached by car at this time, but it is possible either to hire a sailing boat from the main harbor to go to Cleopatra's Bath, or to walk around the shoreline about one mile.

Rommel's Cave is another favorite tourist spot in Mersa Matruh. It is located on the eastern edge of town, and can be found by following the main east-west street, Sharia Galaah, through town to the east, where signs in English point the way. The cave where Rommel, in solitude, drew up his battle plans for Tobruk has been turned into a small museum. In 1978 Rommel's son donated several of his father's personal maps and clothing for display. Beyond Rommel's Cave and around the bend to the east is Rommel's Beach, noted for its excellent snorkeling. Leave your car parked at the little hotel called Marine Fuad and walk out to the beach; the sand is very soft.

Mersa Matruh is the capital of the Matruh Governate, the largest in Egypt. It covers one-third of the nation's land area. There is a large government administration center, and the Ministry of Tourism maintains an office on the second floor of the municipal building located on the corner of the two main streets, Sharia Alexandria and the Corniche.

The town has a population of 60,000, and accommodates over 100,000 summer tourists, mostly Egyptians. At this time foreigners may travel only nine miles west of Mersa Matruh, due to the sensitive situation with Libya. Foreign visitors should carry passports, which must be shown at a checkpoint east of the city. Mersa Matruh has great tourist potential; its nearby beaches are considered among the most beautiful in the world.

The main road to the Libyan frontier at Sollum drops directly south after leaving Matruh and connects with the road to the famous **Siwa Oasis.** Siwa is off limits, mostly as a protection against unprepared travelers' undertaking the grueling 480-mile journey without the necessary water and gasoline. Travel in convoy is necessary.

Some items from Siwa, such as handicrafts, dates and olive oil, are sent to Matruh by plane. These items may be purchased very reasonably in a government-run shop on Sharia Galaah, next to the government drygoods store, called Benzione. The crafts store also sells items made by the bedouins of the Western Desert. Prices are fixed.

West of the main mosque, whose minarets can be seen from any point in town, a secondary road leaves Mersa Matruh from the Corniche, the principal road along the harbor. This road, which is paved part of the way and hard-surface gravel the rest, follows the coastline to the west, and is one of the most picturesque and beautiful drives in all of Egypt. The road parallels the blue-green waters of the sea, framed with stark white sand dunes, and passes through olive and fig orchards.

The road first passes through a village called **Qasr,** which means "palace" in Arabic. It is believed that Anthony and Cleopatra built a magnificent palace here, from which Cleopatra sent out her armies to try to defeat Augustus. Qasr is five miles west of Matruh. Beyond Qasr 7 miles is **Abyad,** a village renowned for its lovely beach. Signs in English on the main road indicate the way.

In the next village, **Om Rakham** (14 miles), at a small grocery store on the north side of the road, you may ask to be taken to the site of a Ramses II limestone temple, a few miles west of Om Rakham. It is situated only a few feet south of the road in an olive-fig grove, but is of marginal interest because the limestone has been severely pitted and eroded by water. Its foundation is now situated in a valley that floods in the winter rainy season. The desert between the temple and the road is overgrown with thistle. Should you undertake the short walk, be sure to wear closed shoes and cover your ankles.

Two miles farther west is **Ageeba Beach,** famous throughout Egypt and said to be one of the most beautiful beaches in the world. The road from Matruh winds up a hill and makes a horse-shoe turn. At this point, you may leave your car and walk to the edge of the hill to see the sculptured cliffs plummeting to the water's edge. This location commands a breathtaking view of the Mediterranean, the beaches east and west, and the rock ledges meeting the blue sea below. A small but easily managed path leads down to the beach and caves. It is a good place for snorkeling; many varieties of fish may be seen. The drive from Ageeba back to Matruh takes a half-hour.

PRACTICAL INFORMATION FOR ALEXANDRIA

HOTELS. Al Agami: *Agami Palace* (west of Alexandria). It's not really a palace, but it is clean and services are adequate. Its advantage is proximity to the beach. Phone: 886430. Double with shower L.E. 13; single w/shower L.E. 7. Breakfast and one meal are compulsory.

Beau Rivage, on the Corniche at 434 al al Gueish St. 62185. L.E. 13 swb; L.E. 16.500 dwb. A small hotel set in a garden facing the Mediterranean Sea. Popular in summer and rooms are difficult to get. Food and service are good. 54 rooms.

Cecil, on the Corniche at 16 Saad Zaghlul Sq. L.E. 15 swb; L.E. 16 dwb. Phone: 807532. Centrally located, overlooking the eastern harbor, the hotel is old but has a certain faded elegance. All 87 rooms are with bath.

Hannoville (the next beach west of Agami): The *Hannoville Hotel,* phone: 800066, charges L.E. 18 for a double with shower and breakfast.

Hotel Delta, 14 Champollion St., Mazarita. Phone: 29820; 805187. Price: L.E. 22.39 swb, 27.15 dwb with breakfast, taxes and service.

A new hotel near the city center, one block of city seafront and convenient to Ramleh train station. Rooms are nicely furnished with twin beds; all have bath, air conditioning, tv and phone. There is a restaurant, bar, telex and photocopying service.

Mersa Matruh: *Beau Site,* located on the beach (west of Alexandria), is the best hotel and is always heavily booked. The owners, the Madpak family, take reservations at their home in Heliopolis, phone: 694500. The phone number in Matruh, 2066, is difficult to reach. The hotel is a collection of buildings along the beach, including the dining room. It has a pleasant and helpful staff, and the food is excellent. The hotel opens in May and closes in October. Rates are L.E. 10 swb; L.E. 12 dwb; compulsory board, L.E. 10 daily. Tents with two beds rent for L.E. 5 per night.

Montazeh Sheraton Hotel, Corniche el Nil, 350 rooms. Approximately L.E. 45 swb; L.E. 49 dwb. The 15-story hotel is located on the grounds of a former palace of Farouk and overlooks the sea and the gardens of Montazeh Palace. This welcome addition is the first major new hotel in Egypt's second largest city in over two decades.

San Giovanni, 205 Algeish Ave., Stanley Beach, 30 rooms. L.E. 23–35 dwb. Phone: 40984. Simple, clean; good location, air conditioning, television, private bath. 24 hr. room service; bar, nightclub and 24 hr. coffee shop. Hotel has one of the best restaurants in town.

San Stefano, on the Corniche at Ar Raml. L.E. 16 swb; L.E. 23 dwb. Phone: 63580. A large, fairly modern hotel about halfway between the heart of the city and Montazah. Rooms are simple but comfortable. 118 rooms.

Sidi Abdel Rahman: *El Alamein,* on a beautiful white sand beach (west of Alexandria), is a popular summer resort open from April to Oct. Reservations may be made at Egyptian Hotel Co., Immobilia Bldg., 26 Sheria

Sherif or call 755715. The government-run hotel has a main building with 70 simply furnished guest rooms and 20 villas—all with private bath and terrace facing sea. Prices start at L.E. 25 plus compulsory half board L.E. 10 per person.

Windsor Palace, on the Corniche at al Shohada St. L.E. 13.50 dwb. Conveniently located hotel with a view of the eastern harbor. Like the Cecil, the hotel was once grand but now faded. Rooms are large and comfortable but old. 85 rooms.

If on a budget, a Greek pension, *Hotel de Roses,* is located on Sharia Galaah, and serves three meals daily in an outdoor tea garden. Tel: 2755.

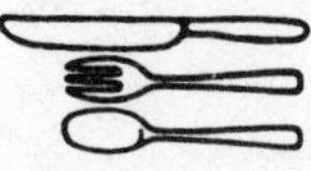

RESTAURANTS. Alexandria is noted for its seafood, especially the large shrimp, which is excellent when grilled and served with lemon or butter. Among the leading restaurants where you can enjoy this specialty is *San Giovanni,* in the hotel by the same name. It is situated at Stanley Beach, overlooking the sea.

Lord's Inn, just off the Corniche, a restaurant around the corner from the San Stefano, specializes in curry. Reservations are required, but since they have no telephone you must stop by to make them.

Among the other leading restaurants are *Au Prive,* 14 El Hurriya St.; *Pastroudis,* 39 al Hurriya St.; *Petrou,* at Beau Rivage by the sea; *Pizzaria,* 14 El Hurriya St.; *Shakespeare Club,* 95 Cornish St.; *Tiki Inn,* Eastern Harbor; *Union,* 1 al Borsa al Kadima St.; and *Santa Lucia,* 40 Sofia Zaghlul; and *Zephyrion,* see Abukir.

SHOPPING. Although its bazaars do not compare with those of Cairo, Alexandria has a lively shopping district located in the area behind Tahrir Square. Many of the well known Cairo department stores, such as *Salon Vert* and *Omar Effendi,* have branches here.

Alexandria is the center of the leather and textile industries and prices might be lower here, especially for those who are good at bargaining.

TRANSPORTATION: Alex Limo has new Mercedes cars driven by English-speaking drivers. Cost is L.E. 22.50 for half-day within a 30-mile radius of city; L.E. 45 full-day up to 12 hours, within 60 miles. For cars with air conditioning add 10%. If you are planning to stay at the Sheraton or at one of the other hotels at Montazeh and are arriving from Cairo by train, it is closer to get off at Sidi Gaber Station, rather than continuing on into Raml Station in the center of Alexandria.

USEFUL ADDRESSES. *Airline Companies:* British Airways, 15 Saad Zaghloul Square; Middle East Airlines, 8 Horreya Street; Sueadan Airways, 6 Talaat Harb Street; T.W.A., 2 Horreya Avenue; EgyptAir, 19 Saad Zaghloul Square. *Consulates:* United Kingdom, 3 Mina Street, Roushdy Pasha, tel. 47166; U.S.A., 110 El Horreya Street, tel. 801911.

Thoth, God of Science

THE SUEZ CANAL AND THE RED SEA

Passage to the Orient

The area of Suez, known as *Goshen* in the Bible, was strategically important in ancient times to the civilizations of the eastern Mediterranean because it formed a bridge of commerce and conquest between Asia and Africa. Many efforts were made to connect the two great bodies of water—the Mediterranean and the Red Seas—which were separated by this narrow strip of land.

The first attempt to cut a channel was made about 2100 B.C. It utilized an ancient branch of the Nile River. A second and different canal was cut about 1900 B.C., running from the Red Sea and Bitter Lakes to meet the Nile at a point north of Bubastis. It was called the "Canal of the Pharaohs" and was used for about a thousand years. This canal is pictured in a stele on the temple at Karnak and shows Seti I returning from victory in Asia by way of a canal at Suez. The same canal, after centuries of disuse, was re-dug in 606 B.C. but not completed until 521 B.C., during the time of Darius I.

A third canal was dug about 286 B.C. during the reign of Ptolemy II and continued to be used as late as the Roman period. In A.D. 98 the Roman Emperor Trajan had the canal changed so that it could meet the Nile near present-day Cairo. This canal came to be known as the River of Trajan. The extent to which the canal was used in the following centuries is not clear, although references to it are found in historical records.

Apparently the last effort to use the canal was about the time of the Arab conquest. It was reopened and became known as the "Canal of the Prince of the Faithful." Historians agree that after the late 8th century the canal was no longer serviceable.

In modern times numerous schemes were suggested to revive the canal, but none were pursued seriously until the arrival of Napoleon's expedition in Egypt in 1798. Napoleon was particularly eager to rebuild the passage as an alternate sea route to India. Preliminary work was undertaken by the expedition but unfortunately abandoned because Napoleon's chief engineer erroneously calculated the level of the Red Sea at 33 feet higher than the Mediterranean and declared that the project was not feasible.

Further efforts to cut a canal were not considered seriously again until several decades later when Ferdinand de Lesseps proved that the two waters were, in fact, at the same level.

In 1854 de Lesseps asked permission from the Egyptian ruler Said to begin work on the canal. Permission was granted two years later, but another two years were needed to raise the money for the project. Finally, construction of the canal was begun in April, 1858. Eleven years later under Khedive Isma'il the canal was formally opened with magnificent ceremony. An opera house was built in Cairo to stage *Aida,* which Verdi had composed for the occasion, and royalty, including the Empress Eugenie, and a host of dignitaries from Europe attended.

For the next century the Suez Canal was the lifeline of the British Empire and the pawn of imperial Europe. In one of the most blatant but brillant manipulations in history, the British gained control of Egypt and the Canal. The events culminated in an agreement in 1882, which gave the British control of the Canal for 99 years.

Suez became the symbol of British imperialism to the Egyptians and the final bone of contention in the country's long struggle for independence. Little wonder that after the revolution of 1952 withdrawal of British troops from the Canal zone became a *cause celebre*. Finally, 100 years after the date of the concession to de Lesseps, the Suez Canal Company was nationalized by the Egyptian government. There followed quickly a series of events which ended in a joint attack on Egypt by the British, French and Israelis in October 1956.

The Canal became embroiled in international politics once again when it was closed for eight years as a result of the Six-Day War in June, 1967. Fifteen ships were trapped in its waters, mines were laid, the Israelis dug in on the east bank, the people fled and the towns on the canal became ghost towns. Then in October, 1973 the Egyptians crossed the canal in a surprise attack, and the war that followed led ultimately to a negotiated settlement worked out by U.S. Secretary of State Henry Kissinger by which Egypt regained the canal.

Again, on June 5, 1975, the Egyptians celebrated the Canal's opening. The occasion was marked by an impressive list of visitors including the great grand-daughter of de Lesseps, some royalty and press from around the world.

The Suez Canal from Port Said on the Mediterranean to Suez on the Red Sea is over 120 miles long. The breadth at water level is 200 meters. Ships drawing 38 feet can transit the canal, and there are plans to deepen it to enable supertankers to pass through it. Transit time for a ship through the canal from Suez or Port Said is about 12 hours. The southern stretch from Suez to Ismailia, including the Bitter Lakes and Lake Timsah, is the most interesting part of the journey.

Port Said

Port Said is located 135 miles northeast of Cairo on the Mediterranean at the western tip of the canal. Passengers on ships transiting the canal may disembark here in order to take an excursion to Cairo and Luxor and to rejoin the ship at either Suez or Safaga further down the Red Sea. Port Said was badly destroyed in the June war of 1967 and all but abandoned during the eight years the canal was closed. The town has been rebuilt but has lost its "old port" atmosphere except for a few buildings directly on the waterfront. There is a small military museum at the west end of town. A branch office of the Tourist Administration is located on the street along the waterfront a few blocks from the Canal Administration building.

There are also several small tourist class hotels, but of the ten we checked, we would only suggest *Holiday Hotel,* Gomhoria St., L.E. 16 swb; L.E. 21 dwb, including breakfast, tax and service. It is air conditioned; rooms have refrigerator/bar, TV, phone. North of town, on the Mediterranean, *Etap Port Said* is under construction and should be a welcome addition. Even now, there are beach houses for rent, L.E. 16 swb; L.E. 18 dwb.

Ismailia

The town skirting the desert and Lake Timsah, halfway between Port Said and Suez was founded by de Lesseps to accommodate the staff of the Suez Canal Company. His home, still kept with his mementos, is used as a government guesthouse and is only opened to visitors on special occasions, although, if you are really interested in seeing the inside, you could probably have it opened by giving some *bakseesh* to the keeper of the keys. The town's Antiquity Museum is nearby and is open daily, except Tues., from 8:30 A.M.–1:30 P.M. Entrance: 50 pts.

The Suez Canal Company is now housed in a large, modern white building, and the town is built around spacious public gardens and wide tree-lined streets.

Ismailia has grown considerably in the past decade, but it's only the beginning. The first of several hotel projects overlooking the lake is nearing completion, launching the town as a new resort area near the capital.

Etap Ismailia, the town's first hotel of international standard, was scheduled to open last summer. The finishing touches were being put on the four-star property when we last visited, and from what we could see, it should be a great addition for local residents and visitors alike.

The 172-room hotel fronts Lake Timseh (one of the Bitter Lakes and part of the Suez Canal waterway) and is designed to serve many purposes—a resort, business and meeting center as well as a traditional hotel. It is situated next door to the headquarters building of the Suez Canal Authority on a small island and is connected by a short bridge to the town.

Built in a half-moon shape around a swimming pool, the seven story building takes full advantage of its wonderful location with all public rooms and restaurants overlooking the pool, lake and beach and an unobstructed view of the ships gliding through the Canal.

Branching off from the cool white marble lobby are two wings, each with a restaurant on the ground floor—a coffee shop at one side; a grill, nightclub and meeting rooms at the other, and shops. A group of beach villas are being built in the grove adjacent to the hotel.

Cross Canal Tunnel: A new tunnel *under* the Suez Canal has been completed, connecting the west and east banks for the first time. It is a first step in the major developments planned for Sinai. The entry-point is 17 miles north of Suez. The tunnel is open from 8:30 A.M. to 6:00 P.M. One must wait to pass through in convoy, as traffic moves in one direction only.

Suez

Located 82 miles east of Cairo on the Red Sea at the southern entrance of the Canal. Suez was the most heavily damaged town in the area during the Suez war and has been slowly coming back. When times are normal it is an important resort area, as the Red Sea is a favorite camping and fishing area. In front of the Suez Canal Authority offices there is a small promenade from which you can view the ships entering the canal at the port of Suez on their way to the Mediterranean Sea.

The coastline along the Red Sea south of Suez is backed by the barren cliffs of the Ataka Mountains, whose colors change from pink to purple at different hours of the day and provide some of the most beautiful scenery in Egypt.

Visitors to the area may stay at *The Summer Palace,* 20 rooms, tel. 2475. The hotel located on the waterfront; sailing and waterskiing available. The *Galal Restaurant,* near the Holiday Hotel, has good fish.

South of the Suez on the Red Sea is an area that has the potential of becoming an important resort, especially for fishing and scuba diving. *Ein Sukhna,* about an hour from Suez, is noted for its beautiful beach. The town, which in Arabic means "Hot Springs," is known for its hot sulphur spring. There is a gasoline station here.

The next major intersection to the south is *Ras Zafarana,* 125 kms. (77 miles) south of Suez. It has a lighthouse which can be seen for many miles north and south along the Red Sea coastal road. There is a gasoline station here, and a road on the west takes off into the desert and leads back to Cairo. Also in the area are the monasteries of St. Paul and St. Anthony.

Ras Ghareb, 235 kms. (146 miles) from Suez, is a large community thriving because of the many oil discoveries in the area. Adequate tire repair facilities may be found here, as well as mechanics and a gas station. This is the last major stop before reaching Hurghada.

At this point the road south deteriorates quickly. At present there is very little traffic on the road, but because of the unpredictable condition of the road surface, and because of the extreme heat from May through September, travelers by car should drive slowly and make sure they are well supplied with drinking water, extra gas, water for the car radiator and battery, and a second spare tire.

While many of the deserted beaches along the way south may seem inviting, it is best to select a swimming area that is frequented by other travelers and local residents. Many of the beach areas are mined from the wars (these areas have chain link fences around them), and there are sharks in the neighborhood that sometimes come in quite close to shore.

After passing several more important oil well sites, the road turns inland until Hurghada.

Hurghada

Located about 237 miles south of Suez, Hurghada is the best place on the Red Sea for scuba diving. The capital of the huge Red Sea province, Hurghada is a small town tucked between the mountains, the desert and the sea. It is made up of one-story houses and dusty streets crowded with children playing and goats and chickens scampering about. The Governor's Palace, as it is called, is far from being palatial; nevertheless, it dwarfs everything else in town except a pretty mosque with twin minarets. There is a student house, frequently full of Americans from Cairo and Alexandria, and an Esso guesthouse used by oilmen and geologists who are involved in the exploration and extraction of oil and minerals in the region.

At the water's edge in a small town called *El Ghadarsqa,* six miles north of Hurghada, a Marine Museum (which has been badly neglected because of the events that have made the area a military zone for the past decade) and an Aquarium contain small fish of unusual shapes and colors. The Museum has a large number of displays of mounted fish covering the Red Sea's wide variety of marine life, as well as shells and coral from the area.

The *Blue Sky,* a 250-ton boat chartered by an Italian company and used mainly by Italian and French scuba divers, is anchored offshore from Sunday through Saturday and returns to harbor once a week for provisions, to disembark passengers and to await new ones arriving from Cairo on the Sunday morning flight. The Italian skipper and others who have dived in these waters say without qualification that no other sea in the world can compare in terms of variety and abundance of marine life, as well as clarity of the water.

The resort area of Hurghada is about three miles south of town at *Abu Menka,* a U-shaped bay with its axis running east-west and sheltered at its southeastern end by several islands that offer some of the best scuba diving in the world. The waters around the islands are so clear that the bottom of the sea is visible at a depth of 60 feet, and they teem with a fantastic variety of shapes, sizes and colors of fish and coral formations.

The bay is framed by a chain of rugged, barren mountains, which protect the area from the desert's westerly winds. At the center of the bay there is an enormous coral formation, so close to the surface of the water that from afar it looks like another island. The reef is only a few hundred yards from shore and within easy reach even for inexperienced swimmers. The sea bottom slopes gently from shore toward the center of the bay, and the absence of strong currents and undertows makes swimming here pleasant and safe. The entire area, undisturbed for so many years, is covered with shells of amazing shapes and colors.

HOTELS: *Hurghada Sheraton,* at the northern end of the bay, 3 miles from Hurghada Airport. Price: L.E. 25 swb; L.E. 30 dwb plus compulsory half board. Originally built in the 1950's and left derelict for over a decade, the hotel has been completely renovated and has become the nucleus of resort activity here. The hotel has 115 rooms with private bath, air conditioning and terrace. Each room is charmingly decorated with Egyptian-made rattan furniture. The hotel is built in the round, with a central garden courtyard providing access to the restaurant, patio and terrace bar and lobby areas. A huge swimming pool with barbecue facilities overlooks the sea. The Acqua Center of the hotel provides fishing, snorkeling, diving and sailing services. Paddleboats and sailfish may also be rented.

Small villas adjoin the hotel house, a beachfront bar and the Acqua Center. The chalets may be rented for groups or large families.

Fresh water for the area is piped in from Qena, across the desert on the Nile; thus the supply of fresh water (and, therefore, the functioning of the central air conditioning) can be erratic.

A chain of hills close to the hotel encloses this part of the bay. The sand here is coarse in comparison to other parts of the coast, where it is powder-fine; but it is easy to walk on. The coarseness is due to the constant erosion of the coral formation, caused by the water and winds.

Magawish, at the southern end of the bay where the craggy mountains rise to their highest peaks. Price: L.E. 45 swb; L.E. 70 dwb, including meals. The resort village is owned by *Misr Travel* and operated in conjunction with *Club Mediterranee*. Each chalet has a small sitting room, bedroom with two single beds and a bath and is air conditioned. The resort has a total of 400 beds, of which 280 will be used by Club Med and must be booked through them. The remainder are sold through Misr Travel, 630 Fifth Ave., New York, N.Y. Misr Travel's clients have full use of all Club Med facilities and sports. The emphasis is on scuba diving, snorkeling and fishing. The walled-in compound roams along 3 kilometers of beach front, and includes a large reception-dining room building, a small theatre, pool and tennis courts. Misr Travel has air-conditioned motorcoaches stationed here for regular tours to Luxor.

EgyptAir has four flights weekly from Cairo to Hurghada: Tues, Thurs, Sat, and Sun, departing Cairo at 7:00 A.M. and arriving at Hurghada at 7:50 A.M. The return is on the same days, departing Hurghada at 8:20 A.M. and arriving at Cairo at 9:10 A.M. The price is L.E. 120 round-trip. Schedules are subject to change and should be confirmed with EgyptAir at time of travel.

With the area off-limits since the 1967 war, Hurghada was left to itself—the inhabitants to their fishing and the fish to their coral. As the late Renzo Brilli of *Tours of Distinction,* New York, described it after his first visit: "There are no oil slicks, no floating cans, bottles, wrappings and the other signs of civilization, nor are there people spoiled by tourists. The blissful silence is broken only by the gentle splashing of the waves and, at times, the murmur of the wind blowing through the mountains in the distance. There is no commercialism, but honest and friendly, smiling people; no billboards or rows of hotels—only the pristine beauty of nature. The incredible colors of the waters contrast yet blend with the ocher of the bleak desert, and are framed by the stark and awesome mountains, beyond which, to the west, are all the wonders of the Nile and Ancient Egypt."

Further south at **Safaga,** 33 miles from Hurghada, the *Safaga Hotel* (operated by the Victoria Hotel in Cairo) is a modern beach hotel with facilities for diving and windsurfing.

Sinai

Sinai, the land of turquoise, is a peninsula east of the Suez Canal and the Red Sea. It was seized by Israel in the Six Day War, and its return to Egypt has been the major subject of negotiations between Egypt and Israel since President Sadat's historic visit to Jerusalem.

Sinai has been an important part of Egypt for as long as the country has existed, creating as it did a natural barrier between Egypt and her traditional Asian enemies.

Many legends of the ancient Egyptians are set in Sinai. Isis went there to search for the body of her murdered husband, Osiris. The goddess Hathor, known to the pharaohs as "Our Lady of Sinai," sanctified the area.

The Bible mentions Sinai often—here Moses received the Ten Commandments, and it was by way of Sinai that the Holy Family fled into Egypt. Later the region became a place of refuge for Christians from Roman persecution.

The best times to visit are late February to May and September through November. The most important and interesting excursion is to the Greek Orthodox **Monastery of St. Catherine,** built in about 250 A.D. and located about 130 miles southeast of Suez.

The Firan Oasis at the foot of Mount Serbal is the site where, according to some authorities, Moses received the Ten Commandments. Beyond, at *Jebel Musa,* lies the monastery dedicated to Catherine, the Alexandrian saint. In addition to the ancient church and other old buildings the monastery's library has some of the oldest and most valuable manuscripts and icons in the world. The church is built on the traditional site of the Burning Bush. Beyond the monastery, 4,000 stone steps lead to the top of the *Mount of Moses* where tradition holds Moses received the Ten Commandments.

Next to the church is a mosque, which tradition holds was built when the Fatimite Caliph el-Hakim bi Amr Illah in the 10th century ordered the destruction of all Christian monasteries. The monks of St. Catherine's outwitted him by adding the mosque, and so the story goes, the slender minaret, which can be seen in the distance, was enough to deter the demolition of the other buildings. A wooden chair with Kufic inscriptions and a mimbar in the mosque date from the 11th century.

During the time of the Israeli occupation, a hostel was constructed that provides for basic accommodations. The Egyptian government is now studying what facilities, if any, should be added to the area.

On the Mediterranean coast at the northern end of Sinai next to the Israeli border, the town of **El-Areesh** is slated for development as a tourist resort. The foundation stone of Marriott's holiday village has been laid, and construction is expected to start this year.

At the south end, plans are in the making to develop Sharm el Sheikh as a resort. A hotel built during the time of Israeli occupation, it was left in very bad condition but will have to do until something better comes along. Resort packages for a week's stay are available through Air Sinai.

The area's waters are noted for their spectacular fish. For those planning to drive, they should take all provisions, including distilled water for the car battery. Gasoline is available in Suez and at El Tur; a full tank from these stops is enough gasoline to reach Sharm el Sheikh under normal circumstances.

A new service from Cairo to St. Catherine's Monastery is available from Shark el Delta Line, Kolai Terminal on Fri., Sun., and Tues. at 9 A.M. and returning the following days at 6 A.M. Fare is L.E. 6 one-way.

APPENDIX

ENGLISH-ARABIC TOURIST VOCABULARY

There are many systems for the transliteration of Arabic words into English equivalents. In the following glossary the system has been made as simple as possible.

—All long vowels appear as double vowels except "a," which is written with a circumflex: â.

—The ع (ain) in Arabic has no English equivalent. Its presence (when necessary to avoid confusion with other words) has been indicated by: ‘.

...The ء (hamza), a glottal stop, is indicated by: ’.

—H, h—the first is hard, the second is like the English "h" in *hat*.

—T, t—the first is hard, the second is like the English "t" in *tip*.

—D or th (like the "th" in *this*) are almost the same sound in Egyptian speech: hatha, ooDa.

—The خ is indicated by "kh," pronounced gutterly as the German "ch" in *Bach*.

—The ج (jim) in Egypt is pronounced hard as the "g" in *go*.

Greetings

Good morning	*saida*
(reply)	*saida*
Good evening	*masa-l khair*
Good day	*naharak sa'eed*
(reply)	*ahlan wa sahlan*
Hello	*zayak*
(reply)	*zayak inta*
Greetings (Peace be with you)	*as-salâm alaikoom*
(reply)	*alaikoom salâm*
Goodbye (the one departing)	*saida*
(the one remaining)	*ma'-salâma*
How are you?	*zayak innaharda*
Well, thank God	*kwayes elHamdu lillâh*
Welcome (host says)	*ahlan wa-sahlan*

Useful Phrases

Yes	*aywa*
No	*lâ*
Please	*min fadlak, min fadlik* (*f.*)
If you please	*tismah*
After you, I beg you to (enter, eat, take)	*tfaDDal, tfaDDali* (*f.*)
If God is willing	*inshallah*
Thank you	*mshakreen awwe, mutashakir geddan*
What is your name?	*ismak eh?*
My name is	*ismi ....*
Do you speak English?	*Bitkallam ingleezi?*
I do not speak Arabic	*ana ma bakallimsh 'arabi*
How? (In what way?)	*izzay?*
How much? (cost)	*aday?*
How many?	*kam?*
What?	*eh?*
What is that?	*eh da?*
What is it? What's the matter?	*fee eh?*
What do you want?	*awiz eh?*
Who?	*meen?*

Why?	*lai?*
For what purpose?	*min shân eh? alla shan eh?*
I do not want	*mish awiz*
I do not have	*ma 'indish*
I am hungry	*ana gu'an, ana gu'ana* (*f.*)
I want to eat	*awiz akul*
Give me	*iddeeni*
Bring me	*hatli*
Excuse me	*bil-izin*
Take care, watch out	*ou'ak*
Go away!	*imshi*
Hurry up	*yallah*
Get up	*oom*
Stop	*wa'if*
Stop, enough	*bass*
Slower please	*'ala mahlak minfadlak*
Slowly	*wish-waysh*
Take me to the hotel	*khudni 'al otel*
Wait here!	*istenna hena*
Open the door!	*iftaH el bâb*
Shut the door!	*ifil el bâb*
Let me see!	*wareeni*
Come here!	*ta'a la hena*
I do not know	*ma arafsh*
See!	*shoof!* I saw· *shuft*
Never mind	*malaish*
Again	*kaman, min gedeed*
Another time	*marra tânya*
Once	*marra*
Twice	*marratain*
Everything	*kulla haga*
All of us	*kullina*
Together	*ma'a ba'th*
Here	*hena*
There	*henak*
Yet	*lissa*
Not yet	*lissa bardu*
When	*emta*
After	*ba'd*
Later	*ba'dain*
Never	*abadan*
Always	*daiman*
Perhaps	*yimkin*
Is it possible?	*mumkin?*
Please wash these	*wahyatak, ighsili dol*
Please press these	*wahyatak, tikwili dol*

At the Airport

Airport	*maTâr*	Porter	*bawwab*
Car, taxi	*arabiyeh, taxi*	Office	*maktab*
Customs	*gumruk*	Suitcase	*shanta*
Handbag	*shanta*	Ticket	*tezkara*
Money	*fuloos*	Trunk	*sanduq kabeera*

In Town

Bridge	*kubri*	Place	*maHal*
Church	*kaneesa*	Hospital	*mustashfa*
District	*Hye*	House	*bait*
Harbour	*mena*	Shop	*dukkân*
Market	*souq*	Square	*midân*
Mosque	*gami'*	Street	*shârhi'*
Museum	*matHaf*	Town	*medineh, balad*

At the Hotel

Ashtray	*manfatha*	Pillow	*makhadda*
Bath	*hammam*	Room	*ooDa*
Bed, mattress	*sarrir*	Sheet	*millaya*
Blanket	*bataneya*	Soap	*saboona*
Door	*bab*	Towel	*foota*
Doorman	*bawwab*	Window	*shubbâk*
Floor (story)	*dor*	Is there air-conditioning?	*fee tabreed?*
Hotel	*otel, lukanda*		
Hot water	*mayya sukhna*	Is there heat?	*al bait medafa?*
Lamp	*nagafa*	Show me a room	*warreeni ooDa*
Light	*noor*	Where is the toilet?	*fain al-hammam?*
Lightbulb	*lamba*		

On the Road

Above, up	*foq*	Left	*shemâl*
Behind	*wara*	Near	*'areeb*
Under	*taHt*	North	*shamal*
East	*sharq*	Over	*'ala*
Far	*ba'eed*	Outside	*barra*
Gasoline	*benzeen*	Right	*yameen*
Go down	*inzal taht*	Road, highway	*tareeq*
Go out	*iTla'barra*	South	*ganuub*
In front	*'uddam*	Straight ahead	*ala tool*
Inside	*gowwa*	Village	*qariya*

Water	*mayya*	Is the road far from here?	*et-tareeq ba'eed min hena?*
Where	*fain*	How many kilometers?	*kam kilometer?*
Where is the road to ......?	*fain et-tareeq 'al ......?*		

In the Restaurant

Bill	*fatoora, hisab*	Lunch	*ghada*
Breakfast	*fatoor*	Matches	*kibreet*
Cigarette	*segayar* (*pl.*)	Plate	*saHn*
Dinner	*'asha*	Restaurant	*mat'am*
Fork	*shawka*	Spoon	*mal'a'a*
Glass	*kubaiyeh*	Table	*tarabayza*
Headwaiter	*rais, garçon*	Table napkins	*foota*
Knife	*sikkina*	Waiter	*sufragi*

Food

Apricot	*mishmish*	Lettuce	*khass*
Banana	*mooz*	Meat	*laHma*
Beef	*laHm ba'ar*	Roast	*rosto*
Beer	*bira*	Skewer	*meshwi*
Bread	*aish*	Melon (yellow)	*shammâm*
Butter	*zebda*	Milk	*leban*
Cabbage	*karomb*	Olives	*zatoon*
Cheese	*gibna*	Olive oil	*zait zatoon*
Chicken	*farkha*	Onions	*basal*
Coffee	*'ahwa*	Oranges	*bortuân*
Cucumber	*khiyar*	Peaches	*khûkh*
Cutlet	*castaletta*	Pepper, black	*filfil*
Eggs	*baid*	sweet	*filfil hellu*
hard boiled	*baid maslooq*	Preserves	*murabba*
soft boiled	*baid brisht*	Rice	*ruzz*
omelette	*omelette*	Salad	*salata*
Eggplant	*batingan*	Salt	*milH*
Figs	*teen*	Soup	*shurba*
Fish	*samak*	Squash	*koosa*
Fruit	*fak-ha*	Sugar	*sukkar*
Garlic	*toom*	Tea	*shy*
Grapes	*'enab*	Tomatoes	*tomatum*
Green beans	*fasulya*	Veal	*laHm 'ijl*
Honey	*'asal*	Vegetables	*khudra*
Ice	*talg*	Vinegar	*Khall*
Lamb	*kharoof*	Watermelon	*baTTeekh*
Lemon	*limoon*	Wine	*nbeet*
Lentils	*'atas*	Yogurt	*leban zabadi*

Weather

Cold	*bard*	Weather	*taqs, gaw*
Hot	*Harr*	Wind	*hawa*
Rain	*matar*		

Colors

Black	*sawda*	Grey	*rumadi*
Blue	*azraq*	Red	*aHmar*
Brown	*bunaya*	White	*abyaD*
Green	*akhDar*	Yellow	*asfar*

Personal Pronouns

I	*ana*	We	*iyHna*
You	*inta, inti* (*f.*)	You	*intu*
He	*huwa, heeya* (*f.*)	They	*huma*

Adjectives

Bad	*baTTâl, wehish*	High	*'ali*
not bad	*mesh baTTâl*	Hot (food)	*sukhn, harr*
Beautiful	*gameel*	Large, big	*kbeer*
Bitter	*murr*	Little (amount)	*shuwaiyeh*
Broad	*'areeD*	Long, tall	*Taweel*
Cheap	*rakhess*	Low	*wâti*
Clean	*naDeef*	Much	*kteer*
Dear, expensive	*ghâli*	Narrow, tight	*Dayyi*
Dirty	*wusikh*	New	*gadeed*
Empty	*fâDi*	Old, antique	*adeem*
Good	*kwayes*	Short, small	*zaghyar*
Not good	*mesh kwayes*	Sour	*had'a kida*
Very good	*kwayes awwe*	Sweet	*Helwa*
Great	*'azeem*	Tired	*ta'bân*

Parts of the Body

Arm	*Dra'*	Head	*râs*
Blood	*damm*	Heart	*alb*
Bone	*'athm*	Kidneys	*klâwi*
Chest	*sadr*	Leg	*rigl*
Ear	*wedan*	Liver	*kibd*
Eye	*'ain*	Mouth	*famm*
Foot	*rigl*	Stomach	*baTn*
Hair	*sha'r*	Tooth	*sinn, snan* (*pl.*)
Hand	*eed*		

Topographical Terms

Coast	*shaTTi*	River	*nahr*
Country	*balad*	Sand	*raml*
Desert	*saHara*	Sea	*baHr*
Earth, soil	*arD*	Spring	*'ain*
Fortress	*al'a*	Tower, fort	*borg*
Garden	*genaina*	Tree	*shagara*
Head, top	*râs*	Valley	*wadi*
Mountain	*gebel*	Well	*beer, saqi*
Plain	*saHel*		

Useful Words

Antiquities	*asar*	Iron (metal)	*Hadid*
Baker	*farrân*	(instrument)	*makwa*
Barber	*Hallâk*	Jar	*olla*
Bedroom	*ooda-t noom*	Judge	*qâDi*
Boat	*safeena*	King	*malak*
Book	*kitâb*	Kitchen	*matbakh*
Bookshop	*maktabi*	Letter	*resâla*
Camel	*gamal*	Lighthouse	*fenar*
Candle	*sham'a*	Living room	*sâlon*
Caravanserai	*khân*	Monastery	*deir*
Cards (playing)	*kusheena*	Moon	*qamar*
Carpet	*siggâda*	New Moon	*hilâl*
Castle	*qasr*	Pain	*waga'*
Chair	*kursi*	Pigeon	*hamam*
Coat	*balto*	Pilgrim	*Hâjji*
Column	*âmood, awamid (pl.)*	Pilgrimage	*Hâjj*
		Policeman	*bolees*
Consul	*'unsul*	Police station	*karakoon, makfar*
Diarrhea	*is-hâl*		
Dining room	*ooda-t sufra*	Prophet	*nebi*
Doctor	*hakeem, doctor*	Prayer-niche	*miHrâb*
Dog	*kalb*	Pulpit	*minbar*
Dome, cupola	*goobah*	Reception room	*diwan, dar*
Donkey	*Hmâr*	Religion	*deen*
Dress	*fustân*	Seamstress	*khayyâta*
Elder man	*sheikh*	Servant	*sufragi*
Eyeglasses	*naddara*	Shirt	*amees*
Fever	*harâra*	Shoes	*gazamadi*
Fire	*nâr*	Stone	*Hajar*
Girl	*bint, benât (pl.)*	Sun	*shams*
Headache	*râsi bewugani*	Tailor	*tarzi*
Heaven, sky	*sama*	Tomb	*turab*
Holiday	*'eed*	Toothpick	*khel*
Horse	*hosân*	Trousers	*bantalon*

PHARAONIC GODS AND SYMBOLS

Pharaonic gods were many, and often had the same or similar characteristics. In addition to possessing all human virtues, each god also possessed a particular attribute of an animal or bird. For example, Sekmet, the god of war, had the strength of the lion; Anubis, the swiftness of the jackal, and Horus, the keen sight of the hawk. During religious ceremonies the priests wore masks of the animals associated with the gods they represented, and the animals and birds associated with the gods were likewise considered sacred.

Supreme among the gods was Re (Ra), the god of the sun, also called Amen-Re. Osiris, his son, ruled on earth until he was murdered by Set, his brother, god of darkness. The mate of Osiris was Isis, goddess of heaven and earth. Their son, Horus, became lord of earth, and Osiris became god of the underworld and judge of the dead.

Some of the major deities and the animals with which they were associated were:

Amen-Re, the sun-god, patron deity of Thebes—the ram, also the hawk.

Anubis, god of the dead, patron deity in certain districts of Upper Egypt—the jackal.

Aton, god of the setting sun, local deity—the lion and the snake.

Hathor, goddess of heaven, joy and love, deity of Denderah and protector of the necropolis of Thebes—the cow.

Horus (and Ha-Rakhte, a form of Horus), usually represented by the winged sun disc—the falcon.

Isis, goddess of heaven and earth, patron goddess of Philae, wife of Osiris and mother of Horus—the vulture.

Khnum, patron god of Elephantine Island and the Cataracts—the ram.

Maat, goddess of justice—the ostrich feather.

Osiris, god of the dead—the "tet."

Ptah, patron god of Memphis and father of the gods—the bull.

Sobek, god of the waters, patron god of Fayoum—the crocodile.

Thoth, god of science and patron god of Hermopolis—the ibis.

With a little practice, you can often recognize the gods by their headdresses in wall paintings. Emblems of rule, sovereignty and dominion were represented by the crook or sceptre and the flail.

The symbol of the key-of-life is known as the *ankh.*

The double crown indicated the union of Upper and Lower Egypt.

INDEX

(The letters H and R indicate Hotel and Restaurant listings.)

FACTS AT YOUR FINGERTIPS

(See also Practical Information sections for each region.)

ALEXANDRIA & VICINITY

Practical Information

Geographical

CAIRO & VICINITY

Practical Information

Geographical

SUEZ CANAL & THE RED SEA

UPPER EGYPT

Practical Information

Geographical